The Vice-Admiralty Courts
and the American Revolution

The Vice-Admiralty Courts
and the American
Revolution

CARL UBBELOHDE

Published for the INSTITUTE OF
EARLY AMERICAN HISTORY AND
CULTURE, *Williamsburg, Virginia,*
by THE UNIVERSITY OF NORTH
CAROLINA PRESS, *Chapel Hill, 1960*

The Institute of Early American History and Culture is sponsored jointly by the College of William and Mary and Colonial Williamsburg, Incorporated. Publication of this book has been assisted by a grant from the Lilly Endowment, Inc.

To Mary

Preface

IN SEPTEMBER 1818, John Adams wrote a letter to William Tudor describing his experiences in and about Boston in the years before the American Revolution. He chanced to mention a case he had pleaded before Judge Robert Auchmuty's vice-admiralty court, and he interrupted his narrative to mourn the loss of that court's records. "The history of this court," he wrote Tudor, "would require volumes. Where are its records and its files? Its libels and answers? Its interrogations and cross interrogatories? All [these records were] hurried away to England . . . never to be seen again."[1]

1. Adams to William Tudor, Sept. 10, 1818, Charles Francis Adams, ed., *The Works of John Adams, Second President of the United States . . .* (10 vols.; Boston, 1850-56), X, 354. Almost all of the records of the Massachusetts Vice-Admiralty Court to 1765 were destroyed by the Stamp Act mob in its attack on the home of William Story, the court register, in that year. The records from 1765 to the beginning of the Revolution were probably carried to England when the British evacuated Boston in 1776. See a Note on Sources, below, 212-14.

A century and more have passed since Adams wrote these words, and only small portions of the records of the Boston and other provincial vice-admiralty courts have been discovered. But searching the newspapers and letter books, journals and diaries of the time yields evidence of the actions which the court records would more fully describe. Pieced together, item by item, they tell the story of the colonial vice-admiralty courts. John Adams would have been able to explain them to us, but now, even the existence of the vice-admiralty courts has been largely forgotten. They are no more, and that they ever were is of small concern to modern law. We have remade admiralty law, as we have remade the common law, to satisfy our particular needs and desires. And we have boldly asserted that because colonial admiralty cases were unrecorded, they provided few examples for the lawmen of our early republic.

This study is not an attempt to seek out the story of the development of American admiralty procedure. That task, better left to lawyers, has in part been done.[2] This is rather an attempt to rescue the story of the last years of the vice-admiralty courts from confusion. Latter-day historians have misunderstood both the changes in the organization of the courts after 1763 and the role that those courts played in the pre-Revolutionary crises. Part of that misunderstanding undoubtedly has resulted from the scarcity of court records. But there are other reasons for the misconceptions.

Many half-truths concocted by patriot propagandists in the decade before the Declaration of Independence have survived historical investigation. Colonial critics severely condemned the vice-admiralty courts, and many of their tales have been unquestioningly accepted and repeated down to the present day. If the courts had been of minor importance

2. Especially by Charles Merrill Hough in his *Reports of Cases in the Vice Admiralty of the Province of New York and in the Court of Admiralty of the State of New York, 1715-1788* (New Haven, 1925), xii-xxi.

in the strife of the times, these errors could be more easily excused. But the vice-admiralty courts, like the council rooms and assembly chambers, were stages upon which one portion of the preliminary struggles with Great Britain were acted. Their history is a segment of the history of the coming of the War for Independence.

In the course of completing this study I have become obligated to many persons. Professor Merrill Jensen of the University of Wisconsin introduced me to Colonial America and guided and encouraged my endeavors in this study. My debt to him is very great. Fellow students Arthur Jensen, Leslie Thomas, Robert Polk Thomson, Katherine Turner, and David Van Tassel shared information and enthusiasms with me. The Graduate School of the University of Wisconsin provided the President Adams Fellowship which made possible further research. The librarians and archivists of the Boston Athenaeum, the Connecticut Historical Society, the Harvard University Library, the Historical Society of Pennsylvania, the Massachusetts Historical Society, the National Archives, the New-York Historical Society, the New York Public Library, and especially the Library of Congress, the State Historical Society of Wisconsin, and Norlin Library of the University of Colorado were all most cooperative. The Council on Research and Creative Work of the University of Colorado provided funds for typing the manuscript. Peter Mitchell helped in the research. To all of these people I am most grateful.

Contents

The Vice-Admiralty Courts
and the American Revolution

I

Salt-Water Courts

HALIFAX Courthouse was crowded to the point of overflowing on the morning of October 2, 1764. In the audience sat the Right Honorable Lord Colville, commander of His Majesty's navy in North America, surrounded by army and navy officers and the gentlemen and ladies of the Nova Scotia seaport. This day had been appointed for the opening of the new court of vice-admiralty for all North America. Only a week before, the brig *Polly* had entered the harbor at Halifax, bringing Doctor William Spry and his family safely from London. Now, in the scarlet robes of his new office, the Right Worshipful William Spry, Doctor of Laws, led the procession into the courtroom. His "Lordship" Jonathan Belcher, chief justice of the Nova Scotia Superior Court, accompanied him. The "Gentlemen of the Law," dressed in gowns and bands, filed into the chamber behind the two judges.

The ceremonies began with a reading of the commission

that Doctor Spry had brought with him from London. Duly passed under the great seal of the High Court of Admiralty of Great Britain and Ireland, the document constituted him "Commissary Deputy and Surrogate in and through all & every the province of America." The commission read, Judge Spry officially opened his new court. First he appointed deputies for the register and marshal, since the men who held these sinecures were in England and intended to remain there. He then admitted the lawyers of Halifax as advocates and proctors in the new court. This done, Judge Spry adjourned his court for two weeks.

Ceremony and society attended the birth of the new vice-admiralty court. That evening the judge and his wife entertained the gentlemen and ladies of Halifax. A "very genteel cold Collation" was served "with elegance and propriety," and the evening concluded "to the general Satisfaction of all present."[1]

The commission that William Spry brought from London was a symbol of a new day of British rule in America. Nine years of war with France had brought England more than great stretches of wilderness. Victorious in arms, she must now arrange her household and prepare to pay the price of her glories. The enormous debt must be liquidated, and the colonial trade must be taxed to contribute its proportionate share. This could be done only with a revitalized customs establishment. The French War had pointed up the weaknesses of both the American revenue collectors and the provincial vice-admiralty courts. The year 1764 became a year of reform. The entire colonial revenue structure was reviewed and revised. As part of this program, Judge Spry had come to Halifax to establish a supercourt with authority

1. *Mass. Gazette,* Oct. 11, 1764; *Providence Gazette,* Nov. 24, 1764; *Penn. Gazette,* Nov. 22, 1764.

extending from Florida to Newfoundland. His court was to serve as a cornerstone in the new imperial rule.

The Courts

There were eleven courts of vice-admiralty in North America at the conclusion of the French and Indian War. These had existed, for the most part, since the closing years of the seventeenth century and had gradually become fixtures of the provincial "constitutions." In the far north, courts had been established in both Newfoundland and Nova Scotia. New Hampshire was included within the territorial boundaries of the Massachusetts court. The crown had only recently divorced Rhode Island from the Massachusetts district and established a separate court there. The boundaries of the New York court encompassed three colonies: Connecticut, New York, and New Jersey. Both of the proprietary colonies, Maryland and Pennsylvania, had separate tribunals, the latter including the three Delaware counties in its jurisdiction. There was a vice-admiralty court in each of the southern provinces: Virginia, Georgia, and the two Carolinas.[2]

These courts were fashioned after their counterparts in the home country. Time and geography had created varia-

2. The origins, organization, and operation of the colonial vice-admiralty courts in the years before 1763 have been carefully described by Helen J. Crump, *Colonial Admiralty Jurisdiction in the Seventeenth Century* (London, 1931); Charles M. Andrews, *The Colonial Period of American History* (4 vols.; New Haven, 1934-37), IV, 222-71; and Joseph D. Doty, *The British Admiralty Board as a Factor in Colonial Administration, 1689-1763* (Phila., 1930), 20-46. There are, in addition, short studies of individual vice-admiralty courts, including "The Courts of Admiralty in New England Prior to the Revolution," *Mass. Law Qtly.*, 17 (1932), 97-100; Frederick Bernays Wiener, "Notes on the Rhode Island Admiralty, 1727-1790," *Harvard Law Rev.*, 46 (1932), 44-90; Charles M. Andrews, "Introduction" to Dorothy S. Towle, ed., *The Records of the Vice Admiralty Court of Rhode Island, 1716-1752* (Washington, 1936); and Carl Ubbelohde, "The Vice-Admiralty Court of Royal North Carolina 1729-1759," *N.C. Hist. Rev.*, 31 (1954), 517-28.

tions, but as in courts of the maritime counties of England, vice-admirals enjoyed nominal supervision over the courts' activities. In the colonies, the royal governors were constituted vice-admirals of their provinces by the Lords Commissioners of the Admiralty in England. As vice-admirals, the governors were commissioned to supervise the crown's interest in all maritime matters. The list of duties was long, but for the most part, unimportant. The crown had rights to certain fish, and it reserved priority to abandoned or wrecked cargoes and vessels, and the governors were expected to make certain that those rights were not ignored. But occasions for action upon such matters seldom occurred. In fact, the commissions as vice-admirals might have become mere titular honors if they had not also granted the governors the right to make temporary appointments to the vice-admiralty courts in their provinces. This appointing power gave the governors an interest in the personnel of the courts. But having selected the officers, the governors seldom interfered with the administration of justice, preferring to allow their protégés to manage the affairs of the courts.[3]

It was the judges who completely dominated the colonial vice-admiralty courts. They were the trial officers, hearing and determining the cases before them without the aid of juries or fellow judges. They fixed the time and the place of trials. They might move the court from one town to another, as the occasion, or their convenience, demanded. Honor and prestige accompanied appointment as vice-admiralty judge, for few institutions were then so controlled by one individual.

The emoluments of the office, however, in no way indicated this prestige. Not one of the provincial judges enjoyed a salary; they were paid by percentages on the goods

3. Leonard Woods Labaree, *Royal Government in America: A Study of the British Colonial System Before 1783* (New Haven, 1930), 26, 31.

they condemned and by fixed fees allowed by colonial statutes.[4] No vice-admiralty judge grew wealthy from his office, and most of them depended on other activities to support themselves and their families. Some judges continued their law practices after elevation to the bench. Others engaged in farming or mercantile ventures to supplement their incomes. Chambers Russell in Massachusetts drew a salary as a Superior Court justice in addition to his income as vice-admiralty judge.[5] In New York and Pennsylvania the judges combined their legal offices with duties as clerks of the common-law courts.[6] Peyton Randolph in Virginia and Egerton Leigh in South Carolina united the offices of attorney general and vice-admiralty judge. Benjamin Green of Nova Scotia tried to combine the offices of vice-admiralty judge and naval officer, but the Board of Trade ordered him to give up one position or the other. Green actually preferred the judgeship, but he had "a large family to care for," and the profits from the admiralty office were "precarious and . . . small." So he elected to retain the naval office, which was "attended with a certain income."[7]

The Lords Commissioners of the Admiralty in England commissioned most of the provincial judges by letters patent from the High Court of Admiralty. Actually, however, all

4. For examples of the fees fixed by provincial statutes, see *Acts and Resolves, Public and Private of the Province of the Massachusetts Bay . . .* (21 vols.; Boston, 1869-1922), II, 245-46; James T. Mitchell and Henry Flanders, eds., *Statutes at Large of Pennsylvania* (17 vols.; Harrisburg, 1896-1915), V, 161-78; William Saunders and Walter Clark, eds., *The Colonial . . . [and State] Records of North Carolina* (26 vols.; Goldsboro and Raleigh, 1886-1907), XXIII, 281-82.

5. William Thomas Davis, *History of the Judiciary of Massachusetts Including the Plymouth and Massachusetts Colonies, the Province of the Massachusetts Bay, and the Commonwealth* (Boston, 1900), 77-78.

6. Petition of Richard Morris to the King, Nov. 28, 1761, Public Record Office, Colonial Office 5, 1141; Governor Penn's Answers to Queries, Jan. 30, 1775, PRO, CO 5, 1286.

7. Benjamin Green to Governor Peregrine Hopson, Apr. 11, 1753, PRO, Admiralty 1, 3818.

of the judges owed their offices to the good favor of the provincial governors, and the appointees in North Carolina and Maryland rarely solicited commissions from England. Even in the colonies where judges requested permanent commissions from the Admiralty, the governors' appointments were accepted and the commissions were issued automatically. Thus, the judgeships became political offices in the hands of the royal governors, to be bestowed upon deserving friends and supporters.[8]

The governors usually selected experienced lawyers as judges, although the rule was unwritten and there were exceptions.[9] The law and procedure of the vice-admiralty courts differed considerably from that of the common-law courts, but the American bar was too unspecialized to limit the positions to men trained in the civil law. Experience in

8. Notwithstanding Andrews' assertion to the contrary, in "Introduction" to Towle, ed., *Recs. of R.I. Vice Admiralty Court,* 19, the fact that the governors controlled the appointments is evidenced by the correspondence of the Lords Commissioners of the Admiralty. See, as examples, the following and their endorsements: Edward Cornwallis to Admiralty, Dec. 2, 1750; James Glenn to Admiralty, Sept. 23, 1752; Peregrine Hopson to Admiralty, Apr. 14, 1753; all in PRO, Admir. 1, 3818. For a sample commission from the High Court of Admiralty of England, see that of Richard Morris, Judge of the New York Vice-Admiralty Court, 1764, Erastus C. Benedict, *The American Admiralty: Its Jurisdiction and Practice with Practical Forms and Directions* (5 vols.; 6th edn., N.Y., 1940-41), IV, 427-33; the original is in the N.Y. Hist. Soc., Misc. Mss., "M." Judge Daniel Dulany's commission from Governor Samuel Ogle, 1734, is an example of a commission issued under the Great Seal of Maryland; in Microfilm Collection of Early State Records, Md., E.1c. Even in New Jersey, where the court was included in the New York district, the governors exercised their appointing powers in the intervals between the death of one judge and the commissioning of his successor. See *Journal of the Commissioners for Trade and Plantations, from April 1704 to [May 1782], preserved in the Public Record Office* (14 vols.; London, 1929-38) [hereafter cited as *Board of Trade Journal*], volume for 1759 to 1763, 315.

9. Governor George Clinton of New York considered appointing Alexander Colden, "not a Lawyer but bred a Merchant," to the judgeship in 1747. See Clinton's letter to Thomas Corbett, May 22, 1747, PRO, Admir. 1, 3818. In Pennsylvania, Thomas Hopkinson, who had been a merchant, sat on the admiralty bench for almost a decade.

any court might aid the promotion of a lawyer to a judgeship.

The governors were not the only parties interested in the
appointments. The vice-admiralty courts were designed to
aid merchants and traders, and most of the business of the
courts concerned salt-water commerce. The merchants were
dependent upon the judges for many services, and they
watched the appointments to the courts with considerable
interest. As a Philadelphia trader cautioned after the death
of Judge Andrew Hamilton: "It behoves the merchts who
trade this way to take some care respecting who is made
Judge of the Admiralty."[10]

The judges were usually residents of the major port cities,
and called their court sessions to order in the courthouse or
some other public building. But trials might take place
wherever the judge desired. Lewis Morris in New York preferred to have the court come to him. As he grew older he
gradually transferred the activities of his provincial court
from the New York City Hall to his private estate at Morris-
ania. In most of the colonies, judges named deputies to act
for them in time of sickness or absence from the province.
And some jurisdictions encompassed an area large enough to
require more than one judge. George Craddock, and later
William Read, acted as deputies of the Massachusetts judge
in the province of New Hampshire. Joseph Cart of New
London served New York Judge Richard Morris as his
Connecticut deputy. And in North Carolina, where a long
seacoast created problems in travel, the judges appointed
surrogates, or deputies, for the distant ports in their juris·
diction.[11]

10. John Reynell to Daniel Flexney, Aug. 8, 1741, John Reynell Letter
Book, Hist. Soc. of Penn.
11. A sample commission from a judge to his surrogate is that of William
Ross to Jasper Charlton of North Carolina, 1757, Records of the N.C. Vice-
Admiralty Court, Microfilm Coll. of Early State Recs., N.C., F.3.

The proctors, or trial lawyers, gathered the evidence in disputes and presented it to the courts.[12]   Merchants and sailors employed colonial attorneys as proctors to plead their causes, but if the British Crown was a party in the litigation, the provincial advocate general prosecuted or defended the king's interest.   There was little uniformity from colony to colony in the appointment of the advocates general.   In Massachusetts, the governors issued temporary commissions, which were followed later by letters patent from the High Court of Admiralty of England.   In Virginia, the governor's commission alone was considered sufficient.   The attorneys general of Georgia and North Carolina were also commissioned as advocates general, while in Pennsylvania and New York the colonial attorneys general prosecuted crown cases as part of their regular duties.

Like the judges, the advocates general could expect little profit from their fees, and neither crown nor colony granted them salaries.   But lawyers were usually willing to accept appointment either for the honor or as a step up the ladder of the governor's patronage.   More than one advocate general was in time promoted to the vice-admiralty bench.   The duties of the office were far from pressing, and it was always possible to rely upon a deputy.

The registers and marshals performed the routine work of the vice-admiralty courts.   The registers acted as the clerks of the courts, keeping the records of the cases and issuing citations and orders on the judges' commands.   The marshals' duties were similar to those of a sheriff: serving processes, taking custody of goods or people, and executing the decrees of the court.   The registers and marshals in Massachusetts, New York, and Pennsylvania solicited commissions from the

12. The distinction then current in England between proctors, who conducted proceedings out of court, and advocates, who represented the party in court, appears to have been unknown in the colonial vice-admiralty courts, probably because of the limited number of professional lawyers.

High Court of Admiralty of England. In other colonies, the governor's commission under the provincial seal sufficed. The judges were allowed to name their own registers and marshals in North Carolina and Maryland.[13]

These offices might be, and often were, deputized. Andrew Belcher held the commission as Massachusetts register for many years, depending upon William Story, and later Ezekiel Price, to perform the duties in return for a percentage of the fees. The fees, however, were no more lucrative than those of the judges, and neither marshals nor registers could live by them alone. In Massachusetts, Ezekiel Price combined a marine insurance enterprise and a public notary's tasks with his duties as deputy register. Charles Paxton, the marshal of the same court, augmented his income with the fees from the profitable post of surveyor of the customs for the port of Boston, and the minor position of crier of the Supreme Court of Judicature.[14]

By 1763 the officers of the vice-admiralty courts, almost without exception, were provincial born. Most of them had never seen the shores of Old England. Except in the newest colonies, they served in courts which had been established for more than half a century. Their duties were seldom exacting; their rewards were never great. Appointment to the vice-admiralty courts, however, carried a certain

13. New York Register Richard Nicholls' commission from the High Court of Admiralty of England, 1745, is in New Jersey Commissions, Microfilm Coll. of Early State Recs., N.J., E.1c. For North Carolina, see William Tryon, "A View of the Polity of the Province of North Carolina," W. L. Saunders, ed., *N.C. Col. Recs., 1662-1776*, VII, 482-83. For Maryland, see PRO, CO 5, 1280.

14. The authority given to officers to name deputies was often criticized. For complaints against Belcher in Massachusetts, see H. Frankland to Admiralty, Feb. 5, 1749, and Robert Auchmuty to Thomas Corbett, n. d., PRO, Admir. 1, 3882 and 3878. For Price's business ventures, see advertisement in the *Mass. Gazette*, Oct. 28, 1773, and his personal papers in the Boston Athenaeum. For data on Paxton, see Josiah Quincy, Jr., ed., *Reports of Cases Argued and Adjudged in the Superior Court of Judicature of the Province of Massachusetts Bay, Between 1761 and 1772* (Boston, 1865), 427.

local distinction, and the pleasant possibility of advancement in the governor's favor. It was a happy combination that few men ever actively sought, or refused, if offered.

The Jurisdiction

The colonial vice-admiralty courts operated on three distinct levels. On the local level they heard and determined disagreements and problems of merchants and seamen. This had been the courts' original function, as it had been the business of English courts centuries before. Late in the seventeenth century, the British Crown had added a second jurisdiction: enforcement of imperial control of trade. In 1696 the colonial vice-admiralty courts were chosen as tribunals for prosecuting offenders against the trade and navigation statutes. And the courts' jurisdiction became international in time of war, when the crown created them prize courts with authority to condemn captured enemy cargoes and vessels.

As local institutions for the convenience of merchants and sailors, the vice-admiralty courts settled a great variety of litigation. The most numerous cases involved questions of seamen's wages and the relations between sailors and their masters and officers. Problems concerning shipwrecks and the salvage of vessels and cargoes were also common. The courts had jurisdiction over a great variety of marine contracts, including charter parties (contracts for leasing part or all of vessels for specific voyages), bottomry (in effect, mortgage of a ship), partnerships, and the building, equipping, and insuring of vessels. Suits over collisions at sea were less common, and questions of the royal rights to whales and other large fish were seldom raised. The courts also performed the quasi-administrative service of conducting surveys of damaged cargoes and vessels, for the convenience of captains, owners, or insurers.[15]

In all of these marine matters, the questions were brought to the attention of the courts by the aggrieved parties. The courts could not act until the person desiring relief presented his case before them. Procedure and terminology varied greatly from colony to colony, but, reduced to its simplest form, the course of litigation through the provincial vice-admiralty courts followed a general pattern. First, the person seeking redress, the *libelant,* filed a *libel* in open court, stating his complaint and prayer for relief. The judge then ordered the marshal to take custody of the vessel, cargo, or person libeled, and to give public notice of his action. A *proclamation,* stating the complaint of the libelant, was issued by the judge when the libel was filed and was repeated at the next session of the court.

At this second reading of the proclamation, the defendant (in admiralty procedure, the *claimant* or *respondent)* filed his *answer* to the libel. The claimant was allowed three opportunities to appear and answer. If he presented no answer, the fourth reading of the proclamation amounted to a *decree* (a judgment) for the libelant by default. If the claimant filed an answer, issue was joined, and the trial proceeded. Both parties were required to "stipulate" (or promise) securities. The opposing proctors examined witnesses outside of court. All testimony was taken in writing in the form of answers to interrogations and cross-interrogations. At a further session of the court, the proctors presented the witnesses' statements and recited their arguments. Then the judge, often after a brief delay for considering the case, delivered his decree.

15. For descriptions and examples of these causes and services, see Andrews, *Colonial Period,* IV, 230-34.

A definitive decree ended the contest, and the marshal executed the punitive measures it ordained. If, however, there was cause for postponing a final judgment, the judge might deliver an *interlocutory decree*. Appeals from either decree required the approval of the judge. If he granted the request, and the appealing side presented security, the judge directed the register to forward the records of the case to either the King in Council or the High Court of Admiralty of England. Both the council and the court heard colonial vice-admiralty appeals. Despite repeated attempts to designate one of these agencies the sole appellate body, a single appeal channel had never been settled. Consequently, the provincial judges were often in doubt as to the correct place to send appeals. A decision on a case by the King in Council was final, but decrees of the High Court of Admiralty might be carried on a further appeal to the High Court of Delegates, composed of members of the Privy Council.[16]

The provincial judge, upon receipt of the decision on appeal, proceeded to execute its provisions. If a libel against a vessel or cargo was successfully prosecuted, the marshal was ordered to sell the forfeited goods at a public auction after appraisers had evaluated them. (In New York, the marshal's role was filled by merchants appointed by the

---

16. For a typical case appealed to the King in Council, see that of *Henry Neuton qui tam* v. *Snow Two Brothers*, from the Nova Scotia Vice-Admiralty Court, June 1762, in W. L. Grant and James Munro, eds., *Acts of the Privy Council of England: Colonial Series, 1613-1783* (6 vols.; London, 1908-12), IV, 540-43. The New York case of *John Brown qui tam* v. *Ship New York* was appealed to the High Court of Admiralty of England in 1764-67, and is reported in Reginald G. Marsden, ed., *Reports of Cases Determined by the High Court of Admiralty, 1758-1774* (London, 1885), 30. Colonial appeals from the High Court of Admiralty to the High Court of Delegates were rare. The progress of a customs seizure (the ship *Betsey*) from the Newfoundland Vice-Admiralty Court, to the High Court of Admiralty, and thence to the High Court of Delegates, is described in the *N.Y. Jour.*, Apr. 21, 1774, and in the *Penn. Gazette*, Apr. 20, 1774. On the whole question of colonial appeals, see Joseph Henry Smith, *Appeals to the Privy Council from the American Plantations* (N.Y., 1950), 88-95, 177-202, and 669-70.

governor.) For failure to meet the decreed judgment, an individual might be punished by fine, attachment of property, or imprisonment.

This was the procedure, reduced to its elemental form, by which individual merchants or seamen gained redress. The trial of offenders against the British trade laws followed the same general pattern. But from the beginning of the eighteenth century the colonial vice-admiralty courts enjoyed a jurisdiction denied to their counterparts in England. Local juries in the colonial common-law courts had proven reluctant to condemn the property of neighbors accused of violating the trade laws. Customs officials and crown officers in America had protested against their dependence on colonial juries. They had warned their superiors in England that they would never be able to enforce the trade laws so long as the innocence or guilt of suspected smugglers rested upon the whims of provincial juries. These protests led to a clause in the Navigation Act of 1696 granting the vice-admiralty courts, which employed no juries, equal jurisdiction with the common-law courts in trade and revenue cases.

After the inclusion of this formula in the comprehensive navigation act of that year, the British Parliament repeated the grant of jurisdiction in subsequent trade laws. Each new statute extended the authority of the colonial vice-admiralty courts to interpret and enforce commercial regulations and restrictions. These acts of trade prescribed the legal manner of conducting colonial commerce. The routines for entering and clearing harbors, registering vessels, and acquiring the necessary certificates, cockets, and bonds were all spelled out in detail. Deviation from the required conduct was cause for seizure and prosecution by customs officials and their aides. Statutes such as the Molasses Act of 1733, which imposed duties as well as regulations of conduct, granted the vice-admiralty courts concurrent jurisdiction with the common-law courts.

The colonial vice-admiralty courts did not hold exclusive jurisdiction in these cases; customs officers were free to choose the tribunal most capable of satisfying their needs, either common-law courts with juries, or single vice-admiralty judges. But the vice-admiralty courts alone controlled one important phase of British policy. The judges at New York and Boston heard and determined trespass cases against the forest preserves of the Royal Navy. Woodsmen and farmers caught violating the statutes that restricted the cutting of the larger white pine trees in New England had to be prosecuted in the vice-admiralty courts.[17]

Customs officers, or the advocates or attorneys general acting for them, brought crown cases before the courts. The judges were guided in their decisions by the applicable statutes of Parliament, which not only stipulated patterns of conduct, but also prescribed punishments for not conforming with the regulations. The most common penalty was forfeiture of ships and cargoes; other offenses were punished by fine. Forfeited property condemned by the vice-admiralty courts was sold at public auction to the highest bidder. From the profits of these sales, the costs of trial might be deducted, and commissions, usually 5 per cent, were awarded to the officers of the court. The remainder was divided according to the formula set down in the governing statute. Usually the informer or prosecutor, the governor of the colony, and the king each received one-third.

The vice-admiralty courts exercised their international jurisdiction only in wartime. In the seventeenth century the inconvenience of carrying enemy vessels, captured in

17. On the white pine laws and their enforcement, see Robert Greenhalgh Albion, *Forests and Sea Power: The Timber Problem of the Royal Navy, 1652-1862* (Cambridge, 1926), 231-74; and below, 171-78.

colonial waters, to England for trial caused much confusion about the proper method of determining prize cases. A statute of Parliament in 1708 legalized what had become by that time the prevailing custom of trying prize cases in the colonial vice-admiralty courts, and it also outlined procedures for the courts to follow. Patterned after the English machinery for trial of captures, it differed considerably from the procedure employed for other causes. Prize decrees might be appealed from the colonial courts to a selected group of privy councilors, the Lords Commissioners for Prize Appeals, rather than to the King in Council or the High Court of Admiralty.[18]

Prize cases comprised more than one-third of the litigation before the American vice-admiralty courts in the years 1702 to 1763. Considering the colonies as a whole, the remaining disputes were more concerned with marine matters than with illegal trading, although this was not true of all the provinces.[19] Together, the three areas of jurisdiction made the courts versatile institutions. Their prize jurisdiction kept them relatively busy in wartime. Their jurisdiction over breaches of the navigation acts brought them fully into the orbit of imperial commercial control. And their authority to determine private litigation of merchants and sailors made them indispensable to the commercial life of the local communities.

18. Piracy and other felonies on the high seas were not tried by the provincial vice-admiralty courts. Offenders for such crimes might be sent to England for trial in the High Court of Admiralty's Court of Oyer and Terminer. Or, a select panel of colonial officials, sometimes operating with a jury, heard and determined such cases. This "special court of admiralty," sometimes titled the "Justiciary Court of Admiralty," usually included the local vice-admiralty judge, but was headed by the governor, and included the chief justice, the attorney general, council members, and other crown officials. For this purpose, the colonies were grouped into eleven districts, with a commission for each. Samuel Seddon to John Cleveland, Mar. 14, 1762, "Extracts of Commissions for Trying Pirates in America," n. d., PRO, Admir. 1, 3678 and 3679.

19. Notably North Carolina. See Andrews, *Colonial Period*, IV, 241.

The Courts and the Common Law

The provincial vice-admiralty courts did not exist in a legal vacuum. During the early years their power was constantly being challenged by the common-law courts, and their relations with these courts were stormy and troubled. Although some of the early colonial judges' excursions into provincial politics probably caused as much general resentment against the courts as any deep-seated antagonism to admiralty procedure or love for common-law procedure, the colonists, nevertheless, turned in times of trouble with the vice-admiralty courts to compare the American courts with those of England.[20] The struggle between the colonial common-law courts and vice-admiralty courts had been similar, in many ways, to the battles between the two systems in the mother country. But the results had been different. The colonists were well aware that the powers of the English admiralty courts had been circumscribed so severely that by the end of the seventeenth century they enjoyed little more than local mercantile jurisdiction.

In the homeland, the admiralty courts had suffered a diminution of power, along with other civil-law courts, during the constitutional upheavals of the early seventeenth century. Sir Edward Coke and others had then so championed the common-law courts as to place them in undisputed control of the kingdom's judicial machinery. The question had been settled by Parliamentary statute. The common-law courts had been given the right to issue writs of prohibition, thereby effectively limiting the powers of the admiralty establishment. A common-law court could issue

20. Especially in North Carolina in the years 1728 to 1734, when Governor George Burrington and Vice-Admiralty Judge Edmund Porter engaged in a vigorous dispute over the court and its powers. See Ubbelohde, "Vice-Admiralty Court of Royal North Carolina," *N.C. Hist. Rev.*, 31 (1954), 524-28.

such a writ, stopping proceedings in the admiralty court, if the latter was overstepping its jurisdictional boundaries. A judge who proceeded in spite of a prohibition could be punished for contempt of court.[21]

Although the English statute did not extend to the colonies, the common-law courts there assumed the right to issue writs of prohibition. In some cases they very effectively circumscribed the activities of the vice-admiralty courts. But none of the colonial common-law courts had carried its cause to such a complete victory as the English courts had won. Moreover, in contrast to the English experience, the powers of colonial vice-admiralty courts were continually increased by Parliamentary legislation. The jurisdiction over breaches of the trade laws granted to the colonial courts was unknown to the English admiralty tribunals. In England, customs cases were taken to London to be tried before the common-law Court of Exchequer.

No court of exchequer existed in most of the American provinces. Various attempts to institute such courts, with or without the object of transferring the jurisdiction in trade causes, resulted in failure. The choice in the colonies was between trial in the common-law or the vice-admiralty courts. The question was not limited to cases under the trade laws, where the powers of the two courts overlapped in a concurrent jurisdiction. The admiralty's authority encompassed only the oceans and rivers and their immediate shores. Thus, if marine contracts were entered into on land, disputes concerning them might be litigated in the common-law courts. Contracts of insurance and shipbuilding, in fact, often were determined before common-law judges. The problem of defining the jurisdiction between the two systems had been, and remained, potentially explosive.

21. On prohibitions, see William Holdsworth, *A History of English Law* (12 vols.; London, 1925-38), XII, 697-98.

The question was more than that of two institutions com-
peting for patrons. Unpleasant as the facts might have been
to common-law judges, ambitious to expand their own jurisdiction, the vice-admiralty tribunals offered positive advantages to the mercantile community. In almost all cases
of marine contracts the merchants tended to favor the vice-
admiralty courts. They had been designed to aid merchants;
it was their principal business rather than a side line. Procedure in the vice-admiralty courts was generally less complex than in the common-law courts, and it was especially
designed to provide speedy justice. Time was extremely
valuable to merchants trading in perishables or attempting
to reach markets at particularly profitable seasons. The
vice-admiralty courts were always open for business, observing
no schedules or terms such as the common-law courts had
arranged.

The use of the process *in rem,* by which an aggrieved
person could be satisfied against a vessel or its cargo, rather
than against the person of the wrongdoer, was an especially
popular feature of the salt-water courts. It was unknown to
the common law. Sailors seeking redress in wage disputes,
or retribution against captains for mistreatment, also favored
the vice-admiralty courts. There they were allowed to unite
in one libel, while at common law they were each required
to seek separate writs.[22] On the other hand, the costs of trial
might be higher in the vice-admiralty courts than in the
common-law tribunals. Each step in the course of a trial
carried a fee, and although the aggregate of these fees might
total only a small percentage of the profits of a large prize
ship with a valuable cargo, in minor litigation they were
proportionately higher.

In many cases, the choice was in the hands of the libelant,
and he chose the court best suited to his needs. The same

22. *Ibid.,* I, 555.

choice was left by statute to the customs officials, or advocates general, in prosecuting trade causes. Here, however,
a different consideration swung the balance in favor of the
vice-admiralty courts. With only one judge to convince,
and with the same judge pronouncing the decree, the customs officials stood a better chance to win their case in a
vice-admiralty court than in a common-law court, which employed a jury. This was one reason why the vice-admiralty
courts had been chosen as the tribunals for prosecuting
violators of the acts of trade and navigation.[23] But the
customs officials also favored the vice-admiralty courts for
the same reasons that caused the merchants to employ them
for their private litigation: simplicity, knowledge of commercial practices, and speedy trials. As John Swift, the
deputy customs collector at Philadelphia, explained it: "If
we prosecute . . . in the Court of Admiralty the charges will
come to as much as the . . . seizure is worth, if we prosecute
. . in the court of Common Pleas, the charges are not so
high, but we can seldom get it condemned in less than six
months, which is inconvenient."[24] In this contest, the vice-
admiralty courts were usually the victors.

This, then, was the structure and practice of the vice-
admiralty courts in the American colonies at the close of the
French and Indian War. During the following decade these

23. Despite trials of maritime disputes and trade act offenses in common-
law courts such as the New York City Mayor's Court (see Richard B. Morris,
ed., *Select Cases of the Mayor's Court of New York City, 1764-1784* [Washing-
ton, 1935]), the court records indicate that by 1763 the provincial vice-
admiralty courts were probably the chief tribunals for determining violations
of the acts of trade.

24. John Swift to American Board of Customs Commissioners, July 20,
1769, Philadelphia Customs House Papers, X, Hist. Soc. of Penn. This tends
to contradict the statement that until 1764 "smugglers were regularly tried
—and acquitted—by sympathetic juries of their peers" because the common-
law courts "denied" the vice-admiralty courts "jurisdiction over the Acts of
Trade." See Edmund S. and Helen M. Morgan, *The Stamp Act Crisis:
Prologue to Revolution* (Chapel Hill, 1953), 24.

courts were subjected to many changes and much abuse.
From relative obscurity, known for the most part only to
merchants and customs officials, they became symbols and
pawns in the political arena, debated and discussed in colonial assemblies and the Parliament of Britain.

2

A War Ends and a Court Begins

THE ERUPTION of hostilities between Britain and France in 1754 shattered the tranquility of the provincial vice-admiralty courts. All along the Atlantic coastline the admiralty judges found themselves powerful agents in the hostilities, authorized by special commissions to pass judgment on the prize cases brought into their provinces. As soon as the war commenced, Whitehall sent instructions to issue letters of marque and reprisal to merchant vessels. Armed with these "licenses that distinguished legitimate plundering from piracy,"[1] the colonial captains roamed the high seas in search of enemy sail and brought an amazing number of ships into the American ports to be condemned

1. Quoted from W. T. Baxter, *The House of Hancock: Business in Boston, 1724-1775* (Cambridge, 1945), 80. On vice-admiralty courts' authority to try prizes, see PRO, Admir. 2, 1056. Virginia D. Harrington, *The New York Merchants on the Eve of the Revolution* (N.Y., 1935), 303-9, discusses provincial privateering in some detail.

by the vice-admiralty judges. This profitable game of privateering occupied the judges and benefited the English Crown,
the privateers, and the merchants sending them forth.

The war also brought an unpleasant duty to the judges.
Captures of hostile ships aided the war effort; trade with the
enemy islands in the Caribbean retarded it, or so the ministry at home believed. In 1756, when authority for determining prize cases was dispatched to the provincial judges, additional instructions went forward to all of His Majesty's customs officials. They were ordered to effect an immediate
and complete prohibition of the trade with the French
colonies in America. A year later Parliament enacted these
demands into a statute.[2]

Customs officials, however, were subject to human frail-
ties. Bribes and threats often deterred them from their
duties. And even the most energetically loyal officer could
not act alone. He might seize a dozen vessels and cargoes
for illegal trading, but without trial and condemnation in
either the common-law courts or vice-admiralty courts, his
actions would be but a temporary victory for the crown.
England and her colonies were lands of law, where no man's
property was confiscated without trial. The customs officials
were required to initiate action in the courts and prosecute
their cases to a final decree in order to secure the desired
punishment.

The difficulties of convincing common-law juries had
driven the customs officers to the vice-admiralty courts, and
new impediments awaited them there. They were faced
with the obstacle of vice-admiralty judges in league with
merchants who, war or no war, intended to continue their
profitable trade with the foreign islands.[3] If such scandalous-

2. 30 George II, c. 9.
3. George Louis Beer, *British Colonial Policy, 1754-1765* (N.Y., 1908), 125-
27; Arthur M. Schlesinger, *Colonial Merchants and the American Revolution*
(N.Y., 1918), 45-49.

ly unpatriotic behavior had been isolated in one or two of the provincial vice-admiralty courts, it might have been a less serious matter. But reports from America indicated that the disloyalty was widespread, and those reports eventually gave birth to the plans and orders that would bring Doctor William Spry from London to Halifax.

Privateers and Smugglers

Charleston, South Carolina, was the fourth largest city in the American colonies and the major port closest to the West Indies. This geographical position gave it a decided advantage in the Caribbean trade over ports further north. In ordinary times Charleston merchants did not consider the West Indies trade of prime importance. The rice crops which formed the bulk of the South Carolina export were sold in Europe. The trade that now sprang up with the islands was designed to capitalize on the opportunities that the war presented. It was the hope of quick gain and high profit that turned merchants to ventures in provisioning the French West Indian islands. The risks were many, but with stouthearted sailing captains, complaisant customs officials, and a sympathetic vice-admiralty judge, the merchants might expect success. The lure of great profits could not be denied.[4]

Three men served South Carolina as vice-admiralty judge during the conflict, and all of them apparently talked the merchants' language. James Mickie, who held the commission at the outbreak of the war, died in 1760, and John Rattray replaced him. Rattray himself died the following year, and Lieutenant Governor William Bull appointed Egerton Leigh, one of his council members, to the seat. Leigh,

4. Leila Sellers, *Charleston Business on the Eve of the Revolution* (Chapel Hill, 1934), 179-82.

the son of a former chief justice, had been "bred to the Law" and had appeared in the vice-admiralty court as proctor for many merchants. Lieutenant Governor Bull could thus justify his choice of judge to the Admiralty in England when he requested a permanent commission for Leigh. But he must also have known that the new judge was an intimate of Henry Laurens and other provincial kings of commerce.[5]

Leigh fulfilled every expectation of the merchants who watched, and probably recommended, his appointment. He could usually find a legal way to decree for the merchants. Lieutenant Governor Bull, who blandly assured Secretary of State William Pitt that he was determined to halt the "artfully managed" trade, did not question Leigh's actions. The Governor hinted that the collector of the customs was not strict enough in enforcing clearances. He blamed the attorney general for refusing to admit the existence of "sufficient Evidence to convict . . . [the offenders] either of high Treason or any illicit Trade." Or, for want of a more convincing argument, he closed his eyes to the local scene and pointed an accusing finger in the direction of the "Northern colonies."[6]

There was a basis for the accusation. Charleston was not alone as a center of trade with the enemy islands. Philadelphia merchants had turned to an ancient device for conducting much of their commerce to the Indies. Governor William Denny had unhesitatingly responded to their requests for commissions as "flags of truce," ostensibly to carry French war prisoners to the islands in exchange for British and colonial captives. The vessels thus commissioned were

5. Admiralty Warrant to High Court of Admiralty, Jan. 7, 1761, and Mar. 8, 1762, PRO, Admir. 2, 1056, 1057; William Bull to Admiralty, Oct. 4, 1761, *ibid.*, 1, 3883.

6. William Bull to William Pitt, Feb. 18, 1761, Gertrude Selwyn Kimball, ed., *Correspondence of William Pitt When Secretary of State with Colonial Governors and Military and Naval Commissioners in America* (2 vols.; N.Y., 1906) , II, 394-96.

free to sail and return with cargoes. These flags of truce were obtained, for a price, until James Hamilton replaced Denny as governor in 1760. Even then, the situation was not easily changed. Hamilton found "the most eminent Lawyers . . . retained in favour of the Trade" and Edward Shippen, the vice-admiralty judge, unwilling to decree against it.[7]

The pattern was much the same in New York. Lewis Morris, Jr., occupied the vice-admiralty bench there until he died in 1762. Long before the outbreak of hostilities Morris had shown that, like Leigh at Charleston and Shippen at Philadelphia, he could be persuaded to shut his eyes when the right pressures were exerted. In 1749 Thomas Hancock had gambled successfully in engaging Oliver DeLancey to free a seized vessel with a cargo of illegal Dutch goods from expected condemnation in Morris' court.[8] The New York judge made little effort to mend his ways now. "After Trifling in the Cause for many Months . . . [he] Refused taking Cognisance, and Dismissed" an action against the brig *Earl of Loudon* for trading with the enemy. The ruling statute provided that offenses might be prosecuted "in the High Court of Admiralty or any chief court of civil or criminal jurisdiction" in the colonies. But Morris claimed "that his Court was only a Court of Vice-Admiralty and not a High Court of Admiralty," and refused to hear the case.[9]

The New York customs officials complained to the Treasury in England that they were doubly handicapped.

7. Governor James Hamilton to Pitt, Nov. 1, 1760, *ibid.*, 351-55; Winfred Trexler Root, *The Relations of Pennsylvania With the British Government, 1696-1765* (N.Y., 1912), 123-25.

8. Baxter, *House of Hancock,* 114-15.

9. Petition of George Spencer to Treasury, May 7, 1763, PRO, Treas. 1, 423; Petition of George Spencer to Governor Robert Monckton, Aug. 2, 1763, Chalmers Papers, N.Y., IV, N.Y. Pub. Lib.; George Spencer to Charles Jenkinson, Feb. 11, 1764, Ninetta S. Jucker, ed., *The Jenkinson Papers, 1760-1766* (London, 1949), 264; Harrington, *New York Merchants,* 274; Beer, *British Colonial Policy,* 126.

The vice-admiralty judge decreed against them, while the common-law courts, their other source of remedy, were equally partial to the merchants. They went on to say that the grand jury of the city of New York was, in fact, made up of traders. Lieutenant Governor Colden joined the customs officials in their complaints, but his actions drowned the sound of his words. However great his concern over the failure to halt the illegal trade during the war, he did not oppose Governor Robert Monckton's decision to appoint Richard Morris to the vice-admiralty post in 1762. Lewis Morris had died, and his son Richard might be expected to conduct the court as his father had done. Richard must have been thoroughly familiar with the problems, for he had sat as his father's deputy in New Jersey and had appeared before his father's court as proctor for several merchants. Like his colleague in South Carolina, Colden's final defense was an accusing finger pointed northward. Rhode Island, he said, was the chief place where "colourings" took place.[10]

More than "colourings" were taking place in Rhode Island. The merchants of Newport and Providence had long been reputed the most crafty of colonial traders, the most notoriously successful in evading regulations that hampered their commercial pursuits. The very nature of the Rhode Island government provided opportunities for such enterprises. The colony was one of the two remaining charter governments in America, retaining the right of electing its own officers, from the governor to the lowliest local official. The crown had done little to reduce the colony to the pat-

10. Richard Morris to Admiralty, Aug. 11, 1762, PRO, Admir. 1, 3883; Admiralty Warrant to High Court of Admiralty, Sept. 28, 1762, *ibid.*, 2, 1057; Lt. Governor Colden to Pitt, Oct. 27 and Nov. 11, 1760, Kimball, ed., *Correspondence of Pitt with Colonial Governors*, II, 348-49, 358-59; Papers from the case of *The Henry and Cargo* (1761), Recs. of the N.Y. Provincial Vice-Admiralty Court, National Archives; Harrington, *New York Merchants*, 274-75; John A. Krout, "Richard Morris," Allen Johnson and others, eds., *Dictionary of American Biography* (21 vols.; N.Y., 1928-44), XIII, 218.

tern of a royal province. Only the customs officials and the
vice-admiralty courts were established and maintained by
His Majesty, and these small islands of imperial control
were almost engulfed in the sea of popular government.

With such political advantages at their disposal, the
Rhode Island merchants were able to employ all the techniques that other traders used for reaching the foreign
islands, with little risk to their property. They prevailed
upon the Assembly to pass legislation allowing a flag-of-truce
commission for each fifteen prisoners, and their privateering
vessels carried the permissible number of French prisoners to
the colony. When this method could not be used, the
merchants relied upon the more dangerous stratagem of
clearing for Jamaica or some other British province, depending on forged papers to cover their actual voyages to
enemy ports. The trade was profitable and less of a risk
than in many provinces. The popularly elected officials
were understanding and helpful. Only the customs and vice-
admiralty establishments remained obstacles, and even the
vice-admiralty court seemed vulnerable.

Since the beginning of the century, Rhode Island had
been included in the jurisdiction of the Massachusetts vice-
admiralty court. Rhode Island causes, however, were not
carried to Boston for trial. The Massachusetts officers appointed deputies to hold court in Rhode Island. The
declaration of war in 1756 caused Rhode Islanders to reconsider the situation of their court: A vice-admiralty judge
dependent upon Massachusetts might prove a stumbling
block to the colony's commercial pursuits. There was little
hope of convincing the British government that no court
was needed, desirable as that would have been. The next
best solution was a court of Rhode Island's own choosing,
with carefully selected officials who would rely on local
support.

Independent Rhode Island, traditionally struggling to keep herself free from crown officers, counted the odds and took the plunge. In 1757, the October session of the General Court instructed Governor Stephen Hopkins to pen a petition to the King asking for a separate court. The merchants had already decided upon a man for the judgeship. They asked Hopkins to recommend that Colonel John Andrews, a Providence planter, head the new establishment. The request was granted with surprising speed; when the General Court assembled the following October, Andrews was ordered sworn into his new office before the governor. The judgeship had been won, but some strange quirk in reasoning led the British to refuse the accompanying request for a register and marshal. These officers remained deputized by the Massachusetts principals. The Rhode Islanders, however, were not unhappy with their hybrid court. They had won a judge who understood their problems, and they relaxed in their self-created security.[11]

The honeymoon lasted less than three years. By that time, the judge discovered himself a servant of two masters, incapable of satisfying either. Matters got out of control in April 1761, when two different *informations*[12] were filed in his court against the same cargo of French sugar. Joseph Wanton, collector of His Majesty's customs, initiated one action; William Metcalf, a mariner, began the other. Andrews was forced to decide between them. There was no question concerning the sugar; it had been illegally imported and could be decreed forfeit. There remained the question of which man deserved credit for informing, and this was not an unimportant issue. The confiscated goods were to be

11. Papers in PRO, Admir. 2, 1056; Petition of Joseph Sherwood to Admiralty, Dec. 7, 1759, *ibid.*, 1, 3819; John Russell Bartlett, ed., *Records of the Colony of Rhode Island and Providence Plantations, in New England* (10 vols.; Providence, 1856-65), VI, 107, 171, 174, 176.

12. An information was used in place of a libel to initiate prosecution in cases involving the trade and revenue laws.

sold, and the profits divided among the crown, the governor, and the informer. One of the informants would receive over £400, Rhode Island currency.

The case was partially settled in April, when Andrews, by interlocutory decree, pronounced the sugar forfeit and assigned shares of the profits to the king and the Rhode Island governor. But it was September before he granted the final third to Collector Wanton, bringing down upon himself a storm of legal actions. Before the division was actually made, Metcalf obtained from a Superior Court justice a writ of prohibition which ordered cessation of all proceedings on the case. The sailor may have been acting only in his own interest, or he may have been used as a tool by people with more sinister designs. A case of illegal importation of sugar was certainly within the jurisdiction of the vice-admiralty court. But Judge Andrews' earlier decision had not pleased many merchants, and this prohibition forced a delay in the execution of the decree, a delay that cleared the path for further actions against the judge.

A writ of prohibition was not an end in itself. The common-law court which issued the writ determined whether or not the vice-admiralty court possessed jurisdiction in the dispute. If the court decided that the case lay outside of the authority of the vice-admiralty court, action must be brought in the common-law tribunals. If, however, the vice-admiralty judge had acted within his jurisdiction, the prohibition was withdrawn, and he was free to continue the case. Metcalf's prohibition was scheduled for argument before the March term of the Superior Court at Providence. March came and went and Andrews' actions were not reviewed. The delay proved to be his undoing. The undecided case remained as a weapon for a further, and more serious, attack upon his court.

Once again the division of the profits from the sale of

the sugar came into question. Most of the trade laws provided the same pattern for dividing forfeitures: one-third
each to the king, the governor, and the informer or prosecutor. But in 1733, when the Molasses Act was written, the
king's third was granted to the provincial treasuries. Curi-
ously, Andrews had divided the money in the traditional
fashion, clearly a violation of the Molasses Act. He thus
had little defense when the "governor and Company of the
Colony" sued him for giving Rhode Island's share of the
profits to the crown. The common-law judgment against
him amounted to over £1,000.

Few provincial judges ever became so entangled in their
own handiwork as John Andrews. Understandably fearful
that further actions as vice-admiralty judge would lead to
similar consequences, he was deterred from his duties. The
prohibition was never decided and Andrews made no move
to satisfy the common-law judgment against himself. Finally, in June 1763, months after the war ended, he pleaded
with the General Assembly to erase the judgment and allow
him to open his court. The Assembly granted his wish,
asking only that the money from the king's third, which remained in the court's custody, be turned over to the colonial
treasurer. There was little reason now to wish the court
closed. The war had ended, and trade had resumed its
normal pattern.[13]

Skillful as the Rhode Island merchants were in their
maneuvers against the vice-admiralty court, they did little
but copy a plan of action from their fellow traders in
neighboring Massachusetts. Ironically, the Rhode Islanders
were successful in their attack, while in Massachusetts the
vice-admiralty court emerged victorious from the contest.
The difference resulted largely from the difference in political structure. In Rhode Island the popularly elected gov-

13. Bartlett, ed., *Col. Recs. of R.I.*, VI, 370-73.

ernors listened to the voice of the colony. Governor Hopkins paid little heed to British suggestions that he wipe out
the illegal trading during the war, replying that it was impossible to know beforehand who intended to break laws,
and that the methods of illicit trade were unknown until
after the mischief had been done.[14] Francis Bernard of
Massachusetts, on the other hand, owed his governorship to
the British Crown and not to the pleasure of the colony's
polls. An attack against the Rhode Island Vice-Admiralty
Court was an attack against a single judge. To assault the
Massachusetts court was to challenge not only a judge, but
the royal governor and his supporters as well. It was not
surprising that Rhode Island succeeded where Massachusetts
failed.

The Massachusetts merchants who had risked trade with
the enemy and got caught suffered the condemnation of
their property in silence until Benjamin Barons, lately dismissed as customs collector for the port of Boston, rallied
them to the attack. In August 1761, they initiated five
separate actions in the common-law courts in what seemed to
Governor Bernard a deliberate and calculated scheme of
wrecking the "Court of Admiralty and the Custom house
which . . . [could not] subsist without the court."[15] Before
the battle was over, Bernard found full employment defending the court, the customs, and himself. Only two of
the cases reached final decision, but they were important
enough to upset the entire structure of customs enforcement
in the colonies.

14. Governor Hopkins to Pitt, Dec. 20, 1760, Kimball, ed., *Correspondence
of Pitt with Colonial Governors*, II, 373-77.
15. Governor Bernard to Board of Trade, Aug. 6, 1761, PRO, CO 5, 891;
Bernard to ————, Jan. 19, 1761, Bernard to ————, Jan. 21, 1761, and
Bernard to John Pownall, June 28, 1761, Bernard Letterbooks, Harvard
Univ. Lib.; Bernard to Lord Barrington, Aug. 10, 1761, Edward Channing
and Archibald Cary Coolidge, eds., *The Barrington-Bernard Correspondence
and Illustrative Matter, 1760-1770* (Cambridge, 1912), 31.

One of these cases involved a vessel belonging to John Erving, a member of the provincial council. The ship had been seized for illegal trade and libeled in Judge Chambers Russell's vice-admiralty court. After the initial proceedings, Erving took advantage of a statutory provision dating back to 1662 and *compounded* the case.[16] In effect, he admitted the charges brought against him by George Craddock, the customs collector. Rather than suffer a total confiscation of the ship and her cargo, Erving agreed to settle for £500. Then he turned to the common-law courts and sued Craddock for damages. The jury was easily convinced by his arguments, and awarded him nearly £600. Craddock thereupon appealed to the Superior Court for relief.

The issue was important. The customs officers and the vice-admiralty court would not dare to enforce the king's law if they were accountable to local juries for all their actions. No collector would risk seizing vessels if the local populace was to review the seizures. And Judge Russell would face the prospect of similar action every time he decreed a forfeiture. Governor Bernard had good cause to spend sleepless nights as the Superior Court term approached. The judges of that court caused him few worries; they were an uncommonly capable group of jurists, well aware of the importance of the issue before them. In fact, Chambers Russell was a member of that court, and could be expected to argue the side of his vice-admiralty decision with ability. But the question would also be put to a Boston jury, and it was impossible to tell how those men would decide the case.

When the trial ended it was obvious that the court had attempted to satisfy everyone. The judges upheld the crown by pronouncing the decrees of the vice-admiralty court to be of equal force with judgments at common law. But, in a

16. 14 Charles II, c. 11.

strange combination of theory and practice, the jury awarded Erving £500 damages. Craddock appealed the case to England, but Erving discharged the judgment and ended the case, rather than suffer the expense of defending the appeal. It was a halfhearted victory for the customs, the court, and Governor Bernard. Meanwhile another legal battle had begun.[17]

In January 1761, some sixty merchants of Boston had presented a petition to the General Assembly requesting an investigation of the financial operations of the vice-admiralty court. Here, as in Rhode Island, the division of profits from the sale of vessels and cargoes condemned under the provisions of the Molasses Act was questioned. The same clause of that statute that granted the king's share to the provinces stipulated that the costs of trial were to be deducted from that third after the division had been made. Usually the trial charges were subtracted from the gross profits of the sale, and the division was made from the remainder. The merchants now charged that the court had allowed illegal fees and costs to be taken from the province's share of the forfeitures.

After hearing a committee report substantiating the merchants' allegations, the Massachusetts Assembly ordered the provincial treasurer Harrison Gray to recover the money for the province. Gray followed this dictate by bringing action in an inferior common-law court against Charles Paxton, the marshal of the vice-admiralty court. The jury decided

17. Account of the composition of brig *Sarah,* Admiralty Book of Accots. of Sales &c., 1743-1765, Supreme Judicial Court of Suffolk County, Boston; Bernard to Board of Trade, Aug. 6 and 27, 1761, PRO, CO 5, 891; Bernard to John Pownall, Aug. 28, 1761, Bernard Letterbooks, Harvard Univ. Lib.; Beer, *British Colonial Policy,* 118-21; Frank Wesley Pitman, *The Development of the British West Indies, 1700-1763* (New Haven, 1917), 323-24; Andrews, "Introduction," Towle, ed., *Recs. of R.I. Vice Admiralty Court,* 51-52; Joseph Edward King, "Judicial Flotsam in Massachusetts, 1760-1765," *New England Qtly.,* 27 (1954), 372-73.

for Gray, but Paxton appealed the case to the provincial
Superior Court where it was tried without a jury. Although
Paxton quashed the proceedings on a legal technicality by
filing a plea of abatement, this did nothing to insure him
against a further trial of the case on issues. Only the ap-
proaching end of the French War deterred the merchants
from further action. Governor Bernard, with the help of
Vice-Admiralty Judge Chambers Russell and his newly appointed advocate general Robert Auchmuty, Jr., had staved
off a frontal attack on the royal prerogative. Together these
men had saved the Massachusetts customs and vice-admiralty
court from the "Machinations of a formidable confederacy."[18]

A Sea Guard Is Established

The American customs establishment was in trouble.
Letter after letter from the colonies told of campaigns against
customs officers, "independent" vice-admiralty judges, and
uncooperative governors. Customs collectors and surveyors
wrote to the Commissioners of the Customs in England, who
passed the dispatches to the Treasury Board. Naval captains
complained to the Admiralty Board, and governors wrote to
the Secretary of State for the Southern Department. As
Whitehall, the Treasury, or the Admiralty received the reports and letters, they read them and passed them around
from department to department. Many of the complaints
were not new to the readers. The difficulties of enforcing

18. Bernard to Earl of Halifax, Dec. 7, 1764, PRO, CO 5, 755; Chambers
Russell to John Cleveland, Aug. 27, 1761, PRO, Admir. 1, 3883; Depositions
of Andrew Belcher and Charles Paxton, Aug. 1761, ibid.; Bernard to Board
of Trade, Aug. 6 and 27, 1761, PRO, CO 5, 891; Journal of the House of
Representatives [Mass.], Jan. 31, 1761, Microfilm Coll. of Early State Recs.,
Mass. A.1b; Thomas Hutchinson, The History of the Colony and Province
of Massachusetts-Bay, edited by Lawrence Shaw Mayo (3 vols.; Cambridge,
1936), III, 65-67.

the navigation and trade acts had been common knowledge for years.

Anyone with a small knowledge of the geography of the New World could easily foresee one source of trouble. The long Atlantic seacoast was a succession of inlets and bays. Customs officials had always complained about the physical impossibility of surveying activities along the entire shore line. In addition, deputies who filled many of the customs posts were negligent in their duties, and the crown appointees remained in England. Those who were active, and attempted to halt illegal trading, often found themselves unable to move because of judgments against them in the common-law courts. Throughout the war some of the governors had cooperated with the merchants in their schemes to evade the trade acts and the wartime restrictions. Many of the customs officers and vice-admiralty judges had also joined the campaigns to circumvent the regulations. The vice-admiralty courts had originally been granted jurisdiction in determining violations of the acts of trade in an effort to evade colonial juries. But this advantage was of little consequence if the judges were as partial to the local merchants as the juries had been.

As long as the war continued the British put aside the letters and remonstrances and memorials for more important problems. But in February 1763, when the peace was signed and reconstruction began, the American revenue establishment became a major topic of consideration. Britain had fought much of the war in the New World, and many of the benefits from the defeat of her enemies would be reaped there. On the other hand, the war had brought Britain the tremendous debt of £140,000,000. No great skill in state planning was required to understand the obvious. The colonies, in return for their newfound safety from the French, might be expected to obey the navigation and revenue laws and, in so doing, contribute part of the cost of defending the empire. If the revenue from America paid for its own collection and the charges of the peacetime army to be stationed in the colonies, it would provide some relief to the sagging exchequer.[19]

A thorough reorganization of the colonial revenue system would take months. Statistics and testimony must be gathered, and all the departments must be solicited for suggestions and advice. In the meantime, a beginning could be made with the appointment of customs establishments and vice-admiralty courts in the new colonies created from the territory won from France. Vice-admiralty courts for Quebec and West Florida were appointed and were operating within a few years. Both establishments followed the pattern of "regular" crown institutions, with a vice-admiral's commission for the governor and commissions from the High Court of Admiralty for the court officers.[20]

This was only a beginning. During the war the officers of the Royal Navy in America had been empowered to seize vessels trading with the enemy and had been surprisingly successful in tracking down violators. Lieutenant Governor

19. On the war debt, see Curtis P. Nettels, *George Washington and American Independence* (Boston, 1951), 24. For a lower estimate, see Morgan, *Stamp Act Crisis,* 21.

20. Doctor Hugh Bailie, who seems to have been a genuine opportunist, was commissioned judge of the Quebec court in December 1763. The following March he reported Richard Morris of New York dead and obtained the commission to that court, only to have it canceled the following month when his "rumor" was found to be false. James Potts succeeded Bailie as Quebec judge. PRO, Admir. 2, 1057; *Md. Gazette,* Dec. 13, 1764. Alexander Duncan was named judge of the West Florida court in July 1766, and Alexander McPherson was commissioned register of that institution the following June. PRO, Admir. 2, 1057. There was no East Florida court until 1771 when Governor James Grant commissioned the Reverend John Forbes as judge, David Yeats, the deputy secretary of the province, as register, and John Haley as marshal. Minutes of Council Meeting, Apr. 30, 1771 PRO, Audit Office 16, 43; Charles Loch Mowat, *East Florida as a British Province, 1763-1784* (Univ. of Calif. Publications in History, XXXII [Berkeley 1943]), 16, 165.

Colden of New York, and probably others, suggested continuing this arrangement to put an end to all smuggling in the colonies.[21] Almost immediately after the French War ended, early in 1763, Parliament enacted the suggestion into a statute.[22] The "hovering" provisions, by which British customs officials had long been empowered to seize vessels that stood offshore, making no move to enter the ports, were extended to the colonies. Even more important, the act provided that captains and officers of men-of-war stationed in North American waters were to be sworn in as customs officers, with the right to seize and prosecute violators of the acts of trade. To insure swift action, the statute granted a portion of the profits from condemned seizures to the officers and crews of the naval vessels. The distribution of these shares was left to the King in Council for decision.[23]

As a result of this statute, the customs service was, in effect, expanded to the high seas. With the line of watch extended beyond the shores, the small creeks and inlets would no longer provide havens for smugglers. The Admiralty stationed forty-four vessels, ranging from ships of fifty guns to sloops, from Newfoundland to the Leeward Islands. Their officers were "impower'd by Commissions in the usual Manner under the Hands of the Commissrs of the Customs to make Seizures as Officers of that Revenue."[24]

The new regulations were scarcely in effect before the colonies protested. Merchants, accustomed to dealing with collectors and comptrollers in port towns, became concerned at this intrusion into an old and understood system. The traders protested that the American trade was "most grievous-

21. Lt. Governor Colden to William Pitt, Oct. 27, 1760, Kimball, ed., *Correspondence of Pitt with Colonial Governors*, II, 348.

22. 3 George III, c. 22.

23. *Ibid.*; Beer, *British Colonial Policy*, 228-30; Oliver M. Dickerson, *The Navigation Acts and the American Revolution* (Phila., 1951), 168-69.

24. *Md. Gazette*, Oct. 6, 1763.

ly embarrassed, by . . . men of war . . . invested with the
power of custom house officers, who . . . so vigorously execute
their office, that no vessel hardly comes in or goes out, but
they find some pretence to seize and detain her . . . and . . .
even . . . should they [be] cleared [in the vice-admiralty
courts] yet it is a great discouragement to the merchants to
have the voyage broke up by the long detention of a trial
at law."[25]

Unfortunately, the naval captains were quite ignorant
of the actual provisions of the laws of trade. Even if they
had studied the statute books and recognized each technical
offense, they could not hope to identify the practices which
were not strictly legal, but had long been sanctioned as part
of the local mercantile pattern. The sea captains were forced
to rely on the regular customs establishment for advice.
John Temple, surveyor general of the customs for the northern district, aided them as best he could, but he confessed
that they had caused him considerable trouble because of
"their Ignorance of Civil Law." He found himself burdened
with many complaints about their activities, and had been
forced to do "much writing . . . on their accounts."[26]

Temple was disturbed not merely by the ignorance of
the captains. The customs officials in North America had
long depended on their third of forfeitures for supplementary
income. The sea captains, with their commissions as customs
officers, were a direct threat to these perquisites. It was
"first come, first seize," and the navy officers could pick up
ships on the high seas, robbing the land-bound customs officials of their prey. No collector or searcher could view this
innovation with much enthusiasm. In theory, the customhouse officers and the captains of the men-of-war were to
collaborate in enforcing the trade laws. But the jealousy

25. *Newport Mercury*, May 21, 1764.
26. Temple to the Treasury, Sept. 10, 1764, PRO, Treas. 1, 429.

over the seizure shares "entirely destroyed and rendered impracticable a Connection" between them. Instead of working together, they became competitors, and the custom-house personnel continued to solicit for coasting vessels of their own.[27]

A third group soon joined the chorus of protest against the sea captains. Just as the customs officials depended on forfeitures as a source of income, the provincial governors had always enjoyed a share of the profits. In some provinces, the governor's shares were estimated to bring in as much as £200 annually. Now the new regulations presented a direct threat to the governors' emoluments. On the first day of June 1763, the King in Council ordered one-half of the forfeitures paid to the officers and seamen of the Royal Navy and the other half reserved for the British Exchequer. Of the half granted to the naval officers, one-fourth was to go to the admiral, or commanding flag officer, on the American station. The remaining three-fourths was to be divided among the officers and crew of the vessel making the seizure. The orders made no mention of the governor's third, and the directed distribution was certain to create difficulties.[28]

Cadwallader Colden, lieutenant governor of New York, was the first governor to fight the new regulation. Captain Hawker, of the sloop of war *Sardoine,* seized a ship and cargo off Sandy Hook late in 1763. He reported his "prize" to Colden and informed him that he intended to claim one-half of the proceeds for his officers and crew. Colden objected, pointing out that the statutes under which the seizure was made promised one-third of the profits to the governor

27. Quotation from Governor Bernard to the Board of Trade, Apr. 28, 1766, PRO, CO 5, 892. See also John Brown to Charles Apthorp and Apthorp to Brown, Dec. 10, 1763, PRO, Admir. 1, 482; Harrington, *New York Merchants,* 272.

28. On governors' thirds, see Francis Bernard's "Observations on the Account of the Expenses . . . ," Dec. 31, 1766, PRO, Treas. 1, 452. For the Orders in Council, see PRO, Admir. 1, 3866.

of the colony. He told Hawker that he could not give up his rights but suggested that they leave the matter to the decision of the vice-admiralty judge Richard Morris.

Captain Hawker, however, had no intention of surrendering his seizure to the whims of a judge. He sought out the advice of Attorney General John Tabor Kempe and lawyer William Smith, Jr. Neither of them assured him of success, warning that the Governor's claim was as good or better than his. Still persistent, Hawker reported his predicament to Admiral Colville at Halifax. The Admiral had dealt with governors before, and came to the Captain's rescue. He dispatched a letter to Judge Morris "so warm that it . . . either intimidated or made him so cautious that he did not as usually decree one-third [each] to King, Governor and prosecutor, but in general terms to His Majesty and such persons as are intituled to the same."[29] The money from the sale was held by the court until the question of distribution was settled.

Governor Colden reported these developments to the Board of Trade and to General Monckton in England, hoping to enlist their aid in the skirmish. He told Monckton that he had heard of a similar case recently tried in Boston where the judge had decreed the old division.[30] He might have heard of the Massachusetts case, but he did not mention

29. Colden to General Monckton, Jan. 21, 1764, Mass. Hist. Soc., *Collections*, 4th ser., 10 (1871), 512-13. Kempe's and Smith's opinions, and Colville's letter to Judge Morris, Dec. 8, 1763, are printed in George Chalmers, *Opinions of Eminent Lawyers on Various Points of English Jurisprudence, Chiefly Concerning the Colonies, Fisheries and Commerce of Great Britain; Collected and Digested, from the Originals in the Board of Trade, and Other Depositories* (London, 1858), 577-79. See also Judge Morris to Colville, Dec. 30, 1763, and Morris to General Monckton, Jan. 28, 1764, Chalmers Papers, N.Y., IV, N.Y. Pub. Lib.; Kempe to Colville, Dec. 31, 1763, John Tabor Kempe Papers, N.Y. Hist. Soc.; and *John Brown qui tam* v. *The Sloop Patience and 92 Hhds of Wine*, Minutes of the Vice-Admiralty Court of the Province of New York, Lib. Cong. Photostats and N.Y. Vice-Admiralty Court Papers, National Archives.

30. Colden to the Board of Trade, Feb. 19, 1764, PRO, CO 5, 1071.

Governor Bernard's troubles, which greatly resembled his own.

Bernard's difficulties began when Admiral Colville claimed the navy's share of a seizure condemned in the vice-admiralty court in Massachusetts. The Governor was indignant at the thought of being deprived of his traditional share. He admitted to the Board of Trade that he would "be extremely glad to receive an annual Sum in lieu of . . . [his] share of forfeitures; for . . . there is no money more hardly earned than what a Governor receives from forfeitures." But without such an "annual Sum" he was ready to do battle to retain the old division.[31] He complained that the "rights" of "all the Governors in America . . . [were being] sacrificed to inrich one Admiral."[32] Other governors echoed his words. In Virginia, Governor Fauquier and Captain Sterling of His Majesty's Ship *Rainbow* were arguing over their shares in a seizure. They finally compromised and agreed to abide by the decision of a similar case that Governor Penn of Pennsylvania was reported to have appealed to the High Court of Admiralty of England. Sea captains and governors in Barbados and the Leeward Islands were embroiled in similar arguments.[33]

Each side was anxious to see the issue determined in its favor. When the governors' complaints reached England, the question was put to Attorney General Charles Yorke. He reported that the meaning was quite unclear from the statutes and advised amending the 1763 act. Until that could be done, Yorke believed that the old division should be continued.[34]

31. Governor Bernard to the Board of Trade, Apr. 10, 1764, *ibid.*, 891; Admiral Colville to Philip Stephens, Nov. 24, Dec. 26, 1763, and Jan. 22, 1764, in PRO, Admir. 1, 482.

32. Governor Bernard to Richard Jackson, Feb. 13, 1764, Bernard Letterbooks, Harvard Univ. Lib.

33. Governor Fauquier to the Board of Trade, Jan. 25, 1765, PRO, CO 5, 1331; Philip Stephens to Charles Jenkinson, Nov. 8, 1764, PRO, Treas. 1, 431.

34. For Yorke's opinion, see PRO, Admir. 1, 4286.

The Revenue Act of 1764 contained an amendment which attempted to differentiate between seizures on land and sea; but the quarrel continued. The wording of the "clarification" was as vague as the original orders had been contradictory. The governors were to receive their third of all forfeitures inflicted under "this, or any other act of Parliament relating to the trade and revenues" of the colonies. "But seizures made at sea by the King's ship" were to be divided between the king and the prosecutors. Admiral Colville, still eager for the profits from the "prizes" and "captures," saw little hope that these words would untangle the problem. He feared "that the American Lawyers, Judges and Governours . . . would say that *nothing is the Sea but that part of the Ocean which is without the Coast.*" His predictions came true. Two years later, the governors and the sea officers were still arguing over the "mercantile plunder."[35]

Parliament Passes the "Black Act"[36]

The squabble between the sea captains and the governors soon disappeared in the confusion of a larger battle. Even George Grenville, who, as First Lord of the Admiralty, had been largely responsible for the Navy Act, viewed the legislation as a stopgap. If the commissioning of naval officers as customs officials reduced illegal trading in the colonies, the scheme might well be continued and expanded.

35. The attempt to divide the cases into two groups in the 1764 Revenue Act is in 4 George III, c. 15, sections xli and xlii. Colville's statement is from a letter to Philip Stephen, Sept. 22, 1764, PRO, Admir. 1, 482. See also Earl of Halifax to Cadwallader Colden, June 9, 1764, PRO, CO 5, 1097; John Watts to Robert Monckton, Feb. 22, 1766, Mass. Hist. Soc., *Collections,* 4th ser., 10 (1871), 589-91; and below, 77-78, 116.

36. John Rowe's Diary, Sept. 29, 1764, Anne Rowe Cunningham, ed., *Letters and Diary of John Rowe, Boston Merchant, 1759-1762, 1764-1779* (Boston, 1903), 64-65.

But greater changes were in the offing, regardless of the success of the sea guard. Grenville had left the Admiralty even before the statute passed Parliament. He now headed the ministry as First Lord of the Treasury and Chancellor of the Exchequer. Mr. Grenville had plans for the American colonies.

Until this time the British navigation acts had been viewed largely as regulatory legislation. The intent of the generations of Englishmen who had devised the measures had been to strengthen the commerce of the empire, to create a self-sufficient world with London as its hub. The colonies, in the traditional mercantile definition, were useful as sources of supply and as markets for the fabrications of the British shops. Trade was confined largely to intercourse between the various parts of the empire: Great Britain, the West Indies, the American colonies, and the rising dominions in the East. The whole complicated, confusing mass of restrictions and regulations, duties and drawbacks had been designed to enhance British commerce.

The fact that enforcing these acts of trade resulted in revenue for the crown had been, until now, a secondary consideration. There was no better way to deter men from breaking rules than to punish them with fines or to confiscate their property. The traditional method of discouraging undesirable commerce, short of outright prohibition, was to tax it with duties. Out of this, quite naturally, annual sums were added to the royal exchequer. As the volume of trade increased through the years, the sums grew correspondingly larger. It had not been unpleasant to the crown to receive this income, but the money was generally regarded as a by-product of a more comprehensive policy.

George Grenville, however, had more immediate problems than abstract theories of empire-building. The tremendous war debt was a reality. A glance at the charges on the annual budget indicated that, in pounds and shillings, the account between the crown and the colonies was unbalanced. The crown was losing money on its colonies, and now, with an even larger area to defend and protect, it would lose even more. There was a limit beyond which no ministry could tax the British people and continue in office, and that limit had already been approximated. The inescapable answer was colonial taxation, if not to the point of contributing to reduction of the war debt, then at least a substantial contribution to the current charges of their own defense.

An indication that the tide had turned, and that the old plantation system was to be remolded into a revenue-producing machinery, was soon apparent. Grenville and Charles Jenkinson his assistant, who was later to be his successor at the Treasury, scanned the customhouse records and the mass of dispatches from the American crown servants. In October 1763, they presented their ideas to the Privy Council. Their memorial has been called one of the most important papers of this critical period. It was a blueprint for the future, changing the course of the customs establishment, the vice-admiralty courts, and, in the end, the British Empire itself.[37]

The facts were plain to read. Through "Neglect, Connivance and Fraud," the revenues from America amounted to less than one-fourth the cost of collecting them. This was the problem. The Treasury officials informed the Privy Council that they had already done their part in closing the gap. They had ordered the officers of the American customs "to their respective Stations and constantly to reside there for the future." They had reviewed the entire colonial establishment and were prepared to "supply the Deficiency" in personnel where necessary. All officers had been sent new orders demanding "the strictest attention of their Duty" and

37. The memorial is printed in *Acts of the Privy Council: Colonial Series*, IV, 569-72. See also Andrews, *Colonial Period*, IV, 217-20.

constant reports of their activities. The Commissioners of the Customs had been ordered "immediately to dismiss every Officer . . . Deficient in his Duty."

This much the Treasury had done by itself, but it requested assistance from the other departments. The colonial governors should be ordered to pay strict attention to suppressing the "clandestine and prohibited Trade . . . and the Improvement of the Revenue." The military and naval commanders in America should be directed to support the officers of the revenue. The sea guard should not only be "continued, but even extended and strengthened as far as the Naval Establishment will allow." Finally, the Treasury Board suggested a "new and better method of condemning Seizures made in the Colonies."

The last suggestion was not spelled out in great detail. The Treasury knew only that the Commissioners of the Customs had reported to them "that they had received various complaints of great Difficulties and Partialities in the Trials . . . and the several Statutes in force . . . vary so much both as to the Mode and Place of Trial, that the Officers of the Revenue when they have made a Seizure cannot but be under great Doubt and Uncertainty, in what manner they should proceed to the condemnation of it." Some new method should be devised: "an Uniform Plan . . . for establishing the Judicature of the Courts of Admiralty . . . under Persons qualified for so important a Trust, in order that Justice . . . [might] in all Cases be dilegently and impartially administered."

The Privy Council approved the memorial immediately and ordered the cooperation of the various departments in arranging the administrative details for effecting its suggestions. Although the Board of Trade, the Admiralty, and the Secretary of State for the Southern Department communicated with each other throughout the winter on various

schemes, most of the planning for changing the vice-admiralty courts was left to the Admiralty Board. In March it
reached a decision. A new court, headed by an eminent
person trained in the civil law appeared to fit the Treasury's
requirements. This court would have jurisdiction over all
the North American colonies, but it would not supersede
the provincial vice-admiralty courts completely. It would
have no more power than the vice-admiralty courts, except
that violations committed in any of the colonies might be
taken to the new court for trial. The old courts would remain as they were, with no increase in jurisdiction.[38]

Just how the Admiralty decided on this scheme is unknown. Perhaps a suggestion from the colonies was the
deciding factor. In 1729 Parliament had passed an act desig-
nating the vice-admiralty courts at Boston and New York
the sole tribunals for prosecuting offenses against the royal
reservations of white pine trees in New England. The enforcement of the pine laws had been far from successful, both
before and after the statute was passed. Benning Wentworth, surveyor general of His Majesty's woods, was greatly troubled by his failure to halt trespassers and was even
more fearful that Jared Ingersoll, an enterprising lawyer, might be appointed judge of a proposed vice-admiralty
court in Connecticut. In 1761 Ingersoll and some of his
associates received a contract for supplying masts for the
Royal Navy; this contract threatened the Wentworth family's
virtual monopoly of the masting business. With this opening
wedge, Ingersoll's faction hoped to divert the trade in ship
timbers from Portsmouth to the Connecticut River. One of
their schemes for accomplishing this "robbery" of a Wentworth family preserve was to have a vice-admiralty court
established in Connecticut, which was then within the jurisdiction of Lewis Morris' New York court. They believed

38. *Acts of the Privy Council: Colonial Series,* IV, 663.

that in this way they might control prosecutions involving the entrenched and active interests of the trade. To forestall such a development, and to release himself from dependence on the judges at New York and Boston, Wentworth suggested that Britain appoint "a judge of Vice Admiralty, whose authority should extend over all the King's colonies, in matters relative to the woods set apart for His Majesty's use."[39]

This may have been the suggestion that determined the scheme adopted by the Admiralty. There are other possibilities. The jurisdiction of the provincial vice-admiralty courts had always been limited to cases arising within the borders of their own province. A seizure in Pennsylvania had to be tried in the Pennsylvania court, regardless of the residence of the ship's owners, or the place of its registry. Naval captains and customs officials alike protested this restriction, arguing that by moving cases to the courts of their choice they could eliminate trials before judges who seemed loath to decree against local merchants.[40]

Regardless of the source of the plan, the Admiralty's single judge over all America promised to be but a figurehead. His court was to have concurrent jurisdiction with the provincial vice-admiralty courts, but no power of hearing appeals from them. With offenses under all of the acts of trade and navigation cognizable only in the courts of the dominion or territory where the offense was committed, the new supercourt waited upon Parliament for a grant of jurisdiction. Such a grant was not long in coming. Grenville's master plan for the collection of colonial revenue had been approved by Parliament, and on April 5, 1764, the bill

39. *Board of Trade Journal [1759-1763]*, 420; Lawrence Henry Gipson, *Jared Ingersoll: A Study of American Loyalism in Relation to British Colonial Government* (New Haven, 1920), 94-110; and below, 171-75.

40. Captain Hawker to Admiral Colville, Dec. 12, 1763; Admiral Colville to Philip Stephens, Oct. 25 and Dec. 21, 1763, PRO, Admir. 1, 482.

which he sponsored was sanctioned by George III. One clause of the new Revenue Act provided that all prosecutions for infringement of any of the acts of trade might be initiated in any court of record (common-law court), any provincial vice-admiralty court, or "any Court of Vice Admiralty which may or shall be appointed over all America." The new court was thus provided with a reason for being.[41]

This Revenue Act did more than grant jurisdiction to the new supercourt. The most familiar of its provisions reduced the duty on foreign molasses from six to three pence per gallon, from which the statute has ever since been known as the "Sugar Act." Because the object of the act was revenue, the regulations of the wine trade, lumber exports, and textile imports were modified to increase the crown's income; the king's share of forfeitures, which had been granted to the provinces by the Molasses Act of 1733, was once again to go to the royal treasury. Furthermore, the customs officials were given new aid in the prosecution of their seizures.

One innovation was the opportunity for the customs officials to carry their cases to the seat of the new court. In addition, the "burden of proof" in trials under the trade acts was passed on to the claimants of the seized property. It was now the duty of the person whose vessel was seized to produce evidence that no statute had been violated, while the customs official merely refuted the points which the claimant raised. Even if no condemnation was decreed, and the ship and cargo were released from custody and delivered to the owner, the vice-admiralty judge could decide if a *probable cause* for seizure had existed. If he decided that there had

41. 4 George III, c. 15. Before the act was passed, the advocate, attorney, and solicitor general warned the Admiralty that "such a judge . . . could not have jurisdiction in cases where particular Acts of Parliament had confined the recovery of penalties to local jurisdiction." *Acts of the Privy Council: Colonial Series,* VI, 365. The orders, memorials, opinions, and warrants for the new court and its officers are conveniently assembled in House of Lords Mss., Item 226, Lib. Cong. Photostats.

been a probable cause, the judge was authorized to tax the costs of trial on the claimant, and no action could be brought against the prosecutor or informer in the common-law courts. In seizing suspected violators, customs officers no longer needed to hesitate for fear of having to pay the costs of dismissed or acquitted cases, or of being hauled before a jury on charges of false arrest. Even if the vice-admiralty judge failed to declare a probable cause for seizure, and a disgruntled merchant or captain attempted to revenge himself by suit at common law, the king's servant could plead the general issue. He could deny by a general plea the whole declaration or indictment against him at once, thereby placing the "burden of proof" upon his opponent. Treble costs were authorized if the jury awarded the revenue officials the verdict, or if cases were nonsuited or discontinued. Furthermore, if an action at common law was begun against a customs officer, and the common-law court decided that a probable cause for seizure had existed, the person bringing suit was allowed no more than two pence damages; the customs officer could be fined not more than one shilling.[42]

These procedural advantages granted to customs officers were not peculiar to the colonies, or even to admiralty law. "In the interests of good government," all courts in England had long operated under statutory rules that allowed the crown's servants freedom of activity not enjoyed by private persons. Beginning with the Poor Relief Act of 1601, various legal benefits had been written into law: pleading the general

42. Governor Bernard of Massachusetts had suggested such protection to crown officers the year before. He warned the Earl of Halifax that if the customhouse officers did "not appear to have the public support of the Crown in what they do according to the best advice they can procure," he was "convinced that a Combination . . . [would] soon be made to distress & embarass them by appeals & actions at common law for doing their duty in the most plain & positive cases." Bernard to Halifax, Dec. 2, 1763, in Quincy, *Massachusetts Reports*, 394. The Revenue Act of 1764 did not, however, "abolish jury trial" as stated by Philip Davidson in *Propaganda and the American Revolution, 1763-1783* (Chapel Hill, 1941), 106.

issue; short periods of limitation; and double and treble costs if judgment was given for officials in actions against them arising from their duties. The English common-law courts were prepared to protect constables in cases where they arrested persons under a "probable and *bona fide* belief that a felony had been committed." Even with these advantages, the liability of local government officials to be sued by aggrieved persons at times proved a hardship to them.[43]

Such a comparison with the English law would have done little to relieve the minds of the colonial merchants when they first saw the new Revenue Act. Rumors and reports of the impending legislation had been heard in the colonies all spring. Now that the actual provisions were known, it was even worse than had been hinted. There was hardly a bright spot in the whole "Black Act," unless it was the enabling clause which set the twenty-ninth day of September for the inauguration of the new duties and regulations. The colonists at least had a few months to decipher the voluminous code, to discover how its requirements would influence each merchant's particular business, and to watch the establishment of the new vice-admiralty court.

The Admiralty was busy that June, determining both a location and officers for the new court. For want of a better suggestion the board accepted Admiral Colville's request that the court be established at Halifax, the headquarters of his North American fleet. Since the sea captains were expected to continue their effective customs work, Colville may have desired the court close at hand, where he could make certain that the fleet officers received their share of forfeitures. The Admiral was convinced that the provincial judges were "too much interested in the Welfare of their Neighbours" and "intimidated . . . by the Threats and well known mobbish Disposition of the Inhabitants" of the col-

43. Holdsworth, *History of English Law*, X, 157, 252-53.

onies. He assured the Admiralty that "all these Inconveniences might be very well avoided, by sending the Prizes" to Halifax for trial.[44]

The ministry was much more concerned with the appointment of a judge than with the place where he would hold his court. A man well-trained in civil law was needed, a lawyer whose reputation was great enough for his decrees and pronouncements to command respect throughout the continent. But the post would carry a respectable salary and afford a certain dignity; it could not be wasted on someone without influence. Such positions were needed to satisfy the incessant demands on the patronage. Fortunately, a man who fulfilled both requirements was discovered. William Spry had married a niece of William Pitt, and deserved to be taken care of. A practicing civilian at Doctors' Commons, he was dignified with the title of Doctor of Laws. On May 28, he was named judge of the new court, with a fixed salary of £800 sterling a year. This stipend was to come from the king's share of forfeitures as provided under the new act, or, if this was insufficient, from the fund accumulated from the sale of old and obsolete naval stores in England.[45]

This salary was not to be paid to Spry until he had settled himself at Halifax. The minor offices, however, were probably viewed as sinecures, capable of deputization, from the very outset. Spencer Percival, to whom the Admiralty had already granted reversionary rights in the registership of the High Court of Admiralty, was named register of the

44. Admiral Colville to Philip Stephens, Oct. 25 and Dec. 21, 1763, PRO, Admir. 1, 482.

45. Minutes of Council Meeting, Mar. 26, 1764, PRO, Treas. 1, 429; Admiralty to High Court of Admiralty, May 29, 1764, PRO, Admir. 2, 1057; *Mass. Gazette*, Aug. 9 and Oct. 4, 1764; *N.Y. Mercury*, July 30, 1764; *Md. Gazette*, Aug. 9, 1764; *Ga. Gazette*, Aug. 23, 1764; Emory Washburn, *Sketches of the Judicial History of Massachusetts from 1630 to the Revolution in 1775* (Boston, 1840), 175; Charles M. Andrews, *Guide to the Materials for American History, to 1783, in the Public Record Office of Great Britain* (2 vols.; Washington, 1912-14), II, 47n.

new court in August. At the same time Charles Howard was commissioned as marshal.[46] The Admiralty pondered the problem of establishing the new court on a regular basis for many weeks. Each of the provincial vice-admiralty courts was nominally headed by the governor, by virtue of his commission as vice-admiral. If this tradition was to be followed, an entirely new office must be established. The Admiralty would have to commission a "Vice Admiral Over All America." In December 1764, the Earl of Northumberland was named to the high-sounding, but empty, position.[47]

Judge Spry understood well enough that he was expected to establish his court in short order. It took several weeks, however, to collect his family and belongings and get under way for Halifax. When he finally arrived in the Nova Scotia seaport in September 1764, the news of his coming quickly passed from colony to colony. Two generations of colonials had conducted their mercantile houses under the old provincial courts, and the presence of a trained doctor of civil law in a far-off naval station, opening a new court with powers stretching southward to the Floridas, was something to be feared. Throughout the mercantile towns, men wondered how much the "Black Act" and the new court would change their businesses and their profits. Time alone would reveal what those scarlet robes in the Halifax Courthouse signified to the American trader.[48]

46. Admiralty to High Court of Admiralty, June 26 and July 19, 1764 PRO, Admir. 2, 1057; *Mass. Gazette,* Oct. 11, 1764; *Conn. Courant,* Oct. 29 1764; *S.C. Gazette,* Oct. 15-22, 1764; *Md. Gazette,* Oct. 25, 1764; *Ga. Gazette* Nov. 1, 1764.

47. Philip Stephens to Samuel Seddon, May 11, 1764, and Admiralty Warrant to High Court of Admiralty, PRO, Admir. 2, 1057; *Acts of the Privy Council: Colonial Series,* IV, 663-64, VI, 364-65; Beer, *British Colonia Policy,* 249-51.

48. *Mass. Gazette,* Oct. 11, 1764; *N.Y. Mercury,* Oct. 22, 1764; *Ga. Gazette* Dec. 6, 1764.

3

From Sugar to Stamps

A SET of fugitives and vagabonds . . . kept in fear by a fleet and an army" inhabited that "obscure Corner of His Majestys Dominions, calld Hallifax."[1] There, the British Admiralty had constructed a lighthouse and a dry dock, and the port was now the rendezvous for the North American fleet. It was also the seat of Doctor William Spry's new court of vice-admiralty. Admiral Colville and William Spry! Naval officer and vice-admiralty judge! This alliance had the effect of making the town suddenly become foreign and distant. To tradesmen in Georgia it was as remote as London itself, and even Boston merchants no longer looked upon Halifax as a neighboring port. It was a cold and distant place to which conspiring sea captains intended to carry vessels and cargoes for condemnation by a powerful new judge. Vice-admiralty judges had always been

1. John Watts to Moses Frank, Dec. 22, 1765, *The Letter Book of John Watts*, N.Y. Hist. Soc., *Collections* (1928), 407; John Adams' Diary, Adams, ed., *Works of John Adams*, II, 173.

colonials, local men who understood the difficulties of commercial ventures. But Doctor Spry had never before set
foot on the continent. Moreover, he had been trained in the
ecclesiastical and admiralty courts at Doctors' Commons, a
place in London that retained something of the ill repute of
prerogative courts and the Star Chamber.

The learned doctor, helping his family off the brig *Polly*
after the passage from England, was unconscious of the
chatter in the coffeehouses of America. The angry talk
would not have concerned him anyway. He had never been
exposed to a struggle more intense than the word-battles at
Doctors' Commons, and he did not anticipate combat as part
of his new duties. He had come to Halifax to sit in judgment according to the law maritime and the statutes of
the British Parliament. The customs officials and naval
captains would bring their seizures before him. His salary
was fixed and secure; whether he tried one cause or a
thousand, his £800 sterling could not be denied him.

The new judge wasted no time, however, in arranging his
work. After the ceremonious reading of his commission in
Halifax Courthouse, he drew up an announcement to adver-
tise that he had opened shop. He began the notice with the
clause of the Revenue Act that established his jurisdiction.
Then he fixed the "term days" for the first and third Wednes-
days of each month, "when and where all Causes, civil and
maritime, arising in any Province of America or maritime
Parts thereof, or thereto adjacent . . . [might] be prosecuted."
When he had finished he handed the announcement to the
printer of the Halifax *Gazette*. By mid-November 1764,
most of the provincial newspapers had copied the notice.
Judge Spry sat back and waited for the seizures to be brought
to Halifax.[2]

2. *Mass. Gazette,* Nov. 1 and 15, 1764; *Newport Mercury,* Oct. 29, 1764;
N.Y. Mercury, Nov. 12, 1764.

Collectors and Captains

Doctor Spry had hurried to ready his court for business, for every event indicated that there would be much work to do. The naval captains and customs officers in the colonies had also scurried about, preparing to enforce the new regulations when they took effect on September 29, 1764. By that time, most of the absentee customs officials had either resigned their posts or settled themselves in the colonies. Released at last from dependence on both colonial juries and provincial vice-admiralty judges, the sea captains and customs officers could hope to do the ministry's bidding and make money at it. The governors had been instructed to lend them every assistance within their power.

Cooperation between customs officers and governors was not easily perfected, however. On the very day before the new statute was to go into effect, Massachusetts resounded with excitement over a quarrel between Governor Francis Bernard and Surveyor General of the Customs John Temple. With almost uncanny timing, a struggle that had been developing for months erupted into open combat at the very time the crown's servants in America were expected to unite in common action. The personal antagonism and jealousy between Temple and Bernard threatened both the revenue and the royal prerogative.

The customs officials in America had never strictly enforced the Molasses Act of 1733. The methods of circumventing the statute varied from colony to colony, but in Massachusetts the merchants' usual procedure was to declare that they carried only British cargoes, while the revenue officers shut their eyes to the foreign molasses and sugar. The customs officers (and the governors themselves) were kept happy in the arrangement by timely presents of wines and fresh fruits. This pleasant understanding had been long established, and few people considered it out of the ordinary. But now, with the ministry in Britain intent on enforcing the new legislation, and with a reputation to establish in his office, Surveyor General John Temple found the practice illegal.

Temple was on good terms with the Massachusetts merchants, and he probably hesitated to endanger those relations. But he looked upon the Masachusetts Governor as his personal enemy. He waited, watching for an opportunity to strike Bernard a blow that would end his days of governing in America. That opportunity came in late September 1764. Temple had decided a month before that the affairs of the Salem customhouse needed investigation. Molasses and sugar shipped from that port were always in excess of the quantities officially entered, and no person could imagine that the farmers around Salem were raising sugar cane. James Cockle, the customs collector of the port of Salem, held his appointment through the good offices of Governor Bernard, with whom he had retained a close and constant contact.

On inspecting the books and records of the Salem customhouse, Temple discovered many discrepancies, but he needed a dramatic and timely event to act upon. Then early in September a vessel arrived in Salem, loaded with foreign sugars and carrying a document purporting to be a clearance from Anguilla, a dot of thirty-five square miles in the Leeward Islands. Shortly after the ship docked, Cockle received news that the document was a forgery, and he hastened to Boston to consult with the Governor. Bernard invited him to spend the weekend at Castle William, and together they drafted a letter to the governor of Anguilla. In the meantime, Temple had heard of the forgery. He delayed action until Monday, when Bernard and Cockle finally informed him of the situation. Then he broke into a rage, charging them with deliberately keeping the knowledge from him so that the ship might escape with little punishment. The king's treasury, he claimed, had been robbed of an immense amount of revenue that would have come from the sale of the ship and cargo if he had been notified in time to begin a proper information in the vice-admiralty court. And he alleged that other vessels had also slipped through his hands because he had not been properly informed.

It was true that the Governor and Cockle had allowed the captain to compound for his ship and cargo in the vice-admiralty court for the legal minimum, one-third of their estimated value. Temple, however, overstated his case. The seizure was made before the new Revenue Act, and the new division of forfeitures, went into effect. It was the Massachusetts Treasury and not the king's exchequer that suffered. The surveyor general did not take time to argue this point; he was after other game. He began to beat the bushes around Salem for further charges against Cockle, anything that might be used to dismiss him from his post. In a short time he found witnesses willing to testify that Cockle had accepted bribes, and on these grounds he suspended him from office on September 28.

The suspension was a direct affront to Governor Bernard, who had shielded and befriended the collector. It caused an open rupture in the Massachusetts customs establishment, and it made Temple a hero to the mercantile community. Bernard never admitted that Cockle had succumbed to bribery or that he had been anything but an honest customs collector. Whatever the truth, the Massachusetts traders were pleased to have him gone. At Salem the merchants celebrated his suspension "by firing guns, making bonfires, entertainments, &c; and the Surveyor General [was] much applauded by the merchants in the town of Boston for his good and spirited behaviour."[3]

Unfortunately, there was little else to celebrate that month, for the new trading regulations indicated a bleak future. The merchants in Massachusetts were not alone in their fear of Mr. Grenville's "Black Act." They would feel the effect of the duties on foreign molasses more than the merchants of other provinces because the molasses commerce was largely in the hands of the New England shippers. But in the southern colonies, where the wide rivers had delayed the growth of seaports, and coasting vessels had long docked at the planters' own wharves, the new procedures for loading and unloading vessels, clearing and entering customhouses soon proved as damaging as any tax on molasses. Some provisions in the Revenue Act would affect all of the colonial traders. The new safeguards against actions at common law granted to customs officials removed a tempering device by which colonials had restrained overzealous officers from indiscriminate seizing.

Furthermore, the customs officers were now freed from accounting for their actions as long as the vice-admiralty judges held that their seizures resulted from a probable cause. And the new vice-admiralty court at Halifax loomed as an agent of oppression. This was more than a question of losing the comfort of acquaintanceship with the vice-admiralty

3. John Rowe's diary, Sept. 29, 1764, Mass. Hist. Soc., *Proceedings,* 2nd ser., 10 (1896), 60. In this matter, the merchants' reactions to Cockle's dismissal are most paradoxical. If, as Bernard maintained, the collector had never deviated from his duties, the merchants' pleasure at his removal is understandable. But Temple's charges, however overstated they might have been, clearly indicated laxness in the Salem customhouse. On the whole episode, see John Temple to Customs Commissioners, Sept. 10, 1764, and other papers, PRO, Treas. 1, 429; Bernard to Earl of Halifax, Dec. 7 and 29, 1764, PRO, CO 5, 755; Temple to Thomas Whately, Sept. 10 and Oct. 3, 1764, Mass. Hist. Soc., *Collections,* 6th ser., 9 (1897), 26-29; *Acts of the Privy Council: Colonial Series,* VI, 372-74, 377-80; Hutchinson, *History of Massachusetts-Bay,* III, 116-18; Joseph Edward King, "Judicial Flotsam in Massachusetts," *New England Qtly.,* 27 (1954), 377-79.

judge. Halifax was a frontier community with which many merchants had no established trading relations. If vessels were to be carried there for trial, a defense must be organized and argued. Where were the lawyers to come from? What merchant could afford the price of court fees and trial charges for so complicated an operation?

Complaining to fellow merchants in coffeehouses and taverns might afford temporary relief to the exasperated colonials, but it would do nothing to change the regulations. More forceful action was needed. In New York, Rhode Island, and Massachusetts the merchants did not wait to observe the execution of the new regulations. They turned to their provincial assemblies and asked for petitions for relief. In these statements of protest, grievances over the methods of enforcing the trade regulations were as prominent as the complaints about the regulations themselves.[4]

The new court at Halifax, key to the enforcement program, was heavily criticized. The merchants found four objections to the new regulations regarding trial procedures. First, Doctor Spry's court was situated at one extremity of the continent, and it was possible that "many persons, however legally their goods may have been imported . . . [would] lose their property, merely from an inability of following after it, and making that defence which they might do if the trial had been in the Colony where the goods were seized."[5] This was an objection to Spry's court alone. The colonists understood what the law stated: that seizures from any place on the continent might be removed to Halifax for trial. They

4. *Md. Gazette,* Dec. 27, 1764; *N.Y. Mercury,* Dec. 10, 1764; *Boston Evening Post,* Mar. 11, 1765; *Providence Gazette,* Jan. 23, 1765; Stephen Hopkins, *The Rights of Colonies Examined* (Providence, 1764), reprinted in Bartlett, ed., *Col. Recs. of R.I.,* VI, 422; see also Oxenbridge Thacher, *Sentiments of a British American* (Boston, 1764), 7-11, for a forceful statement of the American objections to admiralty jurisdiction.
5. Petition of the Massachusetts Council and House of Representatives to the House of Commons, Mass. Hist. Soc., *Collections,* 6th ser., 9 (1897), 33.

knew that the provincial vice-admiralty courts' jurisdiction had not been extended; these courts were still restricted to determining cases arising within their own boundaries.[6]

The second criticism also applied only to Spry's court. The new judge's salary of £800 a year was to be paid out of the proceeds from the seizures he condemned, or, if this sum was insufficient, from the sale of old naval stores in England. The colonial petitioners protested this arrangement. They claimed that it made the judge dependent on his own actions for his salary and inferred that he would always condemn seizures to insure his wages. The argument, however, had little basis in fact. The provincial vice-admiralty judges had always depended on their percentages from condemnations and their fees from trials as their only source of payment. Judge Spry, on the other hand, had been granted a permanent salary, to be paid regardless of the profits of condemnations.

The merchants directed their other two arguments as much against the provincial vice-admiralty courts as the new Halifax tribunal. The clause of the statute authorizing judges to proclaim a probable cause of seizure, and thereby prohibit common-law actions against customs officers, applied to all of the vice-admiralty courts. The merchants viewed the abolition of their legal defense against false arrests and seizures as a major grievance. Perhaps, they said, such actions had been indiscriminately used in the past and had hampered the activities of the customs officers; but to absolve the crown officials of all liability for their actions

6. For examples of confusion among historians on this point, see Edward Channing, *A History of the United States* (6 vols.; N.Y., 1905-25), III, 43; James Truslow Adams, *Revolutionary New England, 1691-1776* (Boston, 1927), 296; and Curtis P. Nettels, *The Roots of American Civilization* (N.Y., 1938), 615: "An act of 1764 authorized the erection of a general vice-admiralty court for all the colonies, with the provision that penalties arising from violation of the acts of trade might be recovered in *any* colonial admiralty or vice-admiralty court. . . ." [italics mine].

would open the door to wanton and unrestricted plundering of the colonial trade. In the same fashion, the power granted to colonial judges to fix the trial costs on the merchants, regardless of the merits of the seizures, threatened to place the traders wholly at the mercy of the customs officials.

The final objection to the new regulations was grounded in constitutional principle. The petition of the Massachusetts legislature stated the argument very clearly: "The extention of the powers of the Courts of Vice Admiralty have . . . deprived the colonies of one of the most valuable of English liberties, trials by juries."[7] In England, violations of the trade laws were tried in the common-law Exchequer Court, with a jury. In America, a single judge would determine the case, following civil-law procedures that made no provision for a jury. Many Americans concluded that this distinction placed them in an unequal position, depriving them of a sacred right, a precious part of the English Constitution. This argument applied to the provincial courts, as well as to Judge Spry's tribunal.[8]

The colonial position was based on the argument that the Revenue Act of 1764 was a clear departure from earlier trade laws. Legislation for regulation and legislation for revenue were two different things, and if the British intended to raise taxes in America (a right by no means agreed to), the Americans should be allowed the same constitutional liberty as Englishmen: they should be tried for infringement of the revenue laws by a jury of their peers. This argument and the British rebuttal were to persist during the pre-Revolutionary years.

From the British viewpoint, the colonial position was an

7. Petition of the Massachusetts Council and House of Representatives to the House of Commons, Mass. Hist. Soc., *Collections*, 6th ser., 9 (1897), 34.
8. This argument is discussed by David S. Lovejoy, "Rights Imply Equality: The Case Against Admiralty Jurisdiction in America: 1764-1776," *Wm. and Mary Qtly.*, 3rd ser., 16 (1959), 459-84.

argument against tradition. Viewing the Revenue Act of 1764 as only an extension of the earlier navigation statutes, the British rejected the contention that an innovation had been introduced.[9] Regulatory laws and revenue statutes were one and the same thing. The history of the enforcement of the trade acts was filled with instances of colonial juries refusing to convict colonists of illegal trade practices, showing clearly why customs officials favored actions in the vice-admiralty courts. The new statute merely continued what had been begun in 1696, and in no way created new inequalities between Americans and Englishmen. Nor did it deprive the colonists of any right they had been enjoying.[10]

In the autumn of 1764, all arguments against the vice-admiralty courts assumed that certain events would take place—they were protests against anticipated, rather than experienced, hardships.

The colonists assumed that seizures would be hurried to Halifax for trial. None had yet been taken. The colonists

9. Thomas Hutchinson's later defense of the British position was probably typical. In his *Strictures Upon the Declaration of the Congress at Philadelphia; In a Letter to a Noble Lord* (London, 1776), 24, he asserted that since impartial trials by juries in the colonies were unobtainable, "the necessity of the case justified the departure from the general rule; and in the reign of King William the Third, jurisdiction, in both . . . [breaches of the acts of trade and trespasses upon the king's woods] was given to the Admiralty by Acts of Parliament; and it has ever since been part of the constitution of the Colonies. . . . Strange! that in the reign of King George the Third, this jurisdiction should suddenly become an usurpation and ground of Revolt."

10. Despite Dickerson's careful analysis in the *Navigation Acts*, he characterizes the establishment of the Superior Court of Vice-Admiralty at Halifax (the only *new* establishment under the provisions of the Revenue Act of 1764) in this way: "An extensive system of admiralty courts had just been created with jurisdiction over trade, revenue, and ordinary admiralty cases and operating under a system of law different from that used in the local provincial courts" (page 183). There was no such "new system" set up, and no new "set" of imperial courts. Actually, the old provincial courts had enjoyed jurisdiction over breaches of the trade statutes since 1696. The Revenue Act of 1764 did not specifically require prosecutions in the vice-admiralty courts alone, but in the traditional manner, granted them concurrent jurisdiction with the common-law courts in the colonies.

assumed that vice-admiralty judges would find probable causes for seizures. No judge had so decreed.[11] Nevertheless, petitions stating these arguments were duly signed and sent on their way to England.

Meanwhile, the new regulations were law, and their execution was closely watched by colonial merchants. The customs officers were as bewildered by many of the required procedures as the merchants themselves, but they had been strongly warned against laxness. In New England, John Temple summoned his collectors and surveyors and swore them anew to their duties. Warnings were printed in the provincial newspapers that enforcement was to be severe and unrelenting.[12] The Boston merchants watched carefully, determined to contest every action that allowed a dispute. Minor arguments were taken to the advocate general for decision, but in December 1764, when a difference of opinion arose over the duties on loaf sugar, the merchants collectively appointed one of their fellow traders to bring a test case against the port collector in the common-law courts. The jury, as expected, decided for the merchants. It was a minor victory which only slightly modified the new regulations; however, it served to impress the customs collector that the common-law courts could still be used against him.[13]

The merchants of Maryland took more forceful action. In late November 1764, Robert Heron, the collector of Pocomoke, seized a brig with a cargo of molasses. After condemnation in the vice-admiralty court, the forfeiture was advertised for sale at public auction at the local tavern. The owner of the vessel, a Scot named Graham, secured a promise from the merchants "not to buy or purchase any sort of

11. On the protest against the new trial regulations, see George Adrian Washburne, *Imperial Control of the Administration of Justice in the Thirteen American Colonies, 1684-1776* (N.Y., 1923), 176-77.

12. *Providence Gazette*, Jan. 21, 1764; *N.Y. Mercury*, Feb. 20, 1764.

13. John Rowe's diary, Oct. 2, 1764, Dec. 3, 1764, and Jan. 11, 1765, Cunningham, ed., *Letters and Diary of John Rowe*, 65, 73.

Goods taken . . . from a Brother Trader." The auction turned into a riot when Graham, after drinking "four or five Bumpers directly one after another," assaulted the collector and tossed him out of the tavern.[14]

Such extreme measures were rare. The southern merchants found cause for complaint in the regulations concerning coasting vessels, but they limited their opposition to letters to England. Lieutenant Governor Bull of South Carolina forcefully seconded their protests.[15] In all the colonies an uneasy quiet settled down over the port towns while the new procedures were interpreted and tested. Even the naval captains, still at odds with the governors over their shares of the seizures, were less eager to make war on the colonial shippers. One of them went so far as to question the Admiralty about the wisdom of the new act and reflect on the possible consequences of enforcing it.[16]

Benjamin Franklin prophesied well when he wrote to friends in England of the "great Stir" among the merchants caused by the new regulations, observing "that more is apprehended than will happen; and that Experience only will inform us clearly, how short it will fall of procuring on one hand the Good, and producing on the other hand the Evil, that People engag'd in different Interests expect from it."[17]

Judge Spry sat at Halifax and waited for cases to be brought to his new court. The cases, however, did not come. By the spring of 1765 the new establishment had proved less of a danger than many had anticipated, and newspaper readers in Rhode Island could laugh at a mythical description

14. Robert Heron to Treasury, Jan. 3, 1765, PRO, State Papers, Domestic 37, 22.

15. William Bull to Board of Trade, Sept. 8, 1765, PRO, CO 5, 378.

16. Sir John Lindsay to Admiralty, Nov. 9, 1764, PRO, State Papers, Domestic 42, 65.

17. Franklin to Richard Jackson, June 25, 1764, Carl Van Doren, ed., *Letters and Papers of Benjamin Franklin and Richard Jackson, 1753-1785* (Phila., 1947), 167.

of the Halifax court that a reader had reportedly "stumbled over" in the streets of Providence. The "epistel, with the Seal and Direction entirely wore off" described the Halifax court as consisting only of a "Most High and Grand Justiciary *OVER ALL AMERICA*," a "Great Register," two "Great Clerks," a "Sublime Provost Martial," two "high Bailiffs, two sollicitors, and six Attornies . . . and seven lesser Officers of the Court." The new establishment was said to have power to determine "all Causes, real personal, and mixt," and the activities of the naval captains were described: "For the great Dispatch of Business, Packets will constantly ply between this Island and *Panama,* and a Number of Others between *Porto Bello* . . . and the different parts of *America.*" Spry's salary of £800 sterling was magnified to "only *Ten Thousand Dollars Per Annum;* an Instance of the Greater O'conomy of the Nation! And his perquisites . . . cannot amount to much more."[18]

The author of this letter left no doubt about his opinion of the Halifax court. He concluded by observing that "this establishment is a Proof of the tender regard which the Mother State hath for their Children in America, for by Means of this Institution, impartial Justice can *Now* be *easily* and *readily* obtained, without much Expence to the Litigants, for I have heard his Lordship graciously observe, that the Cost of Obtaining a final Decree, in a small Cause, will not amount to much above One Thousand Dollars."

Satire in Rhode Island soon ceased to be amusing, however. Within the month, John Robinson, the new collector of that colony, seized the sloop *Polly* in the Swanzey River for smuggling molasses.[19] At first there was little cause for worry and some reason for rejoicing. Robinson left the

18. *Providence Gazette,* Mar. 23, 1765.
19. Robinson began his duties as collector in May 1764. Franklin Bouditch Dexter, ed., *Extracts from the Itineraries and Other Miscellanies of Ezra Stiles, D.D., LL.D., 1755-1794* (New Haven, 1916), 204.

sloop and cargo in the care of two deputies, and in his absence a group of men with darkened faces recovered most of the molasses and stripped and grounded the sloop. Even more to be cheered by the radical populace was a suit for £3,000 damages which Job Smith, the owner of the sloop, initiated against Robinson for seizing the vessel and cargo. Such an action would have been illegal after trial in the vice-admiralty court, if the judge announced that Robinson had acted upon a probability that the sloop had engaged in illicit trade. But Smith did not wait for Robinson to start condemnation proceedings. He applied for a writ against the collector immediately, and Robinson, stranded and without friends to supply bail, was forced to spend a night in the Taunton jail.

Surveyor General John Temple secured his release the next day, and Robinson set out to show the Rhode Islanders the folly of their actions. With the assistance of the man-of-war *Maidstone,* he reseized the stripped sloop. The prize again in his custody, he let it be known that he would not trust his case to the provincial vice-admiralty judge: He was determined to sail the sloop to Halifax for trial before Judge Spry. Robinson alone might not have dared such a maneuver, but Temple was convinced that it was the best policy. The seizure had been made within the province of Massachusetts, in an overlapping district of the Rhode Island customs territory. Temple and Governor Bernard were still at odds with each other, and the Massachusetts Governor cautioned against such extreme action. Because Bernard was against the removal of the seizure to Halifax, Temple automatically took the other side. Robinson followed his superior's advice and carried the case to Judge Spry. The process of condemning the seizure took almost a year. Meanwhile, the sloop, with the small portion of molasses that had been recovered, rode at anchor in Newport Harbor under the protecting guns of H.M.S. *Cygnet*. In June 1766, Robinson had the pleasure of witnessing Richard Beale, deputy marshal of the Rhode Island Vice-Admiralty Court, sell the sloop *Polly* at public auction in Newport.[20]

An Alteration Is Postponed

John Robinson had broken the ice. The Halifax court had proven useful to him in the case of the *Polly*, and it might prove useful to others. However, no great rush of cases was brought before Judge Spry. The new court was open for business; the judge was in attendance at all times for hearing and determining cases. But neither customs officials nor naval captains came northward with their seizures. There was enough opposition from the merchants and citizens to trials in the local courts, and no officer, other than Robinson, had the courage to transport his seizures to Halifax and face the inevitable consequences. So Judge Spry idly sat in his northern outpost, enjoying the comradeship of Admiral Colville and the other officers of the naval base.

As far back as November 1764, Governor Bernard had demonstrated his sympathy with the merchants' fears over the new court. In transmitting to England a copy of the Massachusetts petition against the Revenue Act, he had taken care to point out the justice of some of the protested grievances. He realized that there existed an "obvious occasion for a general court of Admiralty over all America or very large districts of it," in order to negate the prejudices of local judges. But he was as convinced as the merchants that the

20. The necessary papers and documents of the seizure, but not the sloop itself, were taken to Halifax for the trial. See papers in PRO, Treas. 1, 441 and 442; Bernard to Earl of Halifax, May 11, 1765, PRO, CO 5, 755; *Acts of the Privy Council: Colonial Series*, VI, 381-84; *Newport Mercury*, June 30, 1766; Mass. Hist. Soc., *Collections*, 6th ser., 9 (1897), 62; Morgan, *Stamp Act Crisis*, 40-47.

ministry had erred in placing the court at Halifax. He agreed with the merchants' contention that trials there would be handicapped because of the scarcity of able lawyers. He also believed that the location of the court had "contributed to the alarm it . . . [had] occasioned for . . . the inconveniences of persons being obliged to attend a court at great distance . . . would be . . . [avoided] if the Court was held in the middle of its jurisdiction."[21]

Nothing occurred between November and May to change Bernard's opinion. When Collector Robinson seized the *Polly,* the Massachusetts Governor explained at length his opposition to carrying the case to Halifax. He pointed out that the option of prosecuting causes at Spry's tribunal was "certainly intended . . . [to] be used with discretion, and not wantonly abused. That the obvious reason for removing a cause from the provincial Court to the General Court was a suspicion of the provincial judge being subject to popular influence." Bernard was ready to testify to Chambers Russell's character if Robinson did not already know of his "integrity as a Judge and his fidelity as a Servant of the King."

Although Bernard knew that Robinson was following John Temple's orders to move the case to Halifax, he was not convinced that such action was wise or politic. He believed "that at a time when all the Colonies in America have exprest their uneasiness at being liable to have their causes carried to Halifax, it must be highly improper to use that power wantonly, without any real necessity."[22] Other gov-

21. Bernard to the Earl of ————, Nov. 10, 1764, Francis Bernard, *Select Letters on the Trade and Government of America and the Principles of Law and Policy, applied to the American Colonies* . . . (London, 1774), 16-17. Bernard was likewise convinced that it was unwise not to provide salaries for the provincial judges, terming the payments by percentages "an extreme bad method of paying a Judge, as it makes him interested in every prosecution." Bernard to Board of Trade, Aug. 16, 1764, PRO, CO 5, 892. See also Bernard to Board of Trade, Apr. 8, 1765, *ibid.,* 891.

22. Bernard to the Earl of Halifax, May 11, 1765, PRO, CO 5, 755.

ernors and officers were as timid as Bernard about employing the new procedures. There was opposition enough to the new duties and trading regulations without incurring the further wrath of the colonists by carrying cases to Halifax. The provincial vice-admiralty courts could be employed for condemnations more safely.[23]

The reports from America that reached England early in 1765 were read with considerable attention. The argument against the location of Doctor Spry's court sounded reasonable, even to those who had little knowledge of the geography of North America. After all, it mattered little where the court sat if it performed its function. If the colonists preferred to have the superior vice-admiralty court nearer to their major port towns, it would make little difference.

In January 1765, there were rumors in London that the ministry intended to change the jurisdiction of the court and to order "certain beneficial regulations . . . with regard to the prerogative of judges, and the future method of conducting business in his Majesty's superior courts of admiralty."[24] In March, Jared Ingersoll wrote Connecticut's Governor Fitch from London that a major reorganization of the vice-admiralty system was underway. Ingersoll informed Fitch that the colonists' complaints concerning the denial of jury trial fell on deaf ears in Britain; that everyone agreed there was "no safety in trusting the breach of revenue laws to a Jury of the Country where the Offence . . . [was] committed, that they find even in England they never can obtain Verdicts where Smugling is practised & therefore always bring the Causes up for trial to London." But the ministers had viewed the argument against the location of Spry's court

23. Channing's statement that "a Court of Vice-Admiralty had been established at Halifax to which informers and prosecutors naturally turned" is not supported by the facts; *History of the United States*, III, 343. Although the records of Judge Spry's court have been lost, there is no evidence that he determined more than a very small number of causes. See below, 94, n. 22.

24. *Boston Evening Post*, Apr. 1, 1765; *N.Y. Mercury*, Apr. 8, 1765.

more favorably, and were taking steps to remove this cause
for complaint.

The plan for reorganization followed the suggestions of
Governor Bernard and others who had explained the great
distances involved in taking cases to Nova Scotia. They
suggested that the difficulty might be remedied by dividing
the court's jurisdiction between three separate tribunals,
each having substantially the same powers as the Halifax
court. One of these courts might be located at Boston,
another at New York or Philadelphia, and the third at the
South Carolina seaport of Charleston. The Admiralty discussed granting the judges of the new courts appellate power
over the provincial vice-admiralty courts as well as equal
jurisdiction in original causes. It was agreed that the judges
of the proposed courts should be as well-trained as the eminent Doctor Spry, preferably at Doctors' Commons.[25]

Authority for these proposed district courts to hear appeals from the provincial vice-admiralty courts was written
into the draft of the pending Stamp Act. When that measure
passed Parliament in March, the way was cleared to reorganize the Halifax court. The same letters that brought
news of the Stamp Act to the colonies explained the proposed
reorganization of the courts but added that "the division . . .
[was] not yet exactly fixed."[26] It was June before the Treasury Board had established districts for the courts at Boston,
Philadelphia, and Charleston. The Halifax court was to be
abolished, and its work divided among the three new tribunals.

The departments of state moved slowly. The Board of
Trade considered, and then postponed, action on the sugges-

25. Ingersoll to Fitch, Mar. 6, 1765, New Haven Colony Hist. Soc., *Papers*,
9 (1918), 318-19; also printed in the *Providence Gazette*, Nov. 22, 1766.

26. Thomas Whately to John Temple, May 10, 1765, Mass. Hist. Soc.,
Collections, 6th ser., 9 (1897), 56. See also *Boston Evening Post*, May 20,
1765; *Conn. Courant*, May 20 and 27, 1765.

tions in June 1765. The Privy Council took up the Treasury's recommendations in July and ordered a committee to study the scheme. It was October before the committee reported to the Council, and then only to suggest conferences with the attorney general and solicitor general. No one was certain how to proceed. Judge Spry's commission must be revoked and his court abolished before the new tribunals could be established. But by what law could this be done? December was almost over before the two law officers reported that Spry's commission might be legally revoked by the same authority that had originally granted the letters patent.[27]

Meanwhile the colonists heard various rumors and reports of impending reorganization. In July the three courts were reported to have been authorized. In August Judge Spry was said to have been appointed to a supreme vice-admiralty bench at Boston, and the next month the newspapers advised that "a total supression of Vice-Admiralty Courts in America is now . . . pretty confidently asserted, as a measure speedily to take place."[28]

The change never took place. The rumors in America were soon smothered by the outcries of opposition to the Stamp Act. The summer of 1765 was not the time for any colonist to ponder so insignificant a change as the anticipated division of the jurisdiction of Judge Spry's vice-admiralty court. There were stamp officers to watch and resistance to organize. Nor did the British ministry have time to consider the matter further. All other American affairs were forgotten in the torrent of reports on the hostile reception of

27. PRO, CO 5, 67; Charles Jenkinson to John Pownall, June 7, 1765, and accompanying memorial in Board of Trade Papers, Plantations General, Hist. Soc. of Penn. Transcripts; *Board of Trade Journal* [*1764-1767*], 185-86; *Acts of the Privy Council: Colonial Series*, IV, 664, VI, 403.

28. *Boston Gazette*, June 3 and Sept. 9, 1765; *Conn. Courant*, July 29 and Aug. 12, 1765; *Mass. Gazette*, Aug. 8 and Oct. 31, 1765; *Penn. Gazette*, Aug. 22, 1765.

Mr. Grenville's stamp duties. Judge Spry would remain in Halifax, and his court retain its jurisdiction until more peaceful days had returned to America.

Crisis in the Colonies

The petitions and letters from America protesting the provisions of the Revenue Act of 1764 failed to impress the British ministry. There was a halfhearted attempt to divide Judge Spry's vice-admiralty jurisdiction, but the other colonial complaints were treated with even less concern. The act had been drawn to promote the imperial revenue; to change its provisions in any but administrative detail would reduce its chances of success.

The need for revenue had also prompted the Grenville ministry's plans for an American stamp act. Warning had been issued early in the autumn of 1764 that such a measure was under consideration. The colonists were advised to submit an equally productive revenue device or prepare to accept stamp taxes. In February 1765, without so much as a hasty glance at the provincial remonstrances against such legislation, the ministry introduced its stamp bill in Parliament.

The measure stimulated little debate. Colonel Isaac Barré, who had seen America during the French and Indian War, made a plea for consideration of the colonists' rights. He pointed out the difficulties that the Revenue Act of the previous year had brought to American shippers. Among these was the possibility "that a man might be called 1,500 miles from Georgia, to answer an information laid against him in Halifax."[29]   But the ministry was in certain control

29. *Conn. Courant*, May 6, 1765. See also Morgan, *Stamp Act Crisis*, 53-70; and Edmund S. Morgan, "The Postponement of the Stamp Act," *Wm. and Mary Qtly.*, 3rd ser., 7 (1950), 353-92.

of the House of Commons, and their stamp measure was law by March 1765. By May the colonists learned of the wide sweep of its provisions. Within a few months the American provinces were united in their opposition to the notorious statute.

The economic grievances against what was basically a tax measure soon became lost in arguments about constitutional principles, chief of which was the question of Parliament's authority over non-represented areas. But other issues were also raised, and one of these concerned the vice-admiralty courts. The Stamp Act provided for major changes in the concept of the jurisdiction of the provincial vice-admiralty courts and granted appellate powers to the Superior Court at Halifax. In addition, legal papers used in these colonial courts were subject to stamp duties.

The taxes levied upon processes in the vice-admiralty courts were similar to those detailed for trial processes. Thus the new tax requirements did not particularly excite the colonists. Nor did they ever become agitated over the elevation of Judge Spry's tribunal to appellate rank. The Stamp Act gave his court the power to hear appeals, by either party in a contest, from any of the provincial vice-admiralty courts. This appellate jurisdiction applied to all of the trade acts, as well as to the current legislation; but the power was never exercised.

The Stamp Act also extended what the colonists the previous year had objected to as a new and unwarranted power invested in the vice-admiralty courts. Any prosecution for failure to comply with the Stamp Act provisions might take place in either the provincial common-law courts, the provincial vice-admiralty courts, or in Doctor Spry's court at Halifax. In other words, the vice-admiralty courts unquestionably became revenue courts, with powers which in England were delegated to the Court of the Exchequer, a common-law tribunal. Rather than erect a completely new system of exchequer courts in the colonies, the ministry decided to use the vice-admiralty courts as tribunals for determining crown revenue cases.[30]

In the British view this was not an innovation. Most of the provincial vice-admiralty courts owed their birth, in the seventeenth century, to the need for a court of maritime law. Their original jurisdiction had been limited to disputes concerning ocean commerce. It had been logical enough for Britain to extend this jurisdiction by granting these courts cognizance of violations of the trade and navigation acts. Offenses against the trade laws were either committed on water or concerned ocean shipping. From this point, it had been only a short step to add jurisdiction in cases of trespass against the crown's white pine reserves. Although such offenses took place on land rather than water, the pine laws were an integral part of British mercantile policy. The Revenue Act of 1764 and the Stamp Act were continuations of the acts of trade and navigation; there was no distinction between regulatory and revenue legislation.

The colonists did not agree, and the gap between the American and British positions was as great as in the more vocal arguments over taxation and representation. To the Americans the new laws appeared as revolutionary statutes, and the jurisdiction vested in the vice-admiralty courts seemed subversive of their constitutional rights. Causes concerning transactions far removed from the sea and the enterprise of commerce were to be cognizable in the vice-admiralty courts. The procedure of those courts might be familar to merchants and sailors, but farmers and shopkeepers were ignorant of its methods and customs. Cases would be heard by judges who might, or might not, have a knowledge

30. 5 George III, c. 12, section lviii; Channing, *History of the United States,* III, 50.

of common-law practice. They would be decided, not by a jury of the offender's peers, but by a single judge. A monstrous discrimination was erected against the Americans, who were refused their traditional right to a jury trial, still enjoyed by their fellow subjects in England.

The colonists knew the details of the Stamp Act in May. Its provisions would not be enforced until the following November. Five full months remained to prepare a defense and present petitions against the legislation. The early days passed peacefully for Judge Spry, still awaiting seizures that did not come. But the provincial judges heard and determined cases which were brought to them by naval officers and customs officials, cases which mostly concerned infringements of the Revenue Act of the previous year.

The British naval officers were still quarreling with the governors and customs officers. The attempt in the Revenue Act of 1764 to define the division of forfeitures between these crown officers had accomplished little. A further attempt to clarify the division was made in 1765. The words "seizures made at sea" were redefined, to include any place at sea "or upon any river . . . not . . . actually on shore within any British colony or plantation in America."[31] The new definition did little to soothe the situation. Although all customs officials had been instructed to consult with the governors on every seizure, the sea captains were reluctant to seek their aid for fear of losing their shares of forfeited property. In Boston, Captain Bishop of His Majesty's schooner *Fortune* was the only naval officer who cooperated with Governor Bernard. The Massachusetts Governor praised him in his reports, saying that he had "prosecuted and condemned twenty times the value of all the other naval officers put together."[32]

31. 5 George III, c. 45, section xxvi.
32. Bernard to the Earl of Halifax, July 1, 1765, PRO, CO 5, 755.

The antagonism between the customs officers and the naval officers ran equally deep. The Customs Commissioners in England finally sent instructions to the colonial collectors to inform all of the sea captains that they were to report immediately to the customhouses every time they seized a vessel. The collectors had not been consulted, and seizures had been tried and acquitted in the vice-admiralty courts with no probable cause certified. Now the complete facts in each instance were to be put before the customs officials, with applications directed to the advocates and attorneys general for their opinions; and if they cautioned that no probable cause for seizures existed, the vessels were to be dismissed.[33] But such directions were more easily issued than enforced. The naval officers, eager enough to make seizures, were not pleased with the prospect of losing part of their profits by consulting with customs officers. And so the argument continued.

These problems, however did not cause the explosions of the summer of 1765. They were minor irritations, lost in a rapidly gathering storm. The opposition to the Stamp Act had begun early in May, with the first news that the statute had passed Parliament. The objections were first expressed in letters and articles in the colonial newspapers. Then Patrick Henry stirred a remnant of the Virginia House of Burgesses into passing a series of resolutions against the act. The New England towns copied the example, and the provincial assemblies drew up petitions against the "unwarranted" taxation by Parliament. The appended lists of grievances included the denial of trial by jury through the extension of the powers of the vice-admiralty courts.[34] In

33. Commissioners of the Customs to Collectors, Sept. 13, 1765, Philadelphia Customs House Papers, III, Hist. Soc. of Penn.

34. Instructions by the Town of Providence to the deputies in the General Assembly, Aug. 13, 1765, *Conn. Courant*, Sept. 2, 1765; Proceedings of the Town of Little-Compton, R.I., Aug. 27, 1765, *Penn. Gazette*, Sept. 12, 1765; Instructions of Newport, R.I., to Delegates, Sept. 3, 1765, *ibid.*, Sept. 19, 1765; Instructions of the Town of Boston to Representatives, Sept. 18, 1765,

October, less than three weeks before the Stamp Act became law, delegates from nine colonies gathered in New York to draw up petitions to King, Lords, and Commons against the legislation. The handiwork of this extra-legal congress did not fail to take account of the grievance against the vice-admiralty courts.[35]

The petitions and remonstrances were a polite method of representing the opposition. Methods less nice, but more certain, were soon employed. August saw Boston in the hands of the mob, Governor Bernard in asylum at Castle William, Stamp Distributor Andrew Oliver burnt in effigy, and his home ransacked. Later attacks on the houses of Lieutenant Governor Thomas Hutchinson, Customs Comptroller Benjamin Hallowell, and the deputy register of the vice-admiralty court, William Story, showed clearly that someone had unloosed a thunderbolt. The riots were quickly reproduced in Rhode Island, where Augustus Johnston followed Oliver's example and renounced his office of stamp master. In similar fashion, the distributors of stamps in other colonies were educated in the sentiments of their fellow colonists. By the middle of September, the chosen officers had all resigned their places.

Thus ended the first phase of direct opposition. The servants of the crown had been driven from their offices, and

in *A Report of the Commissioners of the City of Boston, containing the Boston Town Records 1758 to 1769* (Boston, 1886), 155-56; Pennsylvania Assembly Resolves on the Stamp Act, Sept. 21, 1765, *Penn. Gazette,* Sept. 26, 1765; Resolves of the Maryland Assembly, Sept. 28, 1765, *ibid.,* Oct. 17, 1765; Instructions of the Town of Hartford to Deputies, *Conn. Courant,* Sept. 23, 1765; Instructions of Braintree, Mass. to Delegates, Sept. 23, 1765, *Mass. Gazette,* Oct. 10, 1765; Resolutions of Cambridge Town Meeting, Oct. 14, 1765, *Boston Evening Post,* Oct. 21, 1765; Resolves of the Massachusetts House of Representatives, Oct. 29, 1765, *Penn. Gazette,* Nov. 21, 1765; Resolutions of New York City Meeting, Nov. 26, 1765, *ibid.,* Dec. 5, 1765; Resolutions of the South Carolina Commons House of Assembly, Nov. 29, 1765, *Conn. Courant,* Jan. 20, 1766; Resolves of the New Jersey Assembly, Nov. 30, 1765, *Penn. Gazette,* Dec. 5, 1765.

35. Morgan, *Stamp Act Crisis,* 102-13; *Penn. Jour.,* May 1, 1766.

no officer remained to distribute the stamps. The provincial governors hastily stored the stamps in the royal forts or aboard men-of-war. The first day of November arrived, and for want of stamps, courts and ports were closed, and business everywhere stood still.

4

Courts and Customs

T HE NEW YEAR had come and gone. Reports of violence and riots in the mainland colonies drifted north to Halifax. Governor Wilmot and Admiral Colville sympathized with the American governors. A noisy radical element in Nova Scotia had attempted to battle against the stamps, but they had not succeeded. Halifax remained loyal to king and Parliament and was using the stamps as directed in the act. Wilmot and Colville could not understand why people should set themselves up against government. Judge William Spry shared their sentiments.[1]

Judge Spry had little to do but discuss American affairs: His court was a dying institution. For a few months there had been almost no activity on the American waters. Merchant ships waited in their home ports until the question of clearances without stamps had been settled. But this had not caused Spry's inactivity, for even after the ports were

1. Wilfred B. Kerr, "The Stamp Act in Nova Scotia," *New England Qtly.,* 6 (1933), 552-66.

opened, seizures were tried in the provincial courts. The only bright spot in all the northern dreariness was his salary from home, and even this had been delayed. The Treasury had refused to honor his first request until he presented a certificate of residence at Halifax. The orders for payment of the £800 annually had specifically stated that the judge must be located at the seat of his court. So Spry had prepared a properly authenticated certificate of his residence at Halifax.

He wished that he could send a report of the activities of his court at the same time—but he had nothing to report. He added a postscript to the dispatch containing the residence certificate: "The Employment I have had *here* in my Court has been too inconsiderable and trifling to be communicated."[2] A year and a half had gone by since he had opened his vice-admiralty tribunal with pomp and ceremony. His original jurisdiction in maritime and trade causes was not employed; no one came north with appeals from the provincial courts. Judge Spry wished he were elsewhere.

An Incident at Cape Fear

The judge was not alone in his unhappiness. Many crown officials in the mainland colonies that previous autumn had wished themselves out of America. It had been an unhappy time to be customs collector, or any royal appointee, in the colonies. After the riots and threats of late summer had forced the resignations of the stamp distributors, and the stamps themselves were safely secured in royal strongholds, the days and nights had passed peacefully enough. November 1, inaugural day for the new duties, had come and gone. Quebec, Nova Scotia, and the two Floridas were the only

2. William Spry to Philip Stephens, June 7, 1766, PRO, Admir. 1, 3883.

mainland colonies where the stamps were available. In the other provinces, customhouses and law courts closed their doors on the last day of October and did not open them the next morning.

The situation had not looked so ominous then. If the opponents of Mr. Grenville's taxes had been content to abstain from the use of any process that required stamps, the storm might have been weathered. But such a pacific resistance did not develop. Instead of boycotting the customhouses and courts, it soon appeared that the colonists were determined to ignore the provisions of the law and proceed with their affairs without stamps. The customhouse officers were the first to face the dilemma.

Most of the colonial ports were empty on November 1. In anticipation of the impending stamp duties, the merchants had sent every vessel they owned to make one final market. Before many weeks, some of these ships were back at their home ports, and the merchants became impatient for a decision about the use of stamps. They might have relied on smuggling in and out of the harbors without stamped certificates, but this was not what they desired. They wanted assurances from the customs officials that their vessels would not be seized for noncompliance with the new regulations. They wanted a notation on their ships' papers, stating that no stamps were available, to be as valid as the stamps themselves. They left the decision to the customs officers.

After hesitations and delays the merchants won their point. Virginia and Rhode Island in November; Pennsylvania, New York, New Jersey, and Massachusetts in December; South Carolina the first week of February, all opened their ports and customhouses, and commerce returned to normal. The stamps remained in the forts and on the men-of-war; the merchants no longer cared where they were. Certificates stating that no stamped paper was available

provided legal entry into all of the major ports of the continent, the West Indies, and even to England itself.[3]

Success made the merchants bold. It was a rude shock
to the captains of the sloop *Dobbs* out of Philadelphia and the
Patience from St. Christopher, when they were detained in
the harbor of Brunswick, North Carolina, for sailing without
stamped clearances. Captain Jacob Lobb, commanding His
Majesty's sloop *Viper*, seized the vessels in January 1766. It
was plain to him that his actions were fully covered by his
customs commission which allowed him to seize and prosecute
vessels violating the trade acts. But he found himself in a
delicate situation. The North Carolinians had determined
to do without stamps, both in their customhouses and in
their provincial courts. Other ports in the colony were operating without stamped clearances, but no North Carolina
court, common or civil law, had opened its doors. Captain
Lobb, with two seizures in custody, could see no channel for
prosecuting his prizes. In despair he sent a statement of the
details of the captures to William Dry, the collector of the
port, and requested him to commence prosecutions against
the two sloops.[4]

Collector Dry, however, relished the chore no more than
Captain Lobb. He, in turn, presented the evidence to
Robert Jones, Jr., the provincial advocate and attorney general, and asked for advice. Before Jones arrived at a decision, Lobb seized a third sloop, the *Ruby,* and this case was
added to the others. On the fifteenth of February, Jones
delivered his answer to the collector's questions.[5]

The first question was easily disposed of. Collector Dry

3. Morgan, *Stamp Act Crisis*, 133, 134-39, 151, 159-68.
4. Jacob Lobb to William Dry, Jan. 14, 1766, PRO, Treas. 1, 453; *Boston
Gazette,* Mar. 24, 1766; *Penn. Gazette,* Feb. 6, 1766; *Conn. Courant,* Feb. 17
and Mar. 3, 1766; Saunders, ed., *N.C. Col. Recs.,* VII, 127-30, 168-83; Morgan,
Stamp Act Crisis, 165.
5. William Dry to Jones, Jan. 16, 1766, and Captain Jacob Lobb to Dry,
Feb. 14, 1766, PRO, Treas. 1, 453.

asked whether or not the failure to obtain clearances on stamped paper was a proper cause for seizing the sloops, and whether a vice-admiralty court would consider this sufficient neglect to decree the vessels forfeit. Advocate General Jones made short work of the answer. "Of Course they are liable to be seized," he wrote, "and I think Condemned by a Court of Admiralty," for clearances on common paper are "the same as if these Vessels had sailed without clearances."

Collector Dry presented the merchants' arguments in his second query. "Will it not be sufficient," he asked, "to show proof that it was impossible to obtain Clearances &c on Stampt Paper of the Officers of the Customs in the Ports from whence the said Vessels sailed?" The advocate general began his response by pointing out that "Reason does not require Impossibilities and Courts of Admiralty often decree favorably on the part of the Owners of Vessells . . . where it does not appear that any Fraud was intended." But in these cases the captains of the sloops had "been Guilty of great Neglect." They should have tendered the duties to the customs officers and demanded proper clearances. They might have been refused, but they should have gone through the formalities of a similar tender and refusal from a notary public. If they had thus secured proof of their offers and the refusals, "the Judge would decree that the Vessels and Cargoes were not forfeited."

This much for theory. The final question concerned the vital problem of the moment. The collector phrased the question cautiously: "If it is necessary to prosecute . . . must the Prosecution be commenced in the Court of Admiralty at Cape Fear?" That court was closed; the required stamps for its operation were not available. Should the collector attempt a prosecution in the vice-admiralty court without stamps? "Or," and the collector mentioned the distasteful alternative, "must the said Vessels be sent to Halifax in Order to be Libelled?" Jones's answer was straight-forward. "If Prosecutions are intended against these Vessels," he wrote, "they must be sent to Halifax, for should they be libelled here, & the Proceedings carried on upon Common Paper, such Proceedings will be meer Nullities and not alter the Property either of the Vessels or Cargoes."[6]

The advocate general had thrown the unpleasant situation directly back into the hands of Collector Dry. The seizures must be prosecuted; they must be prosecuted at Halifax before Judge William Spry. The collector did not have long to consider his next move. He had no sooner received Jones's answers than news of them was known in Brunswick, and in Wilmington, twenty-odd miles up the Cape Fear River from the customhouse. On that same day, February 15, a group of merchants and townsmen gathered in Wilmington and composed a letter to Dry. They cautioned him that "many of the Country Gentlemen" had been in town that morning and had gone away "much dissatisfied" with the report of the advocate general. The mere suggestion of prosecutions at the Halifax Vice-Admiralty Court had caused great concern. The self-appointed committee spelled out their warning: "Should you suffer those Vessels or the Papers belonging to them, to be carried out of the River, if the People from the Country come down in a Body, which we are *informed* they are determined to do, we leave you to judge how far our Properties or your's may be secure."

Caught in a crossfire, the collector answered the communication by requesting a delay. He explained to the Wilmington gentlemen that his duties required him to prosecute the cases. Attacking him personally would accomplish nothing, for if he should give up his office, "another would be immediately appointed . . . perhaps . . . more strict.'

6. Jones's letter in William Tryon's Letter Book, Microfilm Coll. of Early State Recs., N.C., E.1.

The collector promised to come up the river to Wilmington in a day or two, and the difficulties could be settled then.[7]

William Dry's answer did nothing to alleviate the fears of the Wilmington committee, which decided not to wait for his arrival. On the eighteenth of February they formed an anti-Stamp Act organization and started on their way to Brunswick. By the time they reached that port the marchers numbered almost a thousand. Assuring Governor William Tryon that their mission was peaceful and that no violence was intended, the leaders of this "gentlemen's mob" sought out the collector and his colleagues of the customhouse. The group formed a large circle in the center of Brunswick and placed the customs officers in the middle. Thus surrounded, the trembling collector, naval officer, and comptroller promised that they would commence no prosecutions against the seized sloops and that they would take no further actions to enforce the Stamp Act. To ensure their victory, the committee secured the papers of the three seizures and took custody of the sloops. The decorous revolution completed, the mob dispersed, and the *Dobbs* and the *Patience* sailed upstream to Wilmington. The North Carolina ports remained open, "and Entries and Clearances . . . [were] made in the Form that was practised before the Stamp Act was appointed."[8]

Collector Dry's problem of prosecuting the cases had vanished, but he feared his actions would be severely censured by his superiors in England. To explain how untenable his situation had been, he informed the Customs Board that he could see no way to send the vessels to Halifax, "a place at least five Hundred Leagues from this, and a very bad Coast in Winter." Furthermore, he could find no one "to go on this occasion, and was either of the Vessels to be lost . . .

7. *Boston Gazette,* Mar. 24, 1766.
8. Governor Tryon to Treasury, Apr. 5, 1766, PRO, Treas. 1, 445.

[he knew not] where or in what manner they . . . [were] to be made good, provided they were not condemned."[9]

William Dry was not the first to face such a predicament. Shortly after the Stamp Act took effect, John Swift, the collector at Philadelphia, had discovered himself in a similar quandary. The courts of Pennsylvania were securely closed, and there was little indication that the colonists would relax in their determination to keep them closed.[10] Although the merchants had anxiously hurried the opening of the custom-houses, there was no stampede to begin operation of the courts without stamps, as there had been in North Carolina. For the merchants this was probably desirable. With the ports opened and the courts closed, they could conduct their commercial ventures in relative safety from seizures and forfeitures. To be sure, Judge Spry's establishment at Halifax was operating, but the distance involved and the danger of fomenting further violence deterred both customs officials and sea captains from prosecuting there.

The Massachusetts Vice-Admiralty Court had opened late the previous December. The courts in Rhode Island, New Hampshire, Delaware, and Maryland were conducting trials without stamped paper by February 1766. For the most part, however, the colonists proceeded about their business, ignoring the fact that their governments were without tribunals of law. Rumors from England hinted that the ministry was considering a revision of the hated legislation. Any day might bring news that the battle had been won.[11]

9. Dry to Commissioners of Customs, Feb. 24, 1766, *ibid.*, 453.

10. Draft of a letter from John Swift to the Attorney General, Nov. 2, 1765, Philadelphia Customs House Papers, IV, Hist. Soc. of Penn.; Morgan, *Stamp Act Crisis*, 174.

11. Morgan, *Stamp Act Crisis*, 169, 176; *Boston Gazette*, Dec. 30, 1765.

The Stamp Act Is Repealed

When the British Parliament met in December 1765, there was every indication that the stamp legislation would be modified. Grenville's ministry had been defeated. The Marquis of Rockingham, with the aid of General Henry Conway and the Dukes of Newcastle and Grafton, had assumed control of the nation in July. American affairs had never excited the interest of the English people as much as in the following months. The reports of riots and refusals to accept the stamps were discussed everywhere, calling forth numerous newspaper articles and publications. The British merchants, allied with the new ministry and concerned over the agreements of American merchants to import no British goods until the Stamp Act was repealed, recommended a scuttling of the legislation for economic reasons. Others attacked the stamp program on the constitutional principles which the colonists themselves had raised.[12]

Parliament met briefly in December and then adjourned until the middle of January. By that time the Rockingham ministry had determined to attack its opponents by discrediting Grenville's American policy. The action they sought was double-barreled. They would repeal the Stamp Act, and, at the same time, introduce legislation proclaiming the right of Parliament to legislate for the colonies. For a month Parliament listened to testimony of the riots in the colonies, the economic disasters that had resulted from the act, and the colonists' contentions about the right of taxation.

The first legislation to be passed by the Commons and Lords was the Declaratory Act, asserting Parliamentary su-

12. The Americans followed the controversies in Britain over the Stamp Act closely, reprinting many of the dispatches in their provincial newspapers. For example, see the *Boston Gazette,* Jan. 13, 1766; *Penn. Gazette,* Dec. 12, 1765; *Boston Evening Post,* Apr. 21, 1766.

premacy over the colonies. The battle over the repeal of the Stamp Act was longer and more stubbornly fought. In the early morning hours of February 21, the House of Commons finally voted, 275 to 167, to repeal, in toto, the stamp legislation of the previous year. On March 17, the Lords concurred in the repealing statute. The good news reached America in April, touching off a series of banquets and parades, bell ringing and bonfires.[13]

At first glance the victory looked complete. The Stamp Act was gone, and with it the extension of the vice-admiralty jurisdiction into areas traditionally reserved for the common-law courts. Every correspondent in England reported that the ministry was determined to remove all of the "intolerable Restrictions on trade . . . including the burthensome part of the Admiralty Courts . . . to give America Entire Relief."[14] The molasses duty would soon be reduced to a penny a gallon, and the trade laws brought back to their status of 1763.

Later in the year the molasses duty was lowered, but the new penny tax was extended to include British as well as foreign molasses imported into the colonies; the 1764 duty had applied only to foreign molasses. Other modifications were made, including a prohibition of exportation of all goods, whether enumerated or not, to Europe north of Cape Finisterre. But many of the changes that the Americans expected did not come, and many of the grievances that had their basis in the Revenue Act of 1764 remained.

The sea captains retained the rights of customs officers,

13. The repealing statute was 6 George III, c. 11. For an excellent collection of materials on the Stamp Act from its genesis to its repeal, see Edmund S. Morgan, *Prologue to Revolution, Sources and Documents on the Stamp Act Crisis, 1764-1766* (Chapel Hill, 1959).

14. Richard Champion to Caleb Lloyd, Feb. 23, 1766, G. H. Guttridge, ed., *The American Correspondence of a Bristol Merchant, 1766-1776; Letters of Richard Champion* (Univ. of Calif. Publications in History, XXII [Berkeley, 1934]), 14; Dennys De Berdt to Samuel White, Mar. 17, 1766, Albert Matthews, ed., *Letters of Dennys De Berdt* (Publications of the Col. Soc. of Mass., XIII [Cambridge, 1911]), 315.

with no reduction in the number of men-of-war stationed in American waters. The legal protections given to customs officers by the Revenue Act, absolving them of liability from common-law actions, were not removed. Judge Spry still sat at Halifax. The power of hearing appeals from the provincial courts no longer existed, but his court remained otherwise unchanged. Seizures from any place on the continent could still be taken to Nova Scotia for trial and condemnation.

It was reasonable to expect the Rockingham ministry to abolish Spry's court. From the very beginning, some of the arguments against the court had been well received in England. During the controversy over repealing the Stamp Act, many men had seconded the colonists' objections to the changes in vice-admiralty jurisdiction.[15] It was not only the opponents of the Stamp Act who granted the justice of the complaints against the method of enforcing the trade laws. When repeal was debated in the House of Lords, opposing peers claimed that the Stamp Act had no defects "except as the Admiralty Court, which might have been obviated if the present Administration had given proper Attention."[16] They remembered the attempt of the previous summer to divide Spry's jurisdiction between three new courts and censured the ministry heavily for neglecting and disregarding the plan, allowing it to "remain unexecuted in every part of it even to this day."[17]

But the Rockingham ministry made no move to modify the colonial vice-admiralty courts. The Pitt-Grafton minis-

15. For example, see Ray Nicholas, *The Importance of the Colonies of North America, and the Interest of Great Britain With Regard to Them, Considered Together with Remarks on the Stamp-Duty* (London, 1766), 7, 14.

16. Remarks of Lord Halifax, "Debates on the Declaratory Act and the Repeal of the Stamp Act, 1766," *Amer. Hist. Rev.*, 17 (1912), 581.

17. *Correct Copies of the Two Protests Against the Bill to Repeal the American Stamp Act, of Last Session* (Paris, 1766), 17-18; *Boston Evening Post*, June 16, 1766.

try that replaced it in midsummer 1766 seemed at first equally unconcerned. In August, the Admiralty Board reminded
the ministry that the repeal of the Stamp Act had not changed
the location of the court at Halifax. The Admiralty explained that the situation might "expose Merchants trading
in America to unnecessary difficulties" and suggested that
if Doctor Spry's court was to remain the only superior court,
it should be moved to New York, a more central location.[18]

Others suggested modification of the court during these
months. Grey Cooper, the secretary of the Treasury Board,
was convinced that "the Complaints and Clamours that have
been raised against these Courts over all America have
been more owing to the ignorance and corruption of the
Judges than the modes of tryal or determination of Causes."
He supported the plan to divide Spry's jurisdiction between
several courts, but only if "able Civilians" were appointed
judges. He did not believe it necessary to grant these courts
the power to hear appeals, since to do so would probably
abolish appeals to the High Court of Admiralty of England.
And this, Cooper thought, would be "dangerous . . . in the
present state of the spirit and temper of America."[19]

The new ministry would eventually work a change in the
colonial vice-admiralty system, but it took time to gather
facts and arrange the details. In the meantime, Judge Spry
remained in Halifax, and in the colonies a new type of opposition to the revenue establishments had begun. There
should have been only two opponents in the struggle: the
hunters and the hunted. All of the king's servants—the
governors, attorneys and advocates general, custom officials,
vice-admiralty judges, and the sea captains—were expected
to cooperate in prosecuting violators of the trade laws. But
such was not the case.

18. Admiralty to Secretary Conway, Aug. 12, 1766, PRO, CO 5, 66.
19. Cooper to Secretary Conway, Dec. 18, 1766, *ibid.*, 67.

The governors remained unhappy over the loss of their percentage of seizures to officers and crews of naval vessels. The customs officers were also distressed over the grants of forfeitures to the sea captains, although arrangements were often worked out by which seizures at sea were prosecuted by customs officers in exchange for a share of the proceeds. In New England, the continuing battle between Surveyor General John Temple and Governor Francis Bernard precluded any chance of cooperation. But these antagonisms only partially explain the relative inactivity that came to characterize the American revenue establishment.

The Stamp Act troubles had made the customs officers timid. Collectors and searchers who had fled for safety to other provinces or to men-of-war at anchor in the colonial ports were anxious not to bring further hostility upon themselves. And the few seizures that were made suffered from a new strategy of the customs battle. The colonists knew that a seizure recaptured was as valuable as no seizure at all, and they began to keep vessels from condemnation by retrieving them before they could be informed against in the vice-admiralty courts. The work was usually done at night, when men with blackened faces could not be easily identified. In New England, most of the seizures were spirited away, out of the custody of the customs officers and the crown. Governor Bernard complained that what had formerly been "an accidental or occassional affair" was now "the natural and certain consequence of a seizure, and the effect of a predetermined Resolution that the Laws of Trade shall not be executed."[20]

In this way, many seizures were never tried by the vice-admiralty courts. And the captures that were brought before the courts suffered a variety of fates. Nothing had been

20. Bernard to Board of Trade, Aug. 18, 1766, *ibid.*, 892. See also advertisement in *Boston Evening Post,* Mar. 17, 1766.

done to change the probable-cause regulation by which suits at common law were denied to owners of seized vessels. But the vice-admiralty judges had not lost all sense of justice. They were careful to use sparingly the power of proclaiming probable causes. And there were additional methods of mitigating the harshness of the laws. The Virginia Vice-Admiralty Court, as early as 1764, had ruled that in cases where vessels had cleared port after giving bond for enumerated articles but had included additional goods in the cargo, only the unlisted goods were liable for forfeiture. Sea captains and naval officers protested such loopholes in the regulations, but there was little they could do except complain to the ministry in England, or begin to use the Halifax court.[21]

The odium still lingered around Judge Spry's establishment. After the North Carolina episode during the Stamp Act troubles, no customs officer dared invoke the wrath of the seaboard by carrying cases northward. Thus the provincial vice-admiralty courts continued to determine almost all of the trade-law cases. The silent force of fear kept Judge Spry unoccupied and afforded merchants the comfort of trials in their local courts.[22]

The ease of local trials almost wrecked the Rhode Island customs establishment. John Andrews, whom the merchants

21. Benjamin Waller to Captain Morgan, Dec. 15, 1764, and Morgan to Waller, Dec. 19, 1764, PRO, CO 5, 1331. This interpretation of the trade laws was the direct opposite of that decreed by New York Vice-Admiralty Judge Richard Morris. See his opinion on *James Hawker qui tam* v. *Sloop Hummingbird & Lading*, Hough, *N.Y. Reps.*, 219-20.

22. None of Judge Spry's annual salary of £800 ever came from the crown's share of the forefeitures he had been expected to condemn in his court. His salary was to be paid, in the first instance, from those forfeitures, and, if this sum was insufficient, the remainder was to come from the Old Naval Stores Fund in England. He condemned so few vessels or cargoes, or of such small value, that nothing remained for the crown after the costs of prosecution had been deducted. All of his salary came from the Naval Stores Fund; between June 15, 1764, and December 15, 1767, he drew £2,800. Treasury Warrants, PRO, Treas. 28, 1.

had hand-picked during the French War, refused to be managed by Collector John Robinson and Comptroller John Nicholl. In March 1765, the customs officers had seized the brig *Waiscott* and the sloop *Nelly* for illegal trading and had requested Advocate General James Honeyman to secure depositions from witnesses to the seizures. Honeyman not only delayed the chore, but Judge Andrews scheduled the court session only three days after the two seizures had been made. When the customs officers asked for a postponement to interrogate witnesses, Andrews granted them a week's delay.

The seven extra days did little good. Honeyman would neither examine witnesses nor plead the crown's cause, and John Nicholl was forced to "stand his own advocate." Witnesses could not be found, and Andrews decreed both vessels acquitted. The frustrated customs officers wrote home to England about their difficulties in this case and in previous instances as well. They were constantly hampered by Andrews' actions, they claimed, because he refused to condemn their seizures. If he did condemn them, he failed to hand over the forfeiture money. The sales were geared to inflict the least possible penalty on the owners of vessels. One ship worth an estimated three hundred pounds sterling had been seized, condemned, and sold for about twenty pounds.

The customs officials thought they knew the cause of their troubles: Andrews was beholden to his native province for recommending his appointment as judge "with a view of facilitating the condemnation of Prizes made in the war." If he could not be dismissed, perhaps his court could be regulated in some fashion. The officers suggested that the judge be required to hold his court only "in Newport the Capitol of the Colony, and at Certain fixed days" instead of "at his own house, in the Woods or any other private place and at any Hour of any Day in the Year . . . an Inconveniency . . . labor'd under in every Instance" of causes prosecuted before his court.[23]

The Treasury Board read the customs officers' letters and hurried an order to the Rhode Island governor to investigate the charges. Governor Ward demanded a report of the proceedings from the customs officers and then passed the issue to the General Assembly. The Assembly appointed an investigating committee and then dropped the matter. But Judge Andrews, fearing for his position, took up the argument himself by sending a defense of his actions to the Treasury.

His defense contradicted every assertion of the customs officers. Andrews stated flatly that both the collector and the comptroller were in league with the owners of the two vessels; that they had never really intended the ships to be condemned. This, said the judge, was evident, since he had allowed an appeal to the High Court of Admiralty of England which had never been prosecuted. The charge that he favored "the Merchants to the Prejudice of the Crown" because he was a native of Rhode Island, he termed "mere Vapour, which went off in their Heat." For, he wrote, "faithful servants to the Crown are to be found among the Natives of America, and . . . the Geography of a Man's Birth hath nothing to do with his Merit or Demerit." He cited the record of appeals from his court: fifteen to the Lords of Appeals in prize cases and two to the High Court of Admiralty, and not one reversed.[24]

Writing letters to England might provide a defense against the customs officers' attack, but Andrews decided to take the offensive. He filed a bill of indictment in the

23. John Robinson and John Nicholl to Governor Ward, Feb. 22, 1766, and Robinson and Nicholl to Commissioners of Customs, Oct. 30, 1766, PRO, Treas. 1, 459. The first letter is also printed in Gertrude Selwyn Kimball, ed., *The Correspondence of the Colonial Governors of Rhode Island, 1723-1775* (2 vols.; Cambridge, 1903), II, 376-81.

24. John Andrews to Treasury, Sept. 30, 1766, PRO, Treas. 1, 459.

Providence Court of Quarter Sessions, threatening the collector and comptroller with defamation suits. The grand jury returned the indictment, agreeing that the customs officers "not having God before their eyes, but moved by the Instigation of the Devil" had written false statements to England. In April 1767, Judge Andrews sued Robinson in the Superior Court of Rhode Island for £10,000, Rhode Island currency. He won the award of the court. The actual damages, however, were not to be assessed until a jury was called in Providence the following September. Robinson did not wait until autumn to act; he promptly appealed the case to the King in Council. Before the charge was heard, Robinson left his post, and the involved litigation was finally dropped.[25]

Mr. Townshend's Acts

In England, further political developments were shaping the fate of the colonies. The Stamp Act was gone, and the ministry which had repealed it had also been dissolved. When the weak Rockingham administration crumbled in July 1766, the Duke of Grafton became the nominal head of a government chosen by William Pitt. Out of this ministry came a new scheme of colonial taxation.

Pitt himself retired within a few months. He accepted promotion to the chamber of peers as Lord Chatham and in October settled down in Bath for eighteen months of illness and inactivity which finally ended in resignation of his cabinet post. Out of the confusion of personalities that re-

25. John Robinson and John Nicholl to Governor Ward, Dec. 22, 1766, and Joseph Sherwood to Governor Hopkins, Mar. 21, 1768, Kimball, ed., *Correspondence of Rhode Island Governors*, II, 394-95, 401; Report of Commissioners of Customs, Feb. 5, and Robinson to Commissioners of Customs, May 23, 1767, PRO, Treas. 1, 459; Bartlett, ed., *Col. Recs. of R.I.*, VI, 458 ff.

mained, the Chancellor of the Exchequer, Charles Town-shend, soon emerged as leader of the ministry. Townshend was an unlikely choice for leader of Pitt's party, for his op-position to the repeal of the Stamp Act should have placed him in the Grenville camp. Once in office, he soon indicated that his plans for the colonies would follow his own, not Pitt's, convictions.

By the first of the year 1767, Townshend was ready to inaugurate his fiscal policies. A reduction in the British land tax had been carried through by Grenville's faction, and it was obvious that compensatory revenue would be demanded from the colonies. With neither the aid nor support of his ministerial colleagues, Townshend introduced and secured passage of his revenue program in June 1767. Import duties on glass, lead, paper, tea, and paint formed the tax list for the colonies. There could be no cry about the distinction between "internal" and "external" taxation. The duties would be collected in the American ports as the goods ar-rived from England, the only legal source for all of them. The revenue would be used in America to pay the salaries of crown appointees. Royal officials would thereby be re-lieved of their dependence on provincial legislatures.

To ensure collection of these new duties, Townshend pushed a companion measure through Parliament which radically altered the customs establishment in the colonies. Until this time the American collectors and surveyors had been directed by the Commissioners of the Customs in Eng-land, who operated directly under the Lords Commissioners of the Treasury. Control of the widespread establishment had been centered in London, an ocean apart from the outposts. Townshend separated the American establishment from the British completely. A five-man Board of the Commissioners of the Customs for America was authorized to sit at Boston with complete power over the American revenue system.

The energetic John Robinson, former Rhode Island collector, was chosen one of the members of this new board. His colleagues were Henry Hulton, John Temple, William Burch, and Charles Paxton. Temple's old position as surveyor general of the customs for the northern district had been merged with the duties of the new board. Paxton had formerly held the posts of surveyor of the port of Boston and marshal of the vice-admiralty court of Massachuestts. Hulton had served the British Customs Board as its secretary in England.

Charles Townshend died in September 1767, just as his new plan of American taxation was about to be inaugurated. Two months later, the new Customs Board held its first meeting in Boston. As the members began to survey the work before them, they were astounded at the "very great Height" to which violations of the trade laws had been carried. They were even more amazed to discover that only six seizures had been made in the New England provinces since the stamp troubles, and only one of them had been prosecuted successfully. One vessel had been "rescued" at Falmouth, another "at Newbury and the officers greatly abused," another "was carried off clandestinely at New London while under Prosecution," and the other two "were acquitted at Rhode Island through the combination and influence of the People."[26] There was work indeed for the new board.

26. Customs Commissioners to ————, Feb. 12, 1768, PRO, CO 5, 757. These statistics tend to be misleading as to the actual work of the colonial vice-admiralty courts. They apply only to New England and concern only customs cases. The New England courts, during this same time, heard and determined cases of private litigation between merchants and sailors without interruption. Taken as a whole, the American vice-admiralty courts were relatively busy institutions during 1766 and 1767. Records of at least seventy-seven causes of all types of cases are still extant, although many of these are no more than casual notices in newspapers and correspondence. The cases were tried in courts from Quebec and Newfoundland to South Carolina and

Meanwhile, further south a storm was breaking over the issue of Daniel Moore, who had arrived in Charleston, South Carolina, as collector in March 1767. Greedy customs officers had been known in the colonies before, but Moore set a new standard for rapaciousness. As a reward for "assisting in direction the Paper &c for the Stamps," he had been given the Charleston collectorship, which was reputedly capable of producing the fantastic sum of £8,000 annually.[27] In Charleston he met George Roupell, already installed as a customs searcher, and the two officials became allies.

They had hardly begun a program of "tightening-up" the Charleston customhouse before they provoked the wrath of the entire mercantile community. Although they probably had little desire to add to the crown's revenue and certainly would have preferred to retain the good will of the Charlestonians, they found that to maintain good relations with the merchants and fill their own pockets with forfeiture money at the same time was impossible.

Moore began his duties as collector by announcing that breaches of the trade laws would no longer be tolerated in his district. He soon had a chance to show that he meant to follow his words with action. Captain James Hawker, commanding H.M.S. *Sardoine,* seized the large schooner *Active* in May 1767 for sailing from Winyah without register, bonds, or other papers. The vessel, owned by James Gordon, had always been used in the coasting trade, usually within the boundaries of the province. There was little evidence that any fraud had been intended, but Moore, anxious to

West Florida. Many of the notices are too brief to indicate the nature of the cause, but they included customs seizures, salvage, wage disputes, and insurance contracts.

27. George Mercer, "Account for Attendance, Expences, etc.," Nov. 28, 1775, PRO, Treas. 1, 445. Henry McCulloch of North Carolina estimated the place worth the more conservative sum of £600. Jucker, ed., *Jenkinson Papers,* 230.

prove himself to the merchants, advised the naval officer to prosecute his seizure in the vice-admiralty court. The collector furnished the security necessary for the prosecution.

Moore and Hawker soon found themselves engaged in a man-size battle. Neither was a lawyer, and they were well aware that their case should be capably prosecuted. The province was then without an advocate general; William Drayton, who had held the commission, had recently been appointed chief justice of East Florida. When the customs officers sought the advice of Attorney General Egerton Leigh, he refused them counsel. Leigh had added the attorney generalship to his duties as judge of the vice-admiralty court, surveyor general, and council member, two years before. He told the officers he could not advise them in matters that would come before him in his capacity as vice-admiralty judge. Moore and Hawker then turned to the city lawyers, but were again refused aid. "Every lawyer refused positively to be concerned," although they were willing to argue the other side.[28] Finally the Governor appointed a new advocate general, a young inexperienced attorney named John Deering. He proved to be no match for the legal counsel of the *Active*'s owner.

When trial took place in June, every Charleston merchant watched the proceedings closely. Southern commerce was largely concerned in the coasting trade. Much of it took place, as in this case, within the boundaries of a single province. Until 1764, vessels that tramped from plantation to plantation had not been required to enter and clear customhouses while they were collecting or distributing their cargoes. To do so would have been inconvenient and costly. However, section 29 of the 1764 Revenue Act introduced regulations for the coasting trade similar to those formerly prescribed for ocean commerce. All vessels traveling more

28. *S.C. Gazette*, June 23, 1767.

than seven miles from shore were required to carry cockets listing each item of their cargoes. These cockets were issued by customs officials. This requirement alone, if strictly enforced, would inconvenience coastwise shippers, since they would have to visit a customs officer each time they added to their cargo. In the southern colonies, especially, the most secure, and sometimes shortest, routes lay more than seven miles from shore. In addition, the act stipulated that merchants or captains must present bonds and acquire loading certificates before they took cargoes on board their vessels. This was no innovation, but colonial practice had long allowed merchants to secure the bonds after their vessels had completed their loading and were ready to sail.

In the years since 1764 the revenue officers had allowed the old practice to continue. Now, however, the Charleston collector and his colleague threatened to force strict compliance with the trade laws. The merchants soon recognized their common stake in the fight. When this "cause of great weight and expectation" was argued, "the court-house was constantly crowded."[29]

Judge Leigh satisfied no one by his decree. He acquitted the vessel on the grounds that it had not engaged in illicit trade. But he pronounced that a probable cause of seizure had existed and taxed the costs of the case on the owner of the *Active*. Thus, while his decree cleared the question of coasting regulations, the owner was forced to pay court costs of £150 for the release of his schooner, reportedly worth no more than half that sum. And the "probable cause" certification denied him the right to redress his grievance by suing Hawker or Moore at common law. The collector and the naval officer were equally unhappy. They had lost their argument against coasting vessels and received no "prize" money from what had looked like a certain condemnation.

29. *Ibid.*

Moore, who had so openly proclaimed his intentions of strictly enforcing the trade laws, was left to face the wrath of the combined merchants of Charleston.[30]

30. The subsequent episodes are related in the following chapter. On the *Active* case, see James Hawker to Commissioners of Customs, June 13, 1767, PRO, Admir. 1, 4286; Daniel Moore to Treasury, Aug. 25, 1767, *ibid.,* 459; Leigh's opinion and other papers, *ibid.,* 465; *S.C. Gazette,* June 23, 1767; *Penn. Gazette,* July 9, 1767; *N.Y. Jour.,* July 23, 1767; Sellers, *Charleston Business,* 192-94; Dickerson, *Navigation* Acts, 225-26.

5

Some Patriots Are Made, Not Born

JUDGE SPRY decided that he would remain a judge no longer. His court was not consulted; he was bored with the whole arrangement. When Governor Montagu Wilmot, who had ruled over Nova Scotia for less than three years, died in the early summer of 1766, Spry resolved to graduate to a governorship. He wrote to Grenville, asking for his aid in gaining the vacant position. But Grenville was unable to help and could only assure Spry that he believed he deserved a high office and would promote his cause when he could.[1]

It was almost a year before the judge's dream came true. When the Barbados governorship fell vacant in the summer of 1767, Spry was appointed to fill it. He quickly made arrangements to leave his northern outpost for the balmy, southern island in the Caribbean. He was finished with

1. Grenville to Spry, Aug. 19, 1766, Grenville Letter Books, II, Huntington Lib.

vice-admiralty courts and civil law; and he was finished with these rebellious North Americans. Barbados promised to be paradise indeed. In January 1767, the man-of-war *Beaver* cleared Halifax harbor with Doctor Spry and his family aboard. Less than a month later the new governor landed at Barbados. His dismal adventure in the northern colony could now be forgotten.[2]

Before he left Nova Scotia, Spry appointed Joseph Gerrish his surrogate, to act for him in all matters that might come before the vice-admiralty court. Gerrish was already in the pay of the crown as storekeeper for His Majesty's Royal Navy.[3] The new position added little to his duties, and he was assured a part of the income from the judgeship. The arrangements pleased everyone, the only dissatisfactory note being the fact that the court had never performed the function for which it was established. And there was little indication that it ever would. The customs war in the colonies continued, but the provincial vice-admiralty courts were the agencies for prosecution. The new surrogate judge at Halifax might be thankful that he was not party to those struggles. None of them was pleasant, and in South Carolina the battle threatened to ruin the vice-admiralty court forever.

Mr. Laurens Goes to Court

Henry Laurens might have lived his lifetime in South Carolina, conducting his mercantile ventures without opposition to the trade regulations prescribed by the mother country. Laurens was a man of considerable wealth, who

2. Admiralty to Judge Salisbury, June 23, 1767, PRO, Admir. 2, 1057; *Acts of the Privy Council: Colonial Series*, V, 553; *Mass. Gazette*, Sept. 17, 1767, May 12, 1768; *N.Y. Jour.*, Oct. 1 and 29, 1767, Apr. 21, 1768; *Conn. Courant*, Dec. 21, 1767; *Boston Chronicle*, Jan. 25-Feb. 1, 1768.

3. He was also a member of the Nova Scotia Council and a justice of the Court of Common Pleas. *Mass. Gazette*, June 16, 1774; Philip Stephens to Gerrish, Apr. 20, 1768, PRO, Admir. 2. 1057.

by taste and talents might have been expected to uphold the right of Parliament to tax the colonies and place trade restrictions upon the provincials. "The calamity of domestic broils" were "more awful & more distressing [to him] than Fire pestilence or foreign Wars." In 1765 he had shown little enthusiasm for the local opposition to the Stamp Act.[4] But in the course of events he became so embroiled in a private war with customs and vice-admiralty establishments in his home town of Charleston that he became a bitter critic of the crown, its policies, and its servants.

Laurens had watched the actions of Collector Moore and his henchman George Roupell from the moment they began their campaign of customs enforcement. When the issue of coasting vessels had come to a head in the trial of the schooner *Active* in June 1767, Laurens had contributed to the defense of the schooner, and thereby brought himself fully into the customs war in South Carolina. Before the year was out he felt the full effects of that war.

Early in the summer of 1767, Laurens sent two of his coasting vessels, the *Wambaw* and the *Broughton Island Packet,* to one of his plantations in Georgia. They both sailed in the usual manner, without certificates or bonds from the Charleston customhouse. The *Wambaw*'s captain, after unloading a cargo of provisions and tools, filled the vessel with shingles and returned to Charleston. But before clearing Laurens' plantation wharf, the captain traveled to the small Georgia town of Frederica to obtain clearance papers and to post bond. Laurens had decided to take no chances with the revitalized Charleston revenue officers. There was no customhouse at Frederica, but the statutes allowed such bonds to be given before magistrates or "known British merchants."

4. Laurens to Captain Christopher Rowe, Feb. 8, 1764, and Laurens to Joseph Brown, Oct. 11, 1765, Letterbook of Henry Laurens in Hist. Soc. of Penn.

Despite these precautions, Moore directed Roupell to seize the *Wambaw* when she entered Charleston harbor. Laurens was charged with carrying lumber from one colony to another without posting bond and obtaining clearance papers. His defense that the shingles were put aboard solely for ballast was contradicted by his own admission that he intended to sell them after they had served this purpose. The collector refused to admit that the bonds given in Georgia were valid, claiming that Laurens himself had "set up two justices of peace in Georgia as Customs House Officers."[5] But Moore was not especially anxious to face Judge Leigh with the case and suggested that if Laurens would come to the customhouse and agree to observe the acts of trade in the future, he would disregard the seizure. Laurens refused, and the question was put to the vice-admiralty judge.

Before the trial began, however, the second Laurens schooner, the *Broughton Island Packet,* was seized. This vessel had also been sent to Laurens' Georgia plantation with provisions, and it returned without bonds or clearances and with logs and chunks of wood as ballast. Moore disliked seizing a second vessel until the fate of the first had been decided, and he sounded out Egerton Leigh. As attorney general, Leigh might ordinarily have been the proper person to turn to. But in his capacity as vice-admiralty judge, he would decree on the case if a seizure were made. Less than three months before he had refused to aid the customs officers in the *Active* case. Nevertheless, he now advised the collector to seize the *Broughton Island Packet.*

The trials of the two vessels took place in Charleston in September. The *Wambaw* was disposed of first, and probably would have been acquitted if Laurens had not admitted that the shingles were to be sold after use as ballast. Certainly the merchant had the advantage in legal counsel, for, as

5. Daniel Moore to Treasury, Aug. 25, 1767, PRO, Treas. 1, 459.

in the case of the *Active* the previous June, the customs collector "could get no assistance at Bar," but had to rely on young John Deering, the advocate general, who "had not a word to say except that he had marked Acts of Parliament on backs of papers and relied on Judge for opinion."[6] Leigh's opinion condemned the *Wambaw* and ordered the schooner sold and the profits divided between the crown, the governor, and the searcher Roupell. The judge taxed the costs of the trial to Laurens, who repurchased his schooner at the public sale.[7]

One week after the condemnation of the *Wambaw,* the trial of the *Broughton Island Packet* took place in the same court. Laurens had little hope for acquittal when he heard Judge Leigh had announced that "like the two Dromios— they came in together and they must stand or fall together."[8] Much to the disappointment of the customs officers, however, Leigh actually differentiated between the seizures; he accepted Laurens' word that the firewood ballast was for personal use only. He acquitted the *Broughton Island Packet* and did not pronounce a probable cause, even though he had advised the customs officers to make the seizure. Roupell and Deering claimed that the judge had promised them such a certificate in return for their assurance that they would not appeal the case. Now they were unprotected from actions at common law, and Laurens, with the aid of his fellow merchants, acted quickly.

They brought a suit against Moore in the common-law court on charges of illegally taking fees for indigo certificates. He was cleared in this suit, but the merchants started other prosecutions against him, and "he thought it prudent to

6. *Ibid.*
7. George Roupell to Customs Commissioners, Sept. 16, 1767, *ibid.,* 459; David D. Wallace, *The Life of Henry Laurens, with a Sketch of the Life of Lieutenant-Colonel John Laurens* (N.Y., 1915), 137-39.
8. Quoted in Wallace, *Henry Laurens,* 139.

leave the Province in order to represent those matters at home."[9]   Roupell alone was left to face Laurens' revenge. The planter sued him in the common-law courts for £5,000 damages.   Judge Leigh took off his robes and, as attorney general, served as Roupell's counsel at the trial.   Roupell lost the suit.   The jury awarded Laurens a satisfaction judgment of £1,400 currency, approximately £200 sterling.   The searcher eventually prevailed upon the Commissioners of the Customs to pay the judgment from the colonial revenue, but this did little to soothe his discomfort.   In his unhappiness he blamed all of his troubles on the "ignorant Advocate General who seemed to refuse doing his duty."[10]   And he waited for a chance to even the score with Mr. Laurens.

That opportunity came in June 1768, when the ship *Ann* was being readied to sail from Charleston to Bristol.   The vessel, owned by a partnership which included Laurens, was loaded with a cargo of rice.   Roupell was informed that small quantities of rum, wine, cattle horns, and pinkroot were also on board, and that no bonds were given, or permit granted, before the vessel was loaded.   He seized the *Ann* and filed an information against her in the vice-admiralty court.   His chances of success were admittedly slim.   The Charleston port officers had long sanctioned the illegal practice of allowing merchants to load their vessels before securing clearance papers.   But Roupell was seeking revenge, and he offered to release the vessel if Laurens would surrender his verdict in the *Broughton Island Packet* case.   Laurens scornfully refused to be blackmailed, and Leigh's vice-admiralty court heard his case.

9. Memorial of Daniel Moore to Treasury, PRO, Treas. 1, 468; Roupell to Customs Commissioners, Sept. 16, 1767, and Deposition of J. Deering, *ibid.*, 459; Memorial of Charles Garth upon the Conduct of Daniel Moore, *ibid.*, 463; *Mass. Gazette*, Oct. 8, 1767; *Conn. Courant*, Oct. 12, 1767; *S.C. Gazette*, Nov. 3, 1767.

10. Roupell to Customs Commissioners, Sept. 16, 1767, PRO, Treas. 1, 459; *Penn. Gazette*, Oct. 19, 1769; Wallace, *Henry Laurens*, 139-42; Sellers, *Charleston Business*, 194-98; Dickerson, *Navigation Acts*, 226-27.

Judge Leigh was Henry Laurens' nephew, and in the past the two men had been close friends.[11] Their friendship was threatened by the proceedings in the trial of Laurens' two schooners the previous autumn, as well as by their disagreement over a provincial statute concerning the clerk of the circuit court. Leigh's decree in the case of the *Ann* proved to be the final blow to their relationship. Although the judge acquitted the vessel and denied Roupell's motion for appeal, he pronounced a probable cause for seizure and thus blocked Laurens' revenge at common law. In addition, Leigh assessed part of the costs of the trial to the merchant. The contest was over, but Laurens' battle had just begun.[12] His next target was to be Judge Leigh.

Laurens wrote out the facts of the situation as he saw them. He included in his "Observations on American Custom House Officers and Courts of Vice-Admiralty," the records of the cases as they had been argued and decreed in Leigh's court. When he finished his manuscript, he sent it to William Fisher, a Philadelphia merchant who owned a share of the *Ann*. Fisher printed part of the paper in Philadelphia and sent copies to Laurens, along with the opinion of several prominent Philadelphia lawyers to the effect that Leigh's decisions appeared to be questionable.[13]

11. Laurens to William Fisher, Aug. 1, 1768, Etting Mss., Miscellaneous, Hist. Soc. of Penn.

12. The records of the trial are in PRO, Treas. 1, 465. Leigh's decree of acquittal, and his refusal to allow an appeal from his decree, pleased Roupell no more than the assessment of court costs pleased Laurens. For Roupell's attempt to gain an appeal despite Leigh's decision, see Roupell to Commissioners of Customs, Aug. 6, 1768; Roupell to American Customs Board, July 11, 1768; American Customs Board to Treasury, Dec. 16, 1768; and Opinion of Attorney General William De Grey, Mar. 25, 1769, all in PRO, Treas. 1, 463, 465, 472. See also *Mass. Gazette*, Aug. 11, 1768; *N.Y. Jour.*, Aug. 4, 1768; *Boston Weekly Newsletter*, Aug. 18, 1768; Wallace, *Henry Laurens*, 142-45; Sellers, *Charleston Business*, 198-200; Dickerson, *Navigation Acts*, 228-29.

13. Laurens to William Fisher, Sept. 12, Nov. 9, Dec. 14, 1768, and Oct. 16, 1769, Etting Mss., Miscellaneous, Hist. Soc. of Penn.

Laurens waited until February 1769 and then published his work in Charleston under the title: *Extracts from the Proceedings of the Court of Vice-Admiralty.*

His pamphlet contained little more than the actual records of the cases of the two previous years, but this was enough to drive Leigh to the defensive. He answered the pamphlet with a personal attack upon Laurens: *The Man Un-Masked.* The print war continued when Laurens combined his *Extracts* with the "Observations" previously published in Philadelphia and had them printed together in April 1769. Later in the summer he followed this publication with an *Appendix to the Extracts from the Proceedings of the Court of Vice-Admiralty.*[14]

In writing his arguments, Laurens was careful to avoid the appearance of merely stating his own grievances against particular individuals. He admitted that the actions of these men had called forth his protests, but he was writing, he said, to warn others that what had happened in Charleston could as easily take place in New York or Philadelphia. Many of his arguments were not new. The same sentiments had been expressed again and again since the passage of the Revenue Act of 1764. Laurens was opposed to many of the trade restrictions; he was even more opposed to the methods used to enforce them: "Be the laws ever so good and equitable; if bad men are employed as executive officers, who are avaricious, revengeful, and make their private gain the rule and measure of their conduct, under good laws, wrested and perverted by such men, trade must inevitably languish and decay."[15]

The villains in South Carolina, according to Laurens, were the customs officers and Judge Leigh. He was outraged over the powers that had been granted the tyrants who filled

14. Wallace, *Henry Laurens,* 145-48; the "Observations" are reprinted in the appendix to Wallace's book.
15. Quoted in Wallace, *Henry Laurens,* 497.

the customs posts; he viewed the powers reposed in the vice-admiralty judges as abhorrent to the English legal system. This led him to extoll the virtues of the common law and to damn the "extension" of jurisdiction of the vice-admiralty courts. He did not describe the historical development of the American admiralty courts, but rather concentrated his attention on the undeniable fact that trials for offenses under the trade laws took place in different courts in England and America.

The American asks "how causes relating to the revenue are decided in Great Britain? Whether they are given to the Admiral?" Laurens supplied the reply. The American "is answered, No. In Ireland? No. America is the only place where cognizance of such causes is given to the Admirality. And what has America done to be thus particularized, to be disfranchized and stript of so invaluable a privilege as the trial by jury?"[16]

Laurens disclaimed any personal motive in the battle. He wrote to an English correspondent that although "gentlemen may look upon this matter as the effect of a quarrel between Mr. Leigh and Mr. Laurens . . . they are quite mistaken. . . . If nothing but my own interest or nothing but resentment had prompted me to write, my pen should have been otherwise employed." And he warned: "The enormous created powers vested in an American Court of Vice-Admiralty threatens future generations in America with a curse tenfold worse than the stamp act."[17]

However sincere Laurens may have been when he wrote these words, his future actions showed that revenge had partially prompted his writings. The quarrel in Charleston soon sank to dismal levels. In the pamphlets which he sent to the other American colonies, the West Indies, and Eng-

16. *Ibid.*, 500.
17. Henry Laurens to Thomas Smith, Aug. 8, 1769, *ibid.*, 148.

SOME PATRIOTS ARE MADE, NOT BORN

land, Laurens called Leigh a "greedy, coarse, and filthy
wretch," a "polecate." These spirited words did nothing to
modify the vice-admiralty judgeship. That was done months
before Laurens took up his pen.

In the summer of 1767, customs officials in South Carolina had complained to the Commissioners of the Customs in
England that Leigh held both the attorney generalship and
the vice-admiralty judgeship. The logic of these complaints
had been recognized in England. The Admiralty Board realized that it was an undesirable situation which deprived the
customs officials of one source of competent legal aid, and
which constantly placed the judge in awkward, perhaps even
unethical, positions. The board took up the problem immediately and reviewed appointments in all the colonies to
determine if the same situation existed elsewhere. It discovered that John Randolph in Virginia also doubled as
attorney general and vice-admiralty judge. The Admiralty
immediately announced to the governors of South Carolina
and Virginia that Leigh and Randolph would have to resign
one office or the other. Randolph, who had been petition-
ing the ministry for a salary as judge, hesitated, postponed
choosing, and finally contrived to give up neither office.[18]
But Leigh was not so fortunate.

Governor Montagu in South Carolina had received notifi-
cation early in May 1768, a full month before the ship *Ann*
was seized, that Leigh must relinquish one of his offices.
In September Leigh quit the vice-admiralty post. The
judgeship carried no salary, and he had discovered that in
South Carolina the post was also without honor.[19]

Thus Laurens' pamphlets were not the cause of Leigh's

18. See below, 162-63.
19. Treasury to Philip Stephens, Aug. 25, 1767, PRO, Admir. 1, 4286;
Stephens to Governor Montagu, May 4, and to Governor Amherst, May 9,
1768, *ibid.*, 2, 1057; American Customs Board to Treasury, Aug. 25, 1768,
PRO, Treas. 1, 465; *Boston Chronicle*, Oct. 21-Nov. 7, 1768; *N.Y. Jour.*, Nov.
18, 1768.

resignation from the judgeship. Laurens knew when he wrote them that Leigh would no longer decide cases of seizures, but this knowledge did not deter him from publishing his case. Although Laurens certainly experienced inconvenience in the seizure and trials of his vessels, and may have suffered financial loss, there seems little doubt of his chief motive in attacking the customs and vice-admiralty establishments. It was not revenge against Moore and Roupell, for when he wrote his attack the latter had fled the colony and the former had been relieved of his post. Indeed, the Charleston customhouse had undergone a complete change of personnel. Laurens' major target was Egerton Leigh, and his campaign against the customs officers and the vice-admiralty courts had by this time become a personal battle.

Leigh's resignation as vice-admiralty judge left a vacancy that was not easily filled. Odium hung over the office. No lawyer was anxious to accept a position being heartily damned by Laurens. From September 1768 until May 1769, the Governor could find "no Gentleman of the Law . . . that would accept it." Then James Simpson, a promising young attorney who had been admitted to the bar only five years before, agreed to take the post.[20] Leigh remained as attorney general and council member until 1774, when he was created a baronet by the British Crown. And Henry Laurens, by his own actions, found himself at the head of the mercantile community, once more angered by Britain's determination to draw a revenue from her American plantations.

Warfare on the Water Front

In comparison to merchants in the northern cities, the Charlestonians were slow to organize themselves against

20. *N.Y. Jour.*, June 22, 1769; Anne King Gregorie, ed., *Records of the Court of Chancery of South Carolina, 1671-1779* (Washington, 1951), 545.

the Townshend taxes. In October 1767, the Boston town meeting had adopted an agreement by which consumers committed themselves not to purchase British goods. The town's radical leaders hoped to coerce the merchants into an even stronger program: cessation of all imports from Great Britain, excepting only the articles necessary to the fishing industry. Similar schemes at the time of the Stamp Act had been short lived, but they remained as a guide for economic warfare. Perhaps the loss of trade would do what petitions and remonstrances were unable to accomplish.

By March 1768, the pressure of the "non-consumption" agreement had forced the Boston merchants to adopt a non-importation association, conditional upon its acceptance by Philadelphia and New York traders. Strong opposition to this program in Philadelphia caused the attempt at inter-colonial cooperation to collapse. However, the Boston radicals continued their agitation, and in August 1768, the merchants of that city adopted an independent, unconditional nonimportation agreement. The New York merchants subscribed to a similar association within a few weeks, and the Philadelphia merchants belatedly came into line in March 1769.[21]

If these agreements were to be effective, violations could not be tolerated. Selected committees of merchants and radicals accepted the responsibility of carefully watching incoming vessels. The committees became pseudo-customs establishments whose self-imposed duties were quite different from those of the crown's officers. While the royal collectors and surveyors made their daily rounds to ensure obedience to the acts of trade, these new committeemen were equally active in watching for violations of the nonimporta-

21. The southern provinces adopted nonimportation agreements during the summer and fall of 1769. Leslie J. Thomas, The Non-Consumption and Non-Importation Movements 1767-1770 (unpublished master's thesis, Univ. of Wis., 1949), chaps. 1 and 2.

tion agreements. Due to the efforts of the new American customs board, there were more crown servants on the docks and in the harbors than ever before.

Determined to put an end to illicit trade in the colonies, the board immediately exercised its power to appoint additional officers and to create additional customs ports. In three years' time the establishment at Philadelphia trebled in size. And the new board enjoyed the active support of the Royal Navy. The sea captains had finally won their argument over shares of seizures. With ill grace, the governors retreated from their demands for the traditional one-third share of seizures and admitted the legality of the sea captains' claims.[22]

The agreements to cease importation of British goods were long-range plans. Months would pass before the mercantile houses in England would feel the pinch of the loss of the American trade. The program was also conservative, at least in comparison with the treatment of colonial customs and naval officers as the warfare on the water front increased. The techniques of that warfare had been discovered during the Stamp Act days, and a few refinements were now added. To reseize a seizure, and thus keep it from trial in the vice-admiralty court, was still a prime objective. But personal revenge against informers and prosecutors was added as an alternative: the reign of tar and feathers began.

This water-front warfare was concentrated in, but not confined to, the northern provinces.[23] From Pennsylvania northward, the pattern of resistance was repeated in province

22. The governors never completely abandoned the battle. In 1771, William Tryon of New York pleaded with Hillsborough for a share of the king's half of seizures made at sea, claiming that it was unfair to him and to the other American governors not to "be put on the same footing with Admirals." Tryon to Hillsborough, Dec. 4, 1771; William Knox to John Robinson, Jan. 31, 1772, PRO, CO 5, 1103 and 250.

23. In Charleston the "militia drums beat to call a mob" when a British naval officer threatened seizure of an incoming vessel. Captain James Hawker to Lord Charles Montagu, May 30, 1767, PRO, Treas. 1, 459.

after province. Under cover of night and silence, men rowed out of the docks to recapture vessels and cargoes which had been seized, and any capture not securely manned, or protected by the guns of a man-of-war in the harbor, was unsafe.[24] If reseizure was impossible, the informer or prosecutor was threatened. Sometimes notes of warning sufficed. But more often it was necessary to inflict harsher punishments.

The prescribed treatment was a horrible challenge to customs officers and informers. A barrel of tar and a sack of feathers were the only instruments needed. The technique was uncomplicated. Stripped of clothing, smeared with tar, and rolled in feathers, victims of a mob were carried or carted through jeering crowds of townsmen. Occasionally, a more elaborate procedure was used. Peter Oliver outlined a somewhat embellished "Recipe for an effectual Operation": "First strip a Person naked, then heat the Tar untill it is thin, & pour it upon the naket Flesh, or rub it over it with a Tar Brush, *quantum sufficit,*—after which, sprinkle decently upon the Tar, whilst it is yet warm, as many Feathers as will stick to it—then hold a lighted Candle to the Feathers & try to set it all on Fire: if it will burn so much the better: but as the Experiment is often made in cold Weather; it will not then succeed—take also an Halter, & put it round the Person's Neck, & then cart him the Rounds."[25] After such

24. Governor Bernard to Earl of Hillsborough, July 9, 1768, *ibid.,* 465; Commodore Samuel Hood to Philip Stephens, May 8, 1769, PRO, Admir. 1, 483.

25. Peter Oliver, "Origin and Progress of the Rebellion in America, to 1776," British Museum, Egerton Mss., 2671, Lib. Cong. Transcript. See also the descriptions of mob activities in Captain Pryce to Earl of Hillsborough, Feb. 4, 1769, and Thomas Hutchinson to Hillsborough, May 21, 1770, PRO, CO 5, 1073, 759; John Swift to American Customs Commissioners, May 5 and Oct. 13, 1769, Philadelphia Customs House Papers, X, Hist. Soc. of Penn.; *Boston Chronicle,* Sept. 5-12, 1768, Oct. 3-10, 1768, Oct. 26-30, 1769; *Mass. Gazette,* Nov. 17, 1768, Nov. 9, 1769; *Boston Gazette,* Oct. 16, 1769, July 6, 1772; *N.Y. Jour.,* Mar. 30 and Oct. 19, 1769, June 6, 1771.

treatment, few informers were bold enough to repeat their crime, and few customs officers so treated remained in the colony to seek revenge.

Against such attacks, the government appeared powerless. It was almost impossible to discover the ringleaders. Whether done in the dark, or in broad daylight, the violence was accomplished suddenly and efficiently, and the men vanished. Law officers refused to take the offensive; the governors issued proclamations demanding aid from sheriffs and magistrates in putting an end to the tyranny, but with no effect. Rewards for information of the persons involved went uncollected. It seemed impossible to fight back.[26]

Ordinarily, men so mistreated by lawless bands might have revenged themselves in the common-law courts by suing the attackers for assault. But even when the offenders' identity was discovered, and suit brought against them, juries were uncooperative. The process of securing judgment against assaulters took months, and it usually failed because jurymen refused to bring verdicts against their fellow townsmen.[27] In desperation the Customs Commissioners at Boston sought advice from England about possible methods of forcing the "County, Town or District, where such offences . . . [were committed] to make good the damages." But all of the statutory provisions for such compensation depended upon the regular common-law channels, and there was little that could be done.[28]

Stung by these insults to their authority, and more determined than ever to follow their instructions from home, the American Board of Customs Commissioners decided to

26. *Mass. Gazette,* Nov. 10, 1768, Nov. 2, 1769; *Boston Chronicle,* Oct. 30-Nov. 2, 1769.

27. John Tabor Kempe to Andrew Elliot, Sept. 28, 1769, Kempe Papers, N.Y. Hist. Soc.; "Case of Robert Savage," PRO, Treas. 1, 491; *Boston Gazette,* Aug. 5, 1771.

28. American Customs Board to Treasury, Oct. 4, 1768, and Solicitor's Report, PRO, Treas. 1, 465.

set an example that would end, once and for all, the opposition. The man they chose to crucify was John Hancock, among the wealthiest of Boston merchants, already proven a friend to the radical elements in Massachusetts.

Mr. Hancock Loses a Ship

The coming of the commissioners to Boston in the fall of 1767 had inflamed public opinion. While they sat at conference or wandered the streets of the city, they were an ever-present reminder of the duties they were sent to collect. Within six months of their first meeting, the mob forced them to flee, first to the man-of-war in the harbor, and later to Castle William. There they continued to supervise the American customs. The incident that drove them from Boston brought forth one of the strangest trials ever heard in a colonial vice-admiralty court.

John Hancock, who had early made known his opposition to the new duties, was a prime target for the Customs Board. He was a wealthy merchant who had lent his name and his money to the "popular" party in Massachusetts. To humiliate him would perhaps serve as a direct threat to lesser men in the colonies and indicate that the trade regulations would be enforced to the limit. In addition, it seemed to the sensitive board members that Hancock had gone out of his way to pick a quarrel with them. As captain of the local militia, he had refused to lead a parade in their honor when they arrived in Boston. And he had turned down invitations to dinners that he knew they would attend. Early in the winter, he had risen in the General Assembly and announced that he would permit no customs officials "to go even on board any of his London Ships."[29]

29. American Customs Board to Treasury, May 12, 1768, *ibid.;* quoted in Baxter, *House of Hancock,* 260.

Before long, he acted on his challenge. Early in April, Hancock's ship *Lydia* entered Boston harbor from London. Only a few hours after the customhouse sent tidewaiters aboard to watch the unloading of the vessel, Hancock collected a small group of followers and climbed aboard after them. Upon questioning, the two customs officers admitted that they had come aboard to search the vessel on orders of the collector and comptroller. Hancock thereupon ordered the *Lydia*'s captain to make certain that they did not go below deck.

Tidewaiters were legally allowed to board vessels for only two purposes: to search a ship or to watch for running of prohibited or customed goods. The regulations stipulated that tidewaiters were allowed below deck to search, but there was no such permission granted for the purpose of watching. Presumably, they would be able to detect unloading or running from the deck.

After dark on the following night, Owen Richards, one of the tidewaiters, slipped below deck to search out tea or paper or other products bearing an import duty. He was quickly discovered, and within a short time Hancock and his henchmen were again on board the *Lydia*. They questioned the tidewaiter about his intentions and asked him if he meant to search the vessel. Richards, thoroughly frightened, replied that he did not. If he had not come aboard to search, his object must have been to watch—and no statute allowed him below deck for that purpose. Hancock was satisfied that he had put fear into the officer and had still acted within the law.

The Customs Board, however, was certain that they had a case against the merchant. They requested Jonathan Sewall, the Massachusetts attorney general, to institute prosecution against him immediately. And they specifically asked

Sewall to circumvent the difficulties of gaining a grand jury indictment by filing an information in the Superior Court. Sewall did not relish such action; the use of an information would introduce a relatively novel instrument into the Massachusetts common law. Besides, after comparing all of the depositions and testimony, Sewall was convinced that Hancock's "intention was to keep within the bounds of the law." Upon these grounds he refused the commissioners' request.[30]

The board, however, was not satisfied. They sent the papers and reports to the Treasury in London and demanded a reversal of Sewall's opinion. The Treasury upheld the attorney general's decision, but by the time the board received this answer, they had perpetrated another storm.[31]

A month after the *Lydia* was seized, and before the commissioners discovered that Hancock could not be touched for that incident, another of his vessels, the *Liberty,* arrived from Madeira. Her cargo was wine, which she entered at the customhouse on May 10, 1768, paying the legal duties for twenty-five casks. Then, for a full four weeks, Hancock kept his vessel at his wharf reloading her with whale oil and tar for London. On the tenth of June, shortly before she was ready to sail, the customs officers seized the *Liberty* for loading without a permit. The charge was the same as that upon which George Roupell in Charleston had based his seizure of the *Ann.* In Boston, as in South Carolina, the customs officers had never insisted on a strict compliance with the statutes regulating shiploading. However, the Boston

30. Sewall's opinion is in Oliver M. Dickerson, "Opinion of Attorney General Jonathan Sewall Of Massachusetts in the Case of the *Lydia,*" *Wm. and Mary Qtly.,* 3rd ser., 4 (1947), 499-504, and PRO, Treas. 1, 465. The opinion of Samuel Fitch, solicitor of the Customs Board, and the depositions of Tidewaiters Owen Richards and Robert Jackson are also in Treas. 1, 465. See also Baxter, *House of Hancock,* 262; Dickerson, *Navigation Acts,* 232-36.

31. American Customs Board to Treasury, May 12, 1768, PRO, Treas. 1, 465.

customs officers were determined to make an example of Hancock.

They soon discovered the dangers of their scheme: they had got much more than one Boston merchant. For many months there had been no unrescued seizure in New England, and the customs men decided to take no chances. They started to tow the vessel out into the harbor under the protecting guns of His Majesty's man-of-war *Romney.* Their intentions were soon discovered, and a water-front crowd attempted to delay their action and provoke a fight with them. The *Liberty* was finally securely anchored close to the *Romney,* but the customs officers were threatened by the mob on their way home, and that night their houses were stoned, and the collector's pleasure boat was burned on Boston Common.[32]

Less than three years had passed since crown officers' homes were besieged during the Stamp Act riots. The same, or worse, might happen now. That night, the frightened commissioners hid in friends' houses and fled the next morning onto the *Romney.* Governor Bernard soon granted them asylum at Castle William. They moved themselves and their families to the fortress and attempted to conduct their transactions there.

Meanwhile, the *Liberty* seemed lost to John Hancock. The mob had chased the commissioners from town, but the ship, with the king's broad arrow marked on her, still lay under the protection of the *Romney.* Hancock did not relish losing the vessel. On Saturday, the day following the riot, he sent word to the commissioners that he would post bond to abide by the decision of the trial, if they would deliver the *Liberty* to him until the case was decided. The commissioners accepted his proposal and agreed to move

32. The proceedings of the Customs Board, the depositions of witnesses, and accompanying papers are in *ibid.* See also Governor Bernard's "Observations," PRO, CO 5, 757; *Boston Weekly Newsletter,* June 16, 1768.

the *Liberty* back to his dock the following Monday. Before the next week started, however, Hancock changed his mind. After a Sunday night conclave with James Otis, Samuel Adams, and other Boston radicals, Hancock notified the commissioners that he would make no deals with them.[33]

Only one choice remained for the board. They promptly libeled the ship in the vice-admiralty court, and by the first of August the *Liberty* was tried and condemned. Although her cargo of oil and tar was restored to Hancock,[34] the commissioners were not finished. They still had a trump card to play, and they now set about to crush Hancock, once and for all time.

There had been much gossip in Boston about the cargo of the *Liberty* when she arrived from Madeira. The twenty-five casks of wine for which Hancock paid duties at the customhouse were admittedly a small cargo for the vessel, but the two tidewaiters assigned to watch the unloading had reported no suspicious activity. The *Liberty* had stayed at her wharf a full month, taking on her new cargo. Then, on the very day that she was seized for loading without a permit, Thomas Kirk, one of the tidewaiters who had inspected the unloading, made a confession to the commissioners.

The story that he told, under oath, was quite different from the report that he and his colleague had submitted earlier. Kirk now claimed that on the night after the vessel cleared the customhouse, he had been forced below deck and kept there for three hours. While confined, he had heard much noise above him, and the sound of tackle and other unloading machinery at work. Then quietness had again settled over the harbor, and his captors released him,

33. Baxter, *House of Hancock,* 266.
34. Records of Massachusetts Vice-Admiralty Court, Lib. Cong. Photostats; *Boston Weekly Newsletter,* June 23, 1768; *Boston Chronicle,* Aug. 15-22, 1768; *N.Y. Jour.,* Sept. 5, 1768.

promising him that it would "be his life" if he ever disclosed what had happened.

Kirk's confession seemed flawless to the commissioners. His companion could remember nothing and claimed he must have been asleep. But Kirk swore that his colleague had been drinking and had wandered off to home and bed before Hancock's men had boarded the vessel. Captain Marshal, the leader of Hancock's men and the only individual Kirk identified directly, had died in the four-week interval between the incident and the tidewaiter's confession. There was now no one to corroborate and no one to deny Kirk's statement.

If the commissioners could prosecute Hancock on Kirk's charge, they stood a good chance of making him repent his insolence. But the board desired a certain case, and to assure themselves that nothing could go wrong, they sent Kirk's testimony and a description of the incident to the Treasury in London, requesting a legal opinion on their chances of success. The Treasury turned the papers over to William De Grey, the king's attorney general. He reported that although the charge would have to stand solely on Kirk's confession, it should be prosecuted.[35]

The *Liberty* was already forfeited; the wines that Kirk alleged were unloaded from the vessel could never be found. The only alternative was to take action against Hancock himself, and this the board proceeded to do. In late October 1768, with considerable misgivings, the Massachusetts attorney general, Jonathan Sewall, filed suit in the vice-admiralty court against Hancock and five alleged accomplices. The information against them asked judgment for the crown of £9,000 each, or a total of £54,000. The wine had been assessed at the value of £3,000, and £9,000, treble that value,

35. De Grey's report is in PRO, Treas. 1, 463.

was the legal maximum penalty for clandestine unloading.

The case against the accomplices was only a side show compared to the prosecution of Hancock. The marshal of the vice-admiralty court jailed him, and the court required the fantastically large bail of £3,000 sterling for his release. Sewall, who also served as deputy advocate general, prosecuted the crown's case before Robert Auchmuty, the vice-admiralty judge whom Governor Bernard had appointed on Chambers Russell's death in 1766.[36]

Hancock trusted his defense to a rising young lawyer, John Adams. In preparing his brief, Adams found assertions in the information worthy of argument. For example, he contested the statement that Hancock had been personally concerned in the unloading of the wine. During the trial, Adams objected to the procedure the court used in evaluating the testimony of witnesses, and the attempt, as he saw it, to mix civil-law and common-law procedures, whichever fitted best the needs of the prosecutor. But the trial gave Adams a chance to argue more than fine points of interpretation. He moved to the plane of constitutional law when he based his defense partly upon the fact that the statute infringed upon had been enacted by a parliament in which Hancock, and all Americans, were unrepresented. And he argued at length about the inequality inherent in a system which allowed Englishmen their traditional right of trial by jury, but denied that same constitutional right to Americans. This system, Adams asserted, "takes from Mr. Hancock this precious Tryal . . . by jury, and gives it to a Single Judge. However respectable the Judge may be, it is however an

36. Thomas Gage to Earl of Hillsborough, Nov. 3, 1768, *Letters to the Ministry, from Governor Bernard, General Gage, and Commodore Hood . . .* (Boston, 1769), 104; Bernard to Earl of Hillsborough, Dec. 12, 1768, PRO, CO 5, 758; Gage to Hillsborough, Mar. 5, 1769, Clarence E. Carter, ed., *Correspondence of General Thomas Gage with the Secretaries of State, 1763-1775* (2 vols.; New Haven, 1931), I, 220.

Hardship and severity, which distinguishes my Clyant from the rest of Englishmen."[37]

Adams had time to develop his arguments thoroughly, for the trial was tortuously long. From the first of November, all through the Boston winter, Adams and Sewall appeared before Auchmuty, presenting depositions and answers to witnesses' interrogations. Auchmuty himself summoned witnesses to his chambers and privately examined them. Kirk's allegations were denied and refuted by half of the Boston water-front population, and still the commissioners persisted, hoping to find substantiating evidence. The trial became major news in all the colonies, and citizens in New York and Philadelphia followed the twists and turns of the litigation as it was described in the Boston newspapers and reprinted in their local gazettes. By spring the name "John Hancock" was in common parlance along the Atlantic seaboard.[38]

The commissioners' cause, which had looked so bright in October, faded as the months passed by. Even with the help of questionable testimony, the crown's prosecution faltered.[39] The commissioners could only accept Auchmuty's and Sewall's advice to drop the case when a convenient moment arrived. Their surrender was made on the twenty-sixth of March, 1769. On that day, Robert Auchmuty opened his vice-admiralty court with a reading of a new commission

37. The Information and Adams' brief are in Microfilm of The Adams Papers, Part III, reel 184, John Adams Miscellany, Legal Papers, briefs and notes on admiralty cases.

38. The course of the trial can be followed in these newspapers: *Penn. Chronicle*, Nov. 21 and 28, 1768, Dec. 19 and 26, 1768, Jan. 9, 1769, Feb. 20 and 27, 1769, Mar. 6, 1769; *N.Y. Mercury*, Nov. 17, 1768, Dec. 22, 1768; *N.Y. Jour.*, Nov. 24, 1768, Dec. 15 and 29, 1768, Feb. 2 and 23, 1769, Mar. 2, 23, and 30, 1769, Apr. 8, 1769; and in O. M. Dickerson, ed., *Boston Under Military Rule, 1768-69, as Recorded in a Journal of the Times* (Boston, 1936), 18, 19, 28, 31, 34, 43-47, 64, 66-68, 72 and 83.

39. The grand jury of Suffolk County presented an indictment for perjury against one of the crown's witnesses, but he escaped trial by accepting a customs post from the commissioners. *N.Y. Jour.*, May 4 and June 1, 1769.

from the king. He had been promoted from provincial judge to a new district court, with headquarters in Boston. Following this, Jonathan Sewall, who had received a similar commission for a court at Halifax, moved that the prosecution against Hancock and his friends be dropped. There was no opposition, and the advocate general directed the court register to write in his books, "Our Sovereign Lord the King will prosecute no further. . . ."[40]

40. Records of the Massachusetts Vice-Admiralty Court, Lib. Cong. Photostats; *N.Y. Jour.*, Apr. 13 and May 4, 1769. John Adams recorded his memories of the trial in his Autobiography, Adams, ed., *Works of John Adams*, II, 215-16. However, he was mistaken when he wrote ". . . this odious cause was suspended at last only by the battle of Lexington." Baxter, in his *House of Hancock*, 262-68, confuses the case against the *Liberty* and the personal action against Hancock and his friends. Dickerson, in *The Navigation Acts*, 236-56, relates the events more accurately but overstates the "persecution" of Hancock. The commissioners had as much "legal" right to bring action in the vice-admiralty court as in the common-law courts. The "rules of evidence and procedure" were not "highly unusual" but those common to vice-admiralty courts. The action could not "have been begun by an indictment instead of an 'Information'" because the indictment is a common-law form, while the information was a traditional admiralty process. Comparing this civil-law use of the information with the commissioners' request that Sewall start action in the *Lydia* case by a common-law information is fallacious reasoning. Finally, gathering of evidence by written answers to interrogations, however foreign to common law, was customary admiralty procedure.

6

Four New Courts

JOSEPH GERRISH, storekeeper for King George's navy in American waters, had been pleased when Judge Spry appointed him his deputy. It was a signal honor, regardless of the emptiness of the office, to follow in the footsteps of a man lately promoted governor. Gerrish thought so highly of his new position that he determined to secure a permanent commission as the doctor's surrogate, and he wrote to the Admiralty in England, requesting a "confirmation" of his appointment.

The Admiralty, however, could not help him. When his letter arrived in England, plans for altering the American admiralty establishment were well developed. In these new plans, Spry's old court was to be eliminated. Philip Stephens, the secretary of the board, refused Gerrish because "a new regulation . . . [would] probably very soon take place."[1] Governor Spry was greatly disturbed when this news reached

1. Stephens to Gerrish, Apr. 20, 1768, PRO, Admir. 2, 1057.

him in Barbados. He had counted on retaining his double
office, and he hurried a letter to Stephens, asking for further
information.[2] Judge Spry's "old commission," Stephens
wrote, had been revoked. In place of only one superior
court of vice-admiralty in America, there were now to be
four regional establishments. In this new system there was
no place provided for the "eminent civilian" lately turned
governor. Stephens informed Spry that "the patent for the
Revocation . . . [would] be sent to Mr. Gherrish . . . by the
first Safe conveyance in order to be registered in due form at
Halifax."[3] Four new courts and four new judges had come
to take William Spry's place.

The New Establishment

Almost four years had passed since Judge Spry left
England for his Halifax station. Black days had visited the
American dominions since then. The fury against the Stamp
Act ended with its repeal, and for a few months the colonists
had celebrated their victory. Then Townshend's taxes
raised American ire again. The duties were evil enough to
a people who believed their own words about the powers
of taxation and the rights of representation. But the colonists also considered themselves cursed with a high-handed
Boston Customs Board which waged undisguised war on
colonial commerce. Ugly thoughts filled men's minds when
they considered the "tyranny" of the mother country over
her children. Every dispatch from London was quickly
scanned to discover the latest injustices.

It made little difference to the colonists that Charles

2. Spry had continued to receive his salary of £800 as judge in addition
to his salary of £2,000 as governor. Warrants in PRO, Treas. 28, 1.

3. Stephens to Spry, Oct. 5, 1768, PRO, Admir. 2, 1057. Spry retained
the governorship of Barbados until his death in Oct. 1772. Washburn,
Judicial History of Massachusetts, 175.

Townshend had sponsored one measure to answer their grievances, at least in part. The Americans interpreted the alteration in the vice-admiralty establishment as a measure designed to increase the effectiveness of the trade laws. To a certain extent this was true, but the changes were also planned to answer colonial protests against Doctor Spry's Halifax court and the powers vested in that institution.

The suggestions that the jurisdiction of Spry's court be divided, or that the tribunal be moved to a more central location, had never been completely forgotten. The Treasury's plan of July 1765 for superior vice-admiralty courts at Boston, Philadelphia, and Charleston lay gathering dust in departmental offices. But that scheme had been publicized during the debates over the repeal of the Stamp Act in the House of Lords. In the following months both the Admiralty and the Treasury showed signs of interest in the problem.

Thus when Charles Townshend planned alterations in revenue-collecting in America, he incorporated the old Treasury recommendations into the legislation. The import duties took first place in importance and were given priority in the legislative program. Following on the agenda were provisions for collecting these duties which placed the responsibility in the hands of an independent American Customs Board. But before he died, Townshend had approved the draft of a parliamentary bill authorizing the substitution of several superior courts of vice-admiralty in America for Judge Spry's Halifax tribunal.

That bill passed Parliament and became a statute late in 1767.[4] A full six months then lapsed before the Treasury Board completed the details of the new establishment. In July 1768, it presented a memorial to the King in Council outlining the new regulations. In place of the Halifax establishment over which Judge Spry had presided, there

4. 8 George III, c. 22.

were now to be four regional vice-admiralty courts. One
of these would replace Spry's old court at Halifax. The
others would be located at Boston, Philadelphia, and Charleston. The area of jurisdiction of each was specifically detailed.

The Halifax court would encompass the provinces of
Quebec, Newfoundland, and Nova Scotia. The Boston
region would be composed of New Hampshire, Massachusetts, Rhode Island and Connecticut. The Middle Colonies
—New York, New Jersey, Pennsylvania, Delaware, Maryland,
and Virginia—would fall within the jurisdiction of the
Philadelphia court. And to the south, the Charleston tribunal would serve the two Carolinas, Georgia, and the two
Floridas. The sea, as well as its shores, would be divided between the courts. An overlapping region on the water
would be left between the jurisdictions to ensure that every
area was within the new regulations.[5]

Within their own areas, these new courts would be
granted original jurisdiction in all causes that customarily
came under admiralty law and in all breaches of the trade
laws. They would not replace, but rather supplement, the
provincial vice-admiralty courts. In addition, the appellate
power that the Stamp Act had temporarily granted to Spry's
court would be revived and assigned to each of these new
tribunals. They would not, however, be courts of last appeal. Cases could be taken from the provincial courts to
either the new district courts, or to the High Court of

5. The divisions detailed were as follows: Halifax district, from 43° 15' N
northward; Boston district, from 40° 30' N to 44° 30' N; Philadelphia
district from 36° 15' N to 41° N; and the Charleston district, from
36° 15' N southward. Alfred S. Martin, in "The King's Customs: Philadelphia 1763-1774," *Wm. and Mary Qtly.*, 3rd ser., 5 (1948), 212-13, asserts
that these "overlapping spheres of influence . . . aroused antagonism. A
seizure in one district might be carried to another for trial." But no protests against these imaginary lines in the ocean have been found, and since
the boundaries on land did not overlap, but followed the provincial boundaries, it is doubtful if any colonist was antagonized by the division.

Admiralty, or to the King in Council, at the discretion of the appellant. Cases tried on appeal in the new courts could be reappealed to either the King in Council or the High Court of Admiralty in England.[6]

The Treasury's plan was executed in a comparatively short time. No one appeared to oppose the details of the proposal. Establishment of regional courts should not only answer the colonists' complaints about the distance to Halifax and the lack of lawmen there, but it should also ease the task of customs officials and sea captains in prosecuting their seizures. Even the provincial agents could see no danger in the alteration. "No new Extension of Power was intended . . . [and] they concluded that any Application against it would be unnecessary, as well as improper."[7]

Despite common concurrence in the plan, however, several months were consumed in arranging the inevitable legal apparatus. There was no precedent to guide the Admiralty as it prepared to revoke Spry's commission and issue the four new ones. To complicate matters, the board had to decide the fate of the Earl of Northumberland, the figurehead "Vice Admiral Over All America." The members spent some time pondering the necessity of revoking Northumberland's commission. Their legal counsel assured them, however, that the Earl could remain as vice admiral even though Spry's powers were revoked.[8]

Salaries for the judges must also be determined. The Treasury suggested following the example of Spry's establishment and granting an independent sum out of the king's

6. The Treasury representation is printed in *Acts of the Privy Council: Colonial Series*, V, 151-53. See also PRO, CO 5, 216. These tribunals were not "courts of last resort" as asserted by Andrews, *Colonial Period*, IV, 271.

7. *Penn. Gazette*, June 2, 1768; *N.Y. Jour.*, June 4, 1768.

8. Philip Stephens to Samuel Seddon, Aug. 1 and 15, 1768; Stephens to ———— Bishop, Aug. 19, 1768, PRO, Admir. 2, 1057; Seddon to Stephens, Aug. 17, 1768, *ibid.*, 1, 3679; Dr. Harris to Seddon, Sept. 5, 1768, and Queries and Opinions, *ibid.*, 3884.

share of penalties and forfeitures levied in the colonies, or, if this fund was insufficient, from the sale of old naval stores in England. The annual grants to each of the judges was set at £600 sterling, one-fourth less than Spry's salary. The judges were to be cautioned against accepting fees or gratuities.[9]

Finally, everything was in readiness. Spry's commission had been revoked, and the law officers had worked and reworked drafts for the new instruments. On September 22, 1768, the Admiralty Board directed the High Court of Admiralty to issue the four commissions.[10]

Gentlemen of Science and Abilities

Four new courts required four new judges and a dozen minor officers. The judges must be lawyers, but this was the only qualification for appointment. In 1764, when Judge Spry had been chosen to head the Halifax tribunal, the ministry had searched for an "eminent civilian" trained in admiralty law. No such restriction was suggested now, and the ministry was free to pick and choose as it pleased. If, as some persons intimated, it was planned to appoint only "gentlemen of Science and Abilities" from England,[11] such plans were quickly discarded. The salary of £600 attached to the new judgeships made them rewarding positions, even more lucrative than many of the provincial chief justiceships. And the ministry had need of such places.

At the time of the Stamp Act riots, a group of crown officials and supporters had suffered insults and loss of property at the hands of the mobs. In some colonies only

9. *Acts of the Privy Council: Colonial Series*, VI, 466; Papers in PRO, Admir. 2, 1057 and PRO, Treas. 1, 465.

10. Admiralty Warrant to High Court of Admiralty, Sept. 22, 1768, PRO, Admir. 2, 1057. A copy of the commissions is in *ibid.*, 1, 3884.

11. *Penn. Gazette*, June 2, 1768; *N.Y. Jour.*, June 4, 1768.

the stamp distributors had felt the fury of the times; but in
Massachusetts and Rhode Island the vengeance had reached
the homes of customs and court officers as well. Ever since
then the sufferers had pleaded their cases both in England
and America, begging reparations for their losses. The provincial assemblies were slow to act, and despite prodding
from home, the scores had not been settled.

But the king's gratitude for these officers' support of the
Stamp Act could be shown in other ways. Places on the
American establishment would provide them with a fixed
and certain income. Three victims of the Newport mob
had already been recompensed with offices: Thomas Moffat
was now collector of customs at New London; John Robinson was a member of the new American Customs Board in
Boston; and Martin Howard, Jr., had lately been named
chief justice of North Carolina.[12]   When the new courts
were authorized and the offices required appointments, the
ministry turned to scan the list of other Stamp Act sufferers.
Written there was the name of a third Rhode Islander,
Augustus Johnston, former attorney general of the colony.

Augustus Johnston had been a promising young Rhode
Island attorney when the French and Indian War broke out.
New Jersey-born and New York-educated, he had come to
Newport to study law with his stepfather Mathew Robinson.
Appointments had come early to this enterprising lawyer.
After drafting bills for the General Assembly for several
years, he was appointed to the attorney generalship in 1757
to fill a vacancy left by the death of the elected law officer.
From then, until 1766, he had been continuously re-elected
to that office.

The Stamp Act had interrupted Johnston's career, bringing to a conclusion his pleasant relations with both the co-

12. Thomas Moffat to Earl of Hillsborough, June 20, 1769, PRO, CO 5,
1282.

lonial Assembly and the Rhode Island voters. He was named distributor of the stamps for Rhode Island and suffered the burning of his effigy, the destruction of his household furnishings, and, finally, the humiliation of a public resignation from his office. The attorney generalship would never again be his, and his own private law practice suffered considerably. "The Rage of the People . . . against . . . [him] on acct of . . . [his] late Appointment" continued, and Johnston "determind . . . to go for England" to seek advancement from the crown. He was successful in his mission; the ministry named him judge of the new district court at Charleston, South Carolina.[13]

The Philadelphia seat was awarded to Jared Ingersoll of Connecticut. A graduate of Yale at the age of twenty, Ingersoll had settled in New Haven to begin his legal career. Like Johnston, he had risen rapidly as a young attorney. Connecticut had chosen him as London agent in 1758. In England he met Thomas Whately, who later became George Grenville's under-secretary in the Treasury office. By then Ingersoll had returned to America, but when Grenville directed Whately to draft the Stamp Act, the secretary had written to his American friend for advice.

Ingersoll's opinions had first been transmitted by letter, but in October 1764, he sailed for England on private business. The Connecticut Assembly requested him to assist in the London agency while he was in England. In concert with the colonial agents he had known during his earlier mission, he took up the American arguments against the new act. That opposition was unsuccessful, but Ingersoll had persuaded the ministry to remove several items from the

13. Augustus Johnston to Jared Ingersoll, Aug. 13, 1767, New Haven Colony Hist. Soc., *Papers*, 9 (1918), 413; Johnston to Commissioners of Stamps, Dec. 26, 1765, PRO, Treas. 1, 449; Elsie M. S. Bronson, "Augustus Johnston," *DAB*, X, 138-39.

taxable list in the original drafts of the Stamp Act.[14]   When
he found the ministry intent on its course, he had viewed
the situation philosophically and allowed himself to be
named stamp distributor for his home colony, an appointment he owed to Thomas Whately.

Acceptance of that office cut short Ingersoll's political
life as far as the voters of Connecticut were concerned.   Public resignation of the appointment was not atonement enough
to win back his former popularity.   Like Johnston, Ingersoll
must now look to England for political advancement.   His
disappointment at not being named to the American Customs
Board was soon alleviated by the news that he had been
chosen judge for the district vice-admiralty court at Philadelphia.[15]

He owed his new office to Whately.   Although the
Chancellor of the Exchequer, Lord North, decided that
Ingersoll was well suited to the office, it was Whately who
arranged and accepted the judgeship for him.   Whately had
requested the Philadelphia post for Ingersoll months before
the new courts were established; he thought that Charleston
was too far south for Ingersoll's "Northern Constitution."[16]
When the appointments were made, he was pleased that
Augustus Johnston had been named to the southern court,
for he believed that "two more proper men could certainly
not have been chosen."   At the same time, he reported to
Grenville that Lord North had told him "at the King of
Denmark's Levee . . . that, those offices being filled, he feared
the other meritorious sufferers must wait some time for
opportunities to provide for them."[17]

14. Morgan, *Stamp Act Crisis,* 231-32.

15. William Samuel Johnson to Ingersoll, Sept. 30, 1768, William Samuel
Johnson Papers, Conn. Hist. Soc.; Gipson, *Jared Ingersoll,* 294-95; Morgan,
Stamp Act Crisis, 220-37.

16. William Samuel Johnson to Ingersoll, Nov. 30, 1767, New Haven
Colony Hist. Soc., *Papers,* 9 (1918), 418.

17. Whately to Grenville, Oct. 11, 1768, *The Grenville Papers* (4 vols.;
London, 1852-53), IV, 370.

There were, of course, two more judges to be named, but these places had already been claimed by Governor Bernard for his protégés. The court at Boston was to be headed by Robert Auchmuty, Jr., then sitting as judge of the Massachusetts provincial vice-admiralty court. And Jonathan Sewall, acting advocate general and attorney general of the province, was slated to be judge of the Halifax court.

Boston was accustomed to a vice-admiralty judge by the name of Robert Auchmuty. The new appointee's father, a man who could "sit up all night at his bottle, yet argue to admiration the next day,"[18] had served Massachusetts from that bench for almost a decade. When the elder Auchmuty left Boston in 1741 on a mission to England for the colony, Chambers Russell had acted as his deputy and eventually had been named permanent judge. Auchmuty's son Robert, trained in the law by his father, was then too young to hope for such an office, although his father had guided his aspirations in that direction. An attempt to secure the registership of the court for young Robert had failed. Andrew Belcher, the crown appointee, was in England and had easily scuttled the attempt to displace him. Young Auchmuty had yet a few years to wait before he could prove his worth to the crown.[19]

18. John Adams' Diary, Adams, ed., *Works of John Adams,* II, 357. Adams held no such high opinion of the younger Auchmuty as a lawyer. He characterized him in his diary as having "the same heavy, dull, insipid way of arguing everywhere; as many repetitions as a Presbyterian parson in his prayer. Volubility, voluble repetition and repeated volubility; fluent reiterations and reiterating fluency. Such nauseous eloquence always puts my patience to the torture. In what is this man conspicuous?—in reasoning, in imagination, in painting, in the pathetic, or what? In confidence, in dogmatism, &c. His wit is flat, his humor is affected and dull. To have this man represented as the first of the bar, is a libel upon it, a reproach and disgrace to it." *Ibid.,* 198.

19. Russell's commission from the High Court of Admiralty was not issued until 1762, although the elder Auchmuty died in 1750. PRO, Admir. 2, 1056, 1057. For the abortive attempt to displace Belcher, see Robert Auchmuty to Thomas Corbet, n.d., and Andrew Belcher to Admiralty, Oct. 21, 1742, *ibid.,* 1, 3878. There are brief biographical sketches of the two Auchmutys by Edmund Kimball Alden in *DAB,* I, 421-22. See also Annette

Then, in 1761, Governor Bernard had found himself embroiled in the battle over the customs service and the vice-admiralty court. He had needed a talented advocate general to defend the prerogative against the attacks on Judge Russell's court. William Bollan, who held the Admiralty's commission for the office, was in England serving as Massachusetts agent. His deputy James Otis had resigned the post and "put himself at the head of the Attack of the King's Offices."[20] Auchmuty had accepted Bernard's offer of the position, even though there was no salary annexed to it.

Auchmuty had dispatched the crown's business in the court to good effect and won the Governor's unwavering support. He soon proved himself even more valuable championing Bernard's rights to one-third of all seizures, in opposition to the claims of the naval officers. When Chambers Russell had died, late in 1766, Robert Auchmuty, Jr., was the logical candidate for the vacant judgeship. Governor Bernard had appointed him to head the vice-admiralty courts of Massachusetts and New Hampshire in April 1767, and the Lords of the Admiralty confirmed that appointment in July.[21]

The Governor's dependence on his new vice-admiralty judge had increased. He included him, along with Lieutenant Governor Hutchinson and Secretary Oliver, in his "Cabinet Council," commissioned him a justice of the peace,

---

Townsend, *The Auchmuty Family of Scotland and America* (N.Y., 1932), 4, 43-47.

20. Bernard to Board of Trade, May 17, 1765, PRO, CO 5, 891. Bollan had held the office since 1743. See Bollan to Thomas Corbett, June 2, 1743, PRO, Admir. 1, 3878; James T. Adams, "William Bollan," *DAB*, II, 420. The post, however, was not "lucrative" as suggested by John C. Miller in *Sam Adams: Pioneer in Propaganda* (Boston, 1936), 33.

21. Bernard to Philip Stephens, Apr. 10, 1767, Bernard Letterbooks, VI, Harvard Univ. Lib.; Bernard to Board of Trade, Oct. 15, 1766, PRO, CO 5, 892. Russell's death in London was reported in the *Mass. Gazette*, Jan. 15, 1767. For Auchmuty's appointment, see *ibid.*, Apr. 10, 1767; for his permanent commission from the Admiralty see, *ibid.*, Oct. 15, 1767, and PRO, Admir. 2, 1057.

and suggested that he be named a councilor, if and when the crown assumed the appointment of the Massachusetts Council. Bernard left no doubts as to his confidence in Auchmuty, writing that his "Zeal, Fidelity and Ability cannot be suspected."[22]

Thus, when news of the establishment of the four courts reached Bernard, he quickly claimed the Boston bench for Robert Auchmuty. His nominee for the Halifax post, Jonathan Sewall, had surveyed the Massachusetts scene and cast his lot with the Governor and his party some years before. That decision had already earned Sewall two offices, and Bernard now solicited a third post for him.

Jonathan Sewall was born in Boston in 1725. Although he was orphaned early in life, friends took note of his mental abilities and carefully fostered his education. He graduated from Harvard College in 1748, and after a short period of reading law in Vice-Admiralty Judge Chambers Russell's office, he began his own legal practice.[23] Sewall's legal career flourished, but he found time to support the Governor in his ever-increasing quarrels with the General Assembly. In 1767, Bernard rewarded him with a commission as Auchmuty's successor as advocate general, when the latter was promoted to the vice-admiralty bench. William Bollan, still in England and still holder of the Admiralty's commission for the office, objected strenuously. His only satisfaction was a promise of reinstatement when he returned to New England.[24]

In that same year, Bernard further showed his approval of young Sewall by naming him provincial attorney general.

22. Bernard to Earl of Hillsborough, Jan. 24 and Feb. 4, 1769, PRO, CO 5, 758; *Boston Chronicle*, Feb. 2-6, 1769; *N.Y. Jour.*, Mar. 2, 1769.

23. Elizabeth Donnan, "Jonathan Sewall," *DAB*, XVI, 607-8.

24. Admiralty Warrant to High Court of Admiralty, July 1, 1767, and Admiralty to William Bollan, Aug. 13, 1767, PRO, Admir. 2, 1057; Petition of William Bollan to the King, June 5, 1772, PRO, CO 5, 73; *Mass. Gazette*, Oct. 15 and Nov. 26, 1767.

Neither of these two positions was especially lucrative, but by combining the fees from both, Sewall gained a sufficient income. He was, of course, free to conduct his private law practice when he was not prosecuting royal causes. Bernard carefully watched for a more rewarding position for Sewall, and, when the four courts were established, he secured the seat at Halifax for him. Sewall was pleased with the prospect of a yearly salary of £600 sterling and was even more happy with the honor of the judgeship.[25]

It was upon these four men—Johnston, Ingersoll, Auchmuty, and Sewall—that the ministry now depended for punishment of violators of the trade laws. All of the new judges were American-born, and all had been trained in the law. Auchmuty and Sewall had virtually been raised in the provincial vice-admiralty court.

The judges would need help in conducting their courts, and the ministry now turned to select the registers and marshals for the four new establishments. These minor offices could be given to almost anyone; there was no need of special training for the duties they entailed. The Halifax register, Alexander Chorley, remained in England, deputizing his duties to James Brenton, who had held the same post in Spry's court. The marshal's office was deputized to James Brown.[26] Francis Bernard secured the registership of the Boston court for his son John. Judge Auchmuty swore young Bernard to his office in open court in March 1771, but within a few months he resigned the post. His father ex-

25. Bernard explained to the Admiralty Board that Sewall "held these two Offices not with an Intention of keeping them together in one Person . . . but with a View that if Establishments were made for the support of these Offices, he might have his option which he would continue in. . . ." Bernard to Philip Stephens, March 15, 1769, Bernard Letterbooks, VII, Harvard Univ. Lib.; Edward Alfred Jones, *The Loyalists of Massachusetts: Their Memorials, Petitions, and Claims* (London, 1920), 258-59.

26. Warrant from Admiralty to High Court of Admiralty, Oct. 11, 1769, PRO, Admir. 2, 1057; *N.Y. Jour.*, Jan. 18, 1770; *Register for New England and Nova Scotia . . . for 1769* [Mein and Fleming] (Boston, n.d.).

plained to the Admiralty that John had "a valuable Employment in America reverted to him by the Death of his Elder
Brother." The Governor now solicited the place for Thomas,
another of his sons, and the Admiralty cheerfully complied
by issuing new warrants for Thomas.[27]   Neither of the
brothers ever acted as register.   They appointed Ezekiel
Price, the deputy register of the provincial court, to perform
the same duties in the district tribunal.[28]   Charles Howard,
a naval officer at Harwich, England, received the Admiralty's
appointment as marshal for the Boston Superior Court. Upon
Governor Hutchinson's recommendation he deputized the
office to William Sheppard.[29]   Arodi Thayer, the former
marshal of the Massachusetts provincial court, was promoted
to the same position in the new Philadelphia establishment.
Philip Howe was named register for Ingersoll's court.   The
ministry chose Dummer Andrews as register of the Charleston court.   Andrews, an Englishman, had no intention of
moving to South Carolina, so he sent a "Blank Deputation"
to Judge Johnston and asked him "to appoint some proper
Person to act in his Behalf."[30]

   Thus the new courts were staffed.   Although the patronage was in the hands of the ministry in England, rather than
with the colonial governors, the personnel was much the
same as in the provincial courts.   The popular press, how-

   27. Warrants from Admiralty to High Court of Admiralty, Oct. 26, Dec.
28, 1770, and Bernard to Admiralty, Jan. 1, 1770, PRO, Admir. 2, 1058;
Records of the Massachusetts Vice Admiralty Court, Lib. Cong. Photostats.
   28. Commission from John Bernard to Ezekiel Price, Mar. 9, 1771, Boston
Athenaeum Manuscript Scrapbook.
   29. Warrant from Admiralty to High Court of Admiralty, Sept. 1, 1769,
PRO, Admir. 2, 1057; *N.Y. Jour.*, Dec. 14, 1769; Records of the Massachusetts
Vice Admiralty Court, Lib. Cong. Photostats; Lord Sandwich to Thomas
Hutchinson, Aug. 11, 1772, British Museum, Egerton Mss. 2659, Lib. Cong.
Transcripts.
   30. Warrants from Admiralty to High Court of Admiralty, Sept. 1, 1769,
Feb. 22 and Dec. 21, 1770, PRO, Admir. 2, 1057, 1058; *Conn. Courant*, May
7, 1770; *Penn. Gazette*, May 7, 1770; Augustus Johnston to Jared Ingersoll,
Aug. 21, 1770, New Haven Colony Hist. Soc., *Papers*, 9 (1918), 432-33.

ever, did no cheering when the names of the appointees reached America. News of the courts had arrived months before. And as with other innovations in imperial control, the opposition to the new order had begun long before the changes were actually effected.[31]

The Rights of Englishmen

Early in January 1769, a British man-of-war sailed into Boston Harbor, bringing the commissions for the four new judges. It was an inopportune time for the news of the appointments to reach America. After many months' work, the Boston radicals had coerced the merchants to fight the Townshend duties by ceasing importations of British goods. In August of 1768, the Boston traders embarked upon a nonimportation program, and the merchants of New York, Philadelphia, Baltimore, and Virginia hesitatingly followed with similar plans. By autumn 1769, the Atlantic seaboard, from Massachusetts to Georgia, was tense; radicals and Tories jostled for position, and each commercial center suspiciously watched its neighbor.

Imports from Great Britain into the northern colonies decreased more than half between 1768 and 1769.[32] Although the repercussions in England had not been as violent as the colonists anticipated, rumors flowed freely that the ministry contemplated another revision of the revenue. Until those

31. *Conn. Courant*, May 16 and Dec. 3, 1768, Jan. 2, 23, and 30, 1769; *N.Y. Jour.*, June 2, Dec. 1 and 15, 1768, Feb. 2, 1769; *Boston Chronicle*, Nov. 21-28, 1768; *Penn. Chronicle*, Nov. 21, 1768; *Penn. Gazette*, Dec. 8, 1768.

32. While the imports into New England, New York, and Philadelphia dropped by one-half or more, the southern colonies, from Maryland to South Carolina, all increased their imports. These colonies entered into nonimportation agreements later, and in some cases at least, took advantage of the delay to import large quantities. See David MacPherson, *Annals of Commerce, Manufactures, Fisheries, and Navigation, with Brief Notices of the Arts and Sciences Connected with Them* (4 vols.; London, 1805), III, 486, 494-95.

rumors became realities, the Americans remained unhappy. They often forgot the potential economic grievance of the Townshend duties in the heat of their debate over constitutional principles. As in the Stamp Act days, they marshaled a host of arguments supporting their contentions. They remonstrated against employing the duties as salaries for crown officials and contested the methods of enforcing the collection of the revenue. Some colonists asserted that "next to the revenue itself, the late extensions of the jurisdiction of the admiralty . . . [were the] greatest grievance."[33]

The campaign against the vice-admiralty courts had never completely ended. Even after the repeal of the Stamp Act, the provisions of the Sugar Act that outlined the methods of prosecuting violations of the acts of trade continued to be attacked. The Superior Court at Halifax was no longer a direct threat, because neither Judge Spry nor Surrogate Gerrish decreed many revenue cases. But the colonists had never limited their protests to that court. When they complained about the loss of jury trial, the payment of judges by forfeiture shares, or the probable-cause apparatus, they included their provincial vice-admiralty establishments along with the Halifax tribunal.[34]

The publicity attending the Laurens-Leigh controversy in South Carolina and the *Liberty* prosecution in Boston provided a factual framework on which critics hung general indictments of the courts. Yet, despite these well-known examples of collisions between customs officers and merchants, it could be argued that the vice-admiralty courts had

33. *N.Y. Jour.*, May 25, 1769.
34. See, for example, the "Letter" [by George Mason] from Potomack River, Virginia, June 6, 1766, to the Committee of Merchants in London, *N.Y. Jour.*, Jan. 1, 1767, where, after listing the grievances against the "arbitrary civil law court," the writer explains that "these things did not depend altogether upon the Stamp Act, and therefore are not repealed with it." Mason's letter is reprinted in Kate Mason Rowland, *The Life of George Mason, 1725-1792* (2 vols.; N.Y., 1892), I, 381-89.

changed very little. The repeal of the Stamp Act swept away jurisdiction over revenue causes arising on land and reduced the courts to what crown officials would have termed their traditional American status. The provincial courts' powers, in this viewpoint, were much as they had been for the last seventy years. They held authority, equally with the common-law courts, to hear and determine violations of the acts of trade.

The judges' income had not been changed; it still consisted of fees and percentages alone. The probable-cause guarantees granted to customs officers were based in the tradition of English statutory law, despite the injustices they might have created in some cases. Moreover, the common-law courts shared these same procedures whenever they were called upon to determine revenue cases.

In this view of things, what had changed since 1763 was not the courts themselves, but the laws they enforced. The provisions of the Revenue Act of 1764 and the Townshend Revenue Act that the colonists objected to, coupled with the determination of the customs service to enforce those provisions, brought about the opposition to the vice-admiralty courts. But the delegation of jurisdiction to the sea courts in these new statutes actually continued a well-established administrative device, dating back to the Navigation Act of 1696.

Such statements would have neither satisfied nor quieted the Americans in their campaign against the revenue legislation and its enforcement. They gathered arguments and evidence demonstrating the hardships resulting from the import taxes and the provisions for their collection. The enlargement and extension of the vice-admiralty jurisdiction, as well as the payment of judges from the profits of condemnations, were grievous in their eyes. Writers damned the courts as "foreign" to the English Constitution and proclaimed their procedure without jury trial to be an example of insidious "persecution" by a tyrannical ministry.[35]

News of the establishment of the four regional courts arrived in America at a time when criticism was rife. The colonists ignored the fact that earlier grievances against the location of Spry's court had been answered by dividing the court's jurisdiction among regional establishments. To those Americans who demanded the abolition of the extension of jurisdiction to the provincial courts, these new tribunals appeared as only a further indication that Britain was determined to pay no heed to their arguments.

Radicals quickly included the four new courts on the list of British injustices imposed on Americans. Protests of the loss of trial by jury and the extension of the civil law were related to the new tribunals. The selected judges were severely criticized, both because they were political favorites, as in the cases of Sewall and Auchmuty, and because they were proven enemies to "liberty" and had been since the Stamp Act. The salaries of £600 were called "extraordinary" and "enormous," although most of the provincial chief justices enjoyed crown salaries of nearly the same amount. And a case was conjured up against the new salaries by claiming that they were dependent on the forfeitures condemned by the judges.[36] Actually, the stipends were fixed and permanent and would be paid regardless of the number or value of the seizures tried in the new courts.

Whatever the particular point employed to prove the vice-admiralty courts unconstitutional, the reasoning focused on the charge that they denied and deprived the colonists of the "rights of Englishmen." In the homeland, revenue

35. As examples, see Petition of the Merchants of the City of New York Addressed to the House of Commons, *N.Y. Jour.*, Apr. 24, 1767; Address to a Meeting of Philadelphia to Instruct Representatives to the Assembly, July 31, 1768, *Penn. Gazette*, Aug. 4, 1768.

36. *N.Y. Jour.*, Feb. 16 and July 27, 1769; *Penn. Chronicle*, Nov. 20, 1769; *Conn. Courant*, Feb. 12, 1770.

cases were tried by the Court of the Exchequer, a common-law court. In the colonies, they were cognizable in the vice-admiralty courts by civil-law procedures. An unfair, indeed an unconstitutional discrimination thus was placed upon the Americans by depriving them of trial by jury. John Adams had drawn the distinction clearly when he defended Hancock in the Boston court: "The Parliament . . . guarding the People of the Realm, and securing to them the Benefit of a Tryal by the Law of the Land, and . . . depriving all Americans of that Priviledge—What shall we say to this Distinction? Is there not in this . . . a Brand of Infamy, of Degradation, and Disgrace, fixed upon every American? Is he not degraded below the Rank of an Englishman?"[37]

The remonstrators never pointed out that the statutes allowed seizure trials in either the common-law or vice-admiralty courts; this admission would have underscored the crown's assertion that colonial juries refused to give verdicts against trade-law offenders. Nor did the colonists propose the other alternative: the creation of exchequer courts in America. Britain had already rejected this idea as impracticable and probably offensive to the colonists. The American arguments were better maintained without considering alternatives. The "rights of Englishmen" to trial by jury, simply stated, or perhaps adorned with quotations from Coke or Blackstone, served the purpose well enough.[38]

These arguments contributed their expected quota to the attack on the revenue program. Then they were cast aside as quickly as the nonimportation agreements when the

37. John Adams, Admiralty Notebook in Microfilms of The Adams Papers, Part III, Reel 184, quoted in David S. Lovejoy, "Rights Imply Equality," *Wm. and Mary Qtly.*, 3rd ser., 16 (1959), 480-81.

38. *N.Y. Jour.*, May 25, Nov. 2 and 23, 1769; *Boston Chronicle*, Oct. 26-30, 1769; *Boston Gazette*, July 10, 1769; *Conn. Courant*, July 24, 1769; *Observations on Several Acts of Parliament Passed in the 4th, 6th and 7th Years of his present Majesty's Reign . . . published by Merchants of Boston* (Boston, 1769), 12-13.

Townshend duties, with the exception of the tea tax, were repealed in the spring of 1770. The campaign against the vice-admiralty courts subsided. The basic cause for the grievance, the taxes, was gone, and despite occasional outbursts of opposition, the vice-admiralty courts were left in peace for several years. During that time, the older provincial institutions continued to hear and determine the cases brought before them in their traditional manner. And the new district courts spent the interlude establishing themselves and performing the functions for which they were created.

7

The Courts at Work

H ALIFAX, Nova Scotia, was an uncommonly dull
town compared to Boston, Massachusetts. The
prospect of court-keeping there was no more pleasant
to Jonathan Sewall than it had been to William Spry. Sewall thoroughly enjoyed himself in Massachusetts, where his
double office of advocate and attorney general kept him in
the midst of the relentless struggle between crown and
colony. The honor of the vice-admiralty judgeship had been
pleasant to receive, despite the sarcastic tone of the radical
press in announcing the appointment. And the salary of
£600 sterling, more than the best-paid common-law justice
received, added to the pleasurable prospect. But Sewall
dreaded the thought of life in the cold northern outpost of
Halifax.

He read his commission carefully, consulted with Governor Bernard, and probably heard the history of Doctor
Spry's court. Then he decided that he might have his court

without leaving Massachusetts. If William Spry could appoint a deputy to sit for him at Halifax while he governed
Barbados, could not Sewall also arrange for a surrogate? He
could pay the surrogate part of his salary and still have a
good income remaining if he retained his office as Massachusetts attorney general. Then he and his family could
live in their native province.[1]

Sewall was determined to put his scheme into effect. In
late June 1769, he sailed from Boston on the man-of-war
Rose to visit his "maritime seat." In Halifax he sought out
Mr. Joseph Gerrish, who was not in the least adverse to
renewing his connections with an admiralty court. It had
been an honor to substitute for William Spry, and he would
do the same for Mr. Sewall. The details were easily arranged: in return for his work as deputy, Gerrish was to
receive one-fourth of Sewall's salary. On the twelfth day
of July, the Massachusetts attorney general was again in
Boston. And the Halifax Superior Court was once more in
the hands of Joseph Gerrish.[2]

The System Is Completed

The English ministry had intended that the four
new judges would themselves conduct the courts. It was

1. Governor Bernard explained to the Admiralty that Sewall was needed
in Massachusetts to complete important prosecutions in the vice-admiralty
court and that he (Bernard) was "not ready to name fit Persons for either
of [Sewall's] Offices [because] some of the Lawyers, whom . . . [he would]
have been glad to have engaged in his Majesty's service . . . [had] by their
abetting the Factious party rendered themselves unfit objects of the favor of
Government." Bernard to Philip Stephens, Mar. 15, 1769, Bernard Letterbooks, VII, Harvard Univ. Lib.

2. *Mass. Gazette,* July 13, 1769; *N.Y. Jour.,* July 27, 1769; Memorial of
Jonathan Sewall, Oct. 18, 1784, Hugh Egerton, ed., *The Royal Commission
on the Loses and Services of American Loyalists 1783 to 1785: Being the
Notes of Mr. Daniel Coke, M. P. one of the Commissioners during that
Period* (Oxford, 1915), 233.

true that the necessary political connections had sanctioned Doctor Spry's retention of his judgeship after his elevation to the governorship of Barbados. But Spry's court at Halifax had proven itself a rarely used institution. Jonathan Sewall hazarded the ministry's displeasure by his decision to remain in Boston and to allow a deputy to manage his court. But he heard not a word of official censure from England. The American press from time to time spit forth cynical comments on his plural officeholding, but Sewall had already withstood more serious political opposition than this.

Robert Auchmuty had not encountered Sewall's problem: the new promotion changed little in his life. His home, his family, and his professional ties had always been in Boston. He still met his court at the same place and heard the same cases that would have come to him as judge of the old provincial court. Only the name of his court was changed. The newspaper announcements of trials and seizures were now headed "The Court of Vice Admiralty at Boston" rather than the familiar "Province of Massachusetts: Court of Vice Admiralty." Compared with the changes facing the other judges, Auchmuty's problems were simple.

Augustus Johnston was no longer attorney general of Rhode Island, but the small charter colony was still his home. He set out for South Carolina in May 1769 and found on his arrival that James Simpson, the judge of the provincial vice-admiralty court, was trying a seizure of "Considerable consequence." Johnston decided to postpone publishing his new commission and organizing his court until after that "cause should be Issued." By the middle of June he was back in Newport, leaving behind a deputy to act for him during his absence. Although he was happy in his new office, Johnston did not intend to suffer the summer heat of Charleston. From May until November, he lived in Newport, returning each year to South Carolina for the winter months.[3]

Jared Ingersoll at first followed a similar scheme. He traveled from New Haven to Philadelphia in April 1769, published his commission there, and entrusted the affairs of his court to a deputy, James Biddle.[4] He made no move to take up a permanent residence in Pennsylvania, but continued to practice law privately and perform various public services.[5] Friends in England warned him that he could expect no further promotions if he did not move to Philadelphia and conduct his court himself. William Samuel Johnson wrote him of the surprise in London that neither he nor Sewall had moved to their jurisdictions, asking if they imagined that their offices were "to be a sine Cure, Are they to be Non Resident Judges, or is it Consistent with the Dignity of a Judge to Conte in the Pract of the Law?" Ingersoll heeded the advice and prepared to wind up his business affairs in New Haven. But it was not until April 1771 that he and his family arrived in Philadelphia.[6]

Ingersoll's establishment at Philadelphia posed a problem for Edward Shippen, the judge of the provincial vice-admiralty court whose appointment had been solicited by Thomas Penn in 1752. He had conducted the court at Philadelphia for fifteen years and had gained a "reputation for integrity

3. Presumably James Simpson was his deputy. Augustus Johnston to Admiralty, May 17, 1769, PRO, Admir. 1, 3884; Philip Stephens to Augustus Johnston, Aug. 16, 1769, *ibid.*, 2, 1057; Johnston to Jared Ingersoll, Feb. 7, 1769, and Aug. 21, 1770, New Haven Colony Hist. Soc., *Papers*, 9 (1918), 423, 433; *Mass. Gazette*, July 13, 1769; Carl Bridenbaugh, "Charlestonians at Newport, 1767-1775," *S.C. Historical and Genealogical Magazine*, 41 (1940), 44-45.

4. *Penn. Chronicle*, May 1, 1769; "Mentor" letter in *Penn. Gazette*, Jan. 12, 1774.

5. Ingersoll, along with Andrew Elliot, Andrew Oliver, and Samuel Morris, formed a commission for settling the boundary between New York and New Jersey in 1769. See *Mass. Gazette*, Dec. 14, 1769.

6. Johnson to Ingersoll, Dec. 9, 1769, quoted in Gipson, *Jared Ingersoll*, 295-96; *Mass. Gazette*, Apr. 11 and 19, 1771.

and sound judgment . . . among all parties and professions."
When news came that the vice-admiralty courts in America
were to be "under new regulations," Shippen was concerned that his post might be taken from him. He talked to
Chief Justice William Allen, who agreed to write Thomas
Penn. Shippen did not enjoy the prospect of "being super-
ceded," and desired Penn to "obtain for him the same
advantages . . . that the Judges of the Admiralty have in
other provinces."[7]

But Penn could do nothing. Ingersoll's court was to be
located at Philadelphia, and there was room for only one
judge in the new tribunal. The Admiralty had failed to
consider the fate of the old provincial courts in the colonies
where the new regional establishments were located. The
commissions of the provincial judges were not revoked, nor
was it suggested that they close their courts. Rather, the
new institutions were allowed to grow until they replaced
the old vice-admiralty courts. The latter withered away
until they became as barren of activity as Spry's court at
Halifax had been.

In 1775, Governor Penn described the offices of the provincial vice-admiralty court as of "little or no value." Fortunately, Shippen had always depended more upon his £200
salary as prothonotary of the Supreme Court than upon his
fees and percentages as vice-admiralty judge. But he was
not the only officer of the Pennsylvania court affected by the
new regulations. Richard Peters, who had lately been confirmed in the registership that he had executed as his father's
deputy for several years, now found his new office superseded.[8]

7. Allen to Penn, Oct. 8, 1767, Penn Letterbooks, Microfilm Coll. of
Early State Recs., Penn., E.2a. On Shippen's appointment to the court, see
Thomas Penn to [William?] Peters, Mar. 18, 1752, and Thomas Penn to
Governor Hamilton, July 13, 1752, *ibid.*

8. William Peters to Thomas Penn, Jan. 24, and Mar. 30, 1769, and
Thomas Penn to Richard Peters, July 21, 1769, *ibid.*; Penn's answers to

This situation occurred, of course, only in the four cities where district courts were established. In Charleston, there was no particular difficulty, for Johnston and Simpson merged their operations. Simpson sat when Johnston was absent from the province, and when the provincial judge resigned in 1771, the Admiralty immediately commissioned Edward Savage as his successor. Nor did any difficulty exist at Halifax. John Collier, who had retained the provincial judgeship all through the time of Spry's court, died in 1769. Although Sewall had already established his tribunal, with Gerrish as his deputy, the vacant provincial judgeship was transferred to a successor chosen by Governor William Campbell.[9]

At Boston the situation was slightly more complex. Robert Auchmuty had sat as provincial judge, and he, in effect, promoted his whole court into a district tribunal. But New Hampshire was still included in the district of the Massachusetts provincial court, and it was necessary to find a judge for the provincial court at Portsmouth.[10] Thomas Hutchinson, who had inherited the Massachusetts governorship from Francis Bernard, "had no hopes of finding anyone fit for the post." Then, in 1772, Thomas Oliver indicated that he was "not adverse" to becoming the "inferior" judge of vice-admiralty. Hutchinson was pleased, for although Oliver had never practiced law, he had been "designed by

queries, Jan. 30, 1775, PRO, CO 5, 1286; Thomas Penn to Philip Stephens, Mar. 6, 1769, PRO, Admir. 1, 3819; Warrant from Admiralty to High Court of Admiralty, Mar. 14, 1769, *ibid.*, 2, 1057; "Notes of a Conversation between Jared Ingersoll, Arodi Thayer and Richard Peters, September 13, 1770," Peters Mss., Hist. Soc. of Penn.

9. Warrant from Admiralty to High Court of Admiralty, Nov. 26, 1771, PRO, Admir. 2, 1058; Warrant from Admiralty to High Court of Admiralty, Aug. 30, 1769, and Admiralty to William Campbell, Sept. 2, 1769, *ibid.*, 1057; William Campbell to Philip Stephens, June 1, 1769, *ibid.*, 1, 3819.

10. William Parker, a deputy of the Massachusetts judge, conducted the Portsmouth Vice-Admiralty Court during these years. See records in Mass. Hist. Soc., Misc. Mss., XIII.

his education for a Civilian." The fortune he had made in the West Indies would keep him from dissatisfaction with a post offering few emoluments. Even more pleasing was the fact that "although he [was] . . . a near Relation to the City Patriots of the same name, he . . . [was] an advocate for the cause of government."[11]

Hutchinson was surprised that Oliver accepted an appointment from which he would receive little or no profit. But men in the colonies had been serving as vice-admiralty judges for decades with as little chance to collect incomes. It was only of late, since the establishment of the four district courts, that the standard of pay for a vice-admiralty judge had risen. The £600 salary granted to each of the new judges caused considerable discontent. Their salaries were fixed, and, as one critic noted, they were assured of receiving their stipends "for doing no more business than the Superior Court did in one term."[12]

On the other hand, the ministry had designed the salaries to serve two sound purposes. The sums were large enough to provide dignity to the judges and the courts they conducted. And, the stipends were also designed as benefits for men who had supported the crown in former difficulties. The district judges' authority was much greater than that of any of the provincial vice-admiralty judges. Their courts' jurisdiction not only included the right to hear cases that arose anywhere within their districts, but also to determine appeals from the provincial courts within that area.

The number of cases that came before the new judges varied considerably from court to court. Halifax seems to have been fairly active as far as seizures under the trade and revenue laws were concerned. Boston was also a busy port, and Judge Auchmuty probably heard and determined as

11. Thomas Hutchinson to Earl of Sandwich, Nov. 12, 1772, PRO, Admir. 1, 3820; *Mass. Gazette*, Apr. 29, 1773; *Boston Gazette*, May 3, 1773.
12. John Adams' Diary, Adams, ed., *Works of John Adams*, II, 301.

many cases as any of his colleagues. Ingersoll claimed to be "pretty full of business" at his court in the spring of 1773, although from the autumn of 1769 until 1772 there was "little or nothing" to do. Johnston, who had scheduled his time in Charleston so as to spend only the winters there, was the least active of the judges. He wrote to Ingersoll in 1770 that he had "not done any Business in the Office." Two seizures had been made, but they were tried by the deputy in Johnston's absence.[13]

The source from which the judges drew their salaries provides an indication of their activity, since they were paid from the crown's share of forfeitures condemned in their district, or, if this sum was insufficient, from the naval stores fund. Auchmuty was the only judge to condemn sufficient property to make up his £600. Ingersoll's district netted the crown £361 in 1769 and £403 in 1770. It was rumored that Sewall's court at Halifax yielded enough condemnation money by October 1770 to pay his salary for two years "& some to spare over." But at that time the Customs Board at Boston had actually received only £95 from forfeitures in Sewall's district.[14] The remainder of both his and Ingersoll's salaries was paid from the naval stores fund. And in some years all of Augustus Johnston's salary came from that fund. The Customs Board reported that no money from forfeitures and fines had been remitted from the southern district from September 1771 to November 1772.[15]

13. Ingersoll to Jonathan Ingersoll, May 1773, and Augustus Johnston to Ingersoll, Aug. 21, 1770, quoted in Gipson, *Jared Ingersoll*, 299; Arodi Thayer's "Memorial," in which he compares activity in the court before and after 1773, Egerton, ed., *Royal Commission on . . . American Loyalists*, 9.

14. "Account of Application of Monies . . . ," PRO, Treas. 1, 486; Certificate of Customs Board, Dec. 21, 1772, *ibid.*, 447; Secretary of Customs Board to Grey Cooper, Dec. 31, 1772, *ibid.*, 491; Arodi Thayer to Jared Ingersoll, Aug. 13, 1770, New Haven Colony Hist. Soc., *Papers*, 9 (1918), 431.

15. Certificate of Customs Board, Nov. 6, 1772, PRO, Treas. 1, 491. The judges all seem to have drawn their full salaries from the dates of their commissions rather than from the time they established their courts. See

Most of the cases that came before the new judges arose from violations of the trade and revenue acts. But the new judges were also empowered to determine disputes between merchants and between merchants and seamen, as the provincial courts had always done. Seamen's wages, surveys of damaged goods, disputes over charter parties, and all of the varieties of mercantile contracts were litigated in the new courts. Each year, however, saw less of these in comparison with trials for forfeitures under the acts of trade. The latter had become the main business of the vice-admiralty courts, and they remained so until the Revolution.[16]

It is difficult to determine, but relatively safe to assume, that the courts did little business outside of the provinces in which they were located. Just as Spry's court had never made inroads on the activities of the older provincial courts, the new district courts were no competition to them. Almost without exception, the cases they heard would have come to the provincial courts of the colonies in which they were located. In Boston, Auchmuty tried several causes that otherwise would have been determined in Rhode Island.[17] But his court was the exception rather than the rule. In Ingersoll's jurisdiction, for example, the two most active provincial courts, excepting that of Philadelphia, were the courts at New York and Williamsburg, neither of which suffered any decrease in activity. In fact, their cases now numbered more than ever before. There are no records extant of seizures

---

Augustus Johnston to Jared Ingersoll, Aug. 21, 1770, New Haven Colony Hist. Soc., *Papers,* 9 (1918), 432.

16. The remaining records of these courts are very incomplete, but the Boston court in 1770 heard eight trade and revenue cases and three marine cases, in 1771 fifteen trade and revenue causes and no marine causes; in both years there were other causes that cannot be classified. Records of the Massachusetts Vice Admiralty Court, Lib. Cong. Photostats.

17. A seizure by Lieutenant Duddingston, commander of His Majesty's schooner *Gaspee,* in Narragansett Bay, was carried to Boston for trial. See *Boston Gazette,* Aug. 10 and 17, 1772.

from within the boundaries of either of these courts being hauled to Philadelphia for trial.[18]

Again, it is difficult to determine how many causes from the provincial courts were appealed to the new judges. It is probable that the appeal machinery was little used. Auchmuty reviewed no cases until early in 1772, and despite his long acquaintanceship with admiralty procedures, he could not then decide how to proceed. John Adams went to Boston to participate in the appeal and joined the judge and others in a "search of books concerning the nature of appeals by the civil law."[19]

This case, *Samuel Cutt v. George Meserve,* was appealed from the New Hampshire Vice-Admiralty Court. It concerned the brigantine *Resolution* which had been entered at the Portsmouth customhouse on October 26, 1771. George Meserve, the collector of the port, had seized the vessel the following day for importation of 100 hogsheads of undeclared molasses. On the night of October 29, a group of disguised men staged a molasses party and rescued the cargo from the customs guard. The officers retained custody of the ship, however, and Meserve prosecuted his case in the local vice-admiralty court. When the judge decreed the *Resolution* forfeited, the owners appealed to the Boston court. In February 1772, Judge Auchmuty ruled "for affirmation of the former Decree." The following month he decreed in the same manner in the case of *Otis Baker, Esq., and others* v. *George Meserve,* also appealed from the New Hampshire court.[20]

18. Hough, *N.Y. Reps.*, 242; "A List of the Seizures Made in the Colony of Virginia," PRO, Admir. 1, 4286. Although the records of the Virginia court no longer exist, an indication of the activity of that tribunal can be found in the notices of condemnations in the *Virginia Gazette.* In 1771 these totaled thirteen, compared to seven in 1769.

19. John Adams' Diary, Adams, ed., *Works of John Adams,* II, 296.

20. These two cases are described by Lawrence Shaw Mayo in *John Langdon of New Hampshire* (Concord, N.H., 1937), 38-43. See also George

Judge Auchmuty's court at Boston is the only one of the four regional courts for which any records survive, and these end with the year 1772. But up to that time, only these two appeal cases were heard before the Boston judge. Probably the traditional channels of appeal, the High Court of Admiralty, and the King in Council, continued to be used as before.[21]

Thus, the coming of the new courts did less to rearrange vice-admiralty affairs in the provinces than had been expected. In effect, they only superseded the provincial courts in the towns where they sat. The geographical extent of their jurisdiction, their authority to determine cases on appeal, and the judges chosen to preside over them made the four courts appear more important than the local courts they replaced. But, for the most part, the vice-admiralty system was little changed. Disputes and seizures arising within the provinces where the courts sat were tried before them, but in all of the other colonies, the older vice-admiralty courts continued their traditional functions.

The Provincial Vice-Admiralty Courts

The establishment of the four district courts caused little concern to the judges and other officers of most of the provincial vice-admiralty tribunals. Except in Massachusetts, Nova Scotia, Pennsylvania, and South Carolina, where the four courts sat, there was little reason to note the activities of the district judges. Their provincial counterparts probably looked enviously at their salaries and the extent of their

Meserve and Robert Traile to Customs Commissioners, Nov. 15, 1771, PRO, Treas. 1, 491; Records of the Massachusetts Vice Admiralty Court, Lib. Cong. Photostats.

21. The record of a case in 1772, when Judge John Randolph allowed an appeal from his Virginia Vice-Admiralty Court to the High Court of Admiralty in England is in PRO, Treas. 1, 501. See also Smith, *Appeals to the Privy Council*, 192.

jurisdictions. But it soon became clear that the new regulations would not much change the traditional business of the provincial courts.

Like the new courts, the older, local tribunals now found that revenue cases consistently outnumbered maritime disputes. The latter litigations never completely ceased, except perhaps in New York, where merchants had always depended on the Mayor's Court of the City of New York for determination of their differences.[22] In other colonies, the common-law courts were favored over the vice-admiralty tribunals for insurance cases. Other marine contract disputes might also be determined in the common-law courts,[23] but generally these cases were taken before the vice-admiralty judges.

For seamen, who were quite uninterested in the policies of empire-building, the vice-admiralty courts had long been, and continued to be, particular tribunals in case of trouble. When disputes or brawls broke out on shipboard, the courts were applied to for relief. Vice-admiralty judges often determined causes of assault and battery for mariners. But more commonly the sailors' complaints concerned their wages, and the *in rem* process of the civil law allowed them to bring action collectively against the vessel on which they had served to secure their just and promised pay. This was not the only advantage of the salt-water courts over their common-law counterparts. When necessary, trials could be

22. The customs officials prosecuting small seizures favored the mayor's court also, because the costs of trial were generally lower than in the provincial vice-admiralty court. In Nov. 1771, there were five revenue cases pending in the city: three vessels and their cargoes seized by ships-of-war, in the vice-admiralty court; and two small parcels of goods, seized by customs officers, in the mayor's court. PRO, CO 5, 1103. These examples tend to modify Dickerson's assertion that all seizures were tried in the admiralty courts; *Navigation Acts,* 212.

23. For example, see two insurance cases, *McMurterie* v. *Brown* (Supreme Court of Penn.) and *Isaacs* v. *Stead* (Superior Court of R.I.), and a charter party cause, *Long* v. *Harper, Nixon, and Co.* (Supreme Court of Penn.), all appealed to King in Council. *Acts of the Privy Council: Colonial Series,* IV, 724, 745, 759.

conducted quickly in the vice-admiralty courts. For instance, when five sailors libeled the sloop *Charming Jenny* in the New York court for wages, they were satisfied within five days.[24]

Ordinary marine causes sometimes led to revenue causes. In New York, private persons brought action against the ship *Prosperity,* presumably for the recovery of seamen's wages. From the testimony divulged in the trial, the advocate general discovered a breach of the trade laws and "won permission to claim some sugars . . . on board the sd ship for our Lord the King."[25] In other cases, customs officials and seamen sometimes had claims against the same ship. The royal officers might then gain a free hand to prosecute the case by assuring the sailors that their wages would be paid. In this way, the confusion of two separate actions for different purposes against the same vessel was circumvented.[26]

Yet when all of the "marine" cases were added together, they formed only a small portion of the courts' business in comparison with revenue causes. More and more sessions were called to settle customs cases. Since customs officials and sea captains had come to depend on the good judgment and common sense of the provincial vice-admiralty judges, there was no stampede to the newly established district

24. *John Kelly, Matthew Small, John Loller, William Miller and Edward Walsh* v. *Sloop Charming Jenny &c.,* Minutes of the Vice-Admiralty Court of the Province of New York, Lib. Cong. Photostats. On assault and battery cases, see *Patrick Hymes* v. *Moses Linster,* and *Patrick Hymes* v. *John Gillaspie, ibid.; Richard Green* v. *William Shall,* described in *N.Y. Jour.,* Dec. 24, 1767; *Penn. Gazette,* Jan. 7, 1768.

25. *Scull and Others* v. *The Prosperity,* Minutes of the Vice-Admiralty Court of the Province of New York, Lib. Cong. Photostats.

26. Certificate of John Swift, Nov. 25, 1763, Philadelphia Customs House Papers, II, Hist. Soc. of Penn.: "I hereby agree & engage, in order to avoid the expense & trouble of the Mariners belonging to the sloop John arrested by me—libelling the said sloop—that if she is condemn'd in the Court of Vice Admiralty all the wages justly due to the said Mariners from the said sloop shall be paid them—and the settling what wages shall be paid them shall be left & refr'd to Mr Shippen the Judge to be determin'd in such manner as he pleases."

courts. They were used by the revenue establishments in the colonies where they were located. Otherwise, the provincial judges continued as the main prop of the customs gatherers.

The customs officers were faced with a different problem these years. In colony after colony, they were boycotted by members of the legal profession; they could find no lawyers to prosecute their causes for them. Such prosecutions should have been directed by the king's advocate general. But in some colonies such an officer had never existed, and in others the appointees were young and inexperienced and could not hope to compete successfully against the legal counsel of the merchants.

In Massachusetts, Jonathan Sewall retained the office of advocate general after Governor Bernard appointed him attorney general, but when he was named judge of the Halifax district court, Sewall decided to rid himself of the advocate's office. It was not easy to find a successor. Governor Bernard offered the post to John Adams, who refused it as being incompatible with his political views. Finally, Samuel Fitch, who had served the American Customs Board as solicitor, indicated a willingness to accept the office. In November 1768, Judge Auchmuty granted him a temporary appointment, and Governor Hutchinson later secured a permanent commission for him from the Lords of Admiralty.[27]

In those colonies where an advocate general had never been appointed, the situation was more difficult. Customs officers and sea captains looked to the attorneys general to help them prosecute their seizures. In Pennsylvania, Andrew Allen acted as customs counsel reluctantly. At times he

27. John Adams' Autobiography, Adams, ed., *Works of John Adams*, II, 210-12; Records of the Massachusetts Vice-Admiralty Court, Lib. of Cong. Photostats; Warrant from Admiralty to High Court of Admiralty, Nov. 24, 1764, PRO, Admir. 2, 1057; Thomas Hutchinson to Philip Stephens, Aug. 4, 1770, *ibid.*, 1, 3819; Davis, *History of Judiciary of Massachusetts*, 79.

absolutely refused to aid the customs officers, telling them that since "he had no salary from the Crown to make him Independent, he could by no means undertake any Prosecutions of that kind which would Injure him greatly in his Business as a Lawyer."[28] His brother James, also a lawyer, sometimes agreed to prosecute seizures for the customs officers, but he did so with misgivings. In May 1772, when he had undertaken the prosecution of four seizures for Captain Talbot of the man-of-war *Lively,* James Allen confided to his diary that he was doing as a lawyer what he "would not do as a politician; being fully persuaded of the oppressive nature of those laws."[29]

In some colonies the attorneys general were also commissioned vice-admiralty judges and could not conscientiously advise revenue officers on matters which would come before them later in trial. Complaints of this conflict of interests in South Carolina had earlier forced the resignation of Egerton Leigh as vice-admiralty judge. John Randolph in Virginia also held both positions, but he was able to stave off the demands that he resign one or the other; he even secured an increase in his salary. Randolph had been appointed attorney general and judge of the vice-admiralty court in 1767 in place of his brother Peyton, who had resigned. The two offices had "gone together" in Virginia for many years. Almost at the same time as Randolph's appointment, the complaints of customs officers in South Carolina had caused the Admiralty to search for similar situations elsewhere. When they found that Randolph had secured commissions to both offices, they dispatched an order

28. Quoted in Alfred S. Martin, "The King's Customs: Philadelphia 1763-1774," *Wm. and Mary Qtly.*, 3rd ser., 5 (1948), 213; see also Robert Bayard and Thomas Loring to American Customs Board, June 27, 1772, PRO, Treas. 1, 491; John Swift to American Customs Board, Sept. 5, 1771, Philadelphia Customs House Papers, XI, Hist. Soc. of Penn.

29. "Diary of James Allen, Esq., of Philadelphia, Counsellor-at-Law, 1770-1778," *Penn. Mag. of Hist. and Biog.*, 9 (1885), 179.

to Virginia's Governor Botetourt demanding that Randolph relinquish one of his offices.[30]

Randolph was not pleased with the prospect of losing part of his income. As attorney general he received an annual salary of £150, to which the Governor and Council added another £50. As judge, he received an average of five pounds for each case he tried, which might have averaged almost one hundred pounds additional income each year. Rather than lose this, Randolph stalled for time by requesting a salary as vice-admiralty judge, probably with the intention of retaining the more lucrative of the two offices if a division was forced.[31]

When his petitions and requests for the vice-admiralty salary reached London, Lord Hillsborough, then Secretary of State for the Colonies, replied that it was "inconvenient for the attorney general and the Judge of the Admiralty to be the same person." Therefore, instead of granting the requested salary to Randolph as judge, he promised him an additional £200 a year as attorney general if he would give up the judgeship. Governor Botetourt immediately replied that Randolph had accepted the offer "with pleasure."[32] But the attorney general never gave up his judgeship. He was prepared to defend his action by pointing out that Virginia was not comparable to South Carolina, which had been without an advocate general to whom the customs and sea officers could apply for aid in prosecutions. Virginia had been, and was now, served by an advocate general.

30. Admiralty Warrant to High Court of Admiralty, Mar. 26, 1767, and Philip Stephens to Governor Amherst, May 9, 1768, PRO, Admir. 2, 1057; N.Y. Jour., Nov. 5, 1767; Philip Stephens to Richard Sutton, Oct. 7, 1767, PRO, CO 5, 68; Maud H. Woodfin, "John Randolph" and "Peyton Randolph," in DAB, XV, 367-68.

31. John Randolph to Lord Botetourt, Dec. 20, 1768, and Petition of Edward Montagu on behalf of John Randolph to the Earl of Hillsborough, n.d., PRO, CO 5, 1347.

32. Hillsborough to Botetourt, July 17, 1769, and Botetourt to Hillsborough, Sept. 23, 1769, ibid.

Advocate General Benjamin Waller was himself having difficulties in the service of the crown. A practicing attorney, he had reluctantly accepted appointment from Governor William Gooch in 1742 and had never been pleased with the office. Other men before him had held the post "tacked, as an Incumbrance . . . to easy and profitable Places, with handsome Salaries, & Fees," while he, holding only the "naked Office of Advocate had neither Privilege, Salary or handsome Fee to boast of."[33]

After twenty-nine years as advocate general, Waller resigned in 1771. He was succeeded by a young attorney, Richard Starke, who immediately attempted to make the position pay. He petitioned the Admiralty Board in England for a salary and at the same time indicated that he had been promised the judgeship of the vice-admiralty court when Randolph had been requested to resign. The Admiralty, however, could not aid him. The suggestion that he had been recommended to the office of judge was answered by claiming that "such recommendation" never came to the Admiralty. And as for a salary as advocate general, he was notified that the vice-admiralty court of Virginia was "precisely on the same footing as the other Provincial Courts of Admty" and could not be established differently.[34]

Starke complained that the impecuniousness of his office was out of balance with the great responsibilities vested in the provincial advocates general. He probably would have been seconded by his counterparts in other provinces. The governors of Massachusetts had long attempted, without success, to gain a salary from the crown for their law officers. Finally, in 1772, Governor Hutchinson prevailed up-

33. Benjamin Waller to Richard Starke, Mar. 17, 1771, PRO, Admir. 1, 3884.

34. Starke's petition, Mar. 12, 1771, ibid. See also Admiralty to Richard Starke, Feb. 5, 1772, ibid., 2, 1058.

on the American Customs Commissioners to allow Samuel
Fitch 5 per cent of the king's third of forfeitures. He
planned to donate 5 per cent of his shares and attempted to
influence informers to do the same. In this way, a small
purse was gathered for the prosecuting attorney in revenue
cases.[35]

The dependence of the customs officers on crown officials
to prosecute their cases increased the importance of the advocates general. Securing competent legal advice and assistance
was now the major difficulty faced by the customs officers.
They had begun to limit their activities to cases where they
were fairly certain of securing convictions, or at least probable-cause certificates from the vice-admiralty judges. Seized
vessels were no longer certain of recapture by mobs, and
the reign of tar and feathers, although never completely
ended, had subsided. Despite continuing antagonism in
certain localities and sporadic outbreaks of mob action and
violence, the customs officers encountered less direct opposition. Other methods had been found to discipline them.

Common-law suits for trespass or false seizure were extremely damaging to customs officers before the Revenue Act
of 1764 was passed and in cases after its enactment when
judges forgot, or refused, to certify a probable cause. Captain John Brown, the commander of His Majesty's Ship
Hawke, was under indictment in a New York common-law
court for three years before he was convicted and presented
with a damage judgment of more than £4,000 for a seizure
he had made before the Revenue Act of 1764 was passed.
At least part of that time he was not allowed to leave the
province, and he had to turn the command of his vessel over

35. Governor Bernard to Earl of Hillsborough, Dec. 12, 1768, PRO, CO 5,
758; Hutchinson to Earl of Sandwich, Dec. 8, 1772, PRO, Admir. 1, 3820;
Admiralty to Hutchinson, Feb. 3, 1773, *ibid.,* 2, 1058. Jonathan Sewall was
granted a royal salary of £150 as attorney general of Massachusetts in 1772.
PRO, Treas. 28, 1.

to his lieutenant.[36]   In South Carolina, the Charleston merchants had disciplined George Roupell with similar damage suits in the common-law courts.

Thus the customs collectors looked to the judges for certification of probable cause. And the judges, as a rule, seem to have given this protection to the crown servants whenever possible. It was not difficult to find a rationalization for certification; in a Boston trial, Judge Auchmuty allowed a probable cause because the claimant of a seized cargo "had not at the time of Seizure . . . any Evidence of its having been legally imported."[37]   But the judges also retained a considerable degree of independence and sometimes refused the requests of customs officials for certification. The revenue men were then left to face the merchants' litigation in the common-law courts.

Hampering activities of the customs officials by suits at common law had long been a defensive weapon at the disposal of aggrieved merchants. The probable-cause provision ended much of its effectiveness, but such actions were not

36. The case in the vice-admiralty court, *John Brown qui tam* v. *Ship New York,* is reported in Hough, *N.Y. Reps.,* 215-21. Brown appealed the decree (which acquitted both the vessel and her cargo of rum, molasses, wine, and soap) to the High Court of Admiralty of England. That court reversed the decree as to the wine and soap, but affirmed it as to the ship. Thomas White, a merchant of New York and owner of the rum and molasses, brought suit in the Supreme Court against Brown for detaining the cargo. The jury awarded the large damage judgment to White. See Admiral Colville to Philip Stephens, Sept. 22, 1764, PRO, Admir. 1, 482; Customs Commissioners to Captain John Brown, Jan. 19, 1765, PRO, Treas. 1, 441; *N.Y. Jour.,* Nov. 6, 1766; *Conn. Courant,* Nov. 10, 1766; *Boston Gazette,* Nov. 17, 1766.

37. Decree of Judge Robert Auchmuty, May 9, 1768, in *George Dawson* v. *Lighter and Molasses,* PRO, Treas. 1, 465. Auchmuty ruled similarly in his decree on *George Dawson* v. *Sloop Dolphin & Cargo,* Mar. 2, 1773, Samuel Adams Papers, IV, Lib. Cong. Photostats. Dickerson, in his *Navigation Acts,* 212, asserts that "even if the seizure was made unjustly and the goods or ship awarded to the owner, it was the practice of the judge to certify on the record 'probable cause' for the action of the customs officer." Just how widespread or consistent this "practice" was is not shown, nor can it be accurately determined from available records.

stopped completely. When John Temple, the surveyor general of the northern district, attempted to establish a customhouse upriver from New York at Albany, the Albany merchants brought suit against the unwanted official on the basis of a provincial statute of 1724 designed to protect river traffic between New York and Albany from raids by the royal customs officers. Temple's subordinate at Albany, faced with judgments of costs and damages for seizing two vessels, fled his newly created post.[38] In Charleston, South Carolina, common-law judgments threatened Collector Daniel Moore until he left his office and the province. John Swift, the deputy collector at Philadelphia, was more stubborn. When he lost three suits in the common-law courts for money he allegedly owed on importation bonds, he appealed to the King in Council and secured a reversal of the decisions.[39]

These legal games sometimes developed into an art. The naval captains had special cause for concern in the Delaware River, where shippers had devised a scheme which threatened to defeat the Royal Navy. George Talbot, commanding the man-of-war *Lively*, explained the procedure: "When we Board . . . [the merchant vessels], the Master with every one on board, take to their boat & go away then the Vessel is to be left by us, and an Action is brought on for Damages." If the crew of the man-of-war stopped the exodus, "a Writ . . . [was] issued for confining them [the merchantmen] on board their own Vessel." In either case a suit at common law took place which automatically spelled conviction of the captains. Talbot claimed that "when an Action is laid, Justice is out

<hr />

38. "An Act to prevent Boats and other Vessels and the Goods put on board of them from being Interupted or Molested Whilst their Navigation is Confined within this Colony," in *The Colonial Laws of New York from the Years 1664 to the Revolution* . . . (5 vols.; Albany, 1894), II, 214-15; John Temple to Commissioners of the Customs, Apr. 10, 1766, PRO, Treas. 1, 452.

39. *Acts of the Privy Council: Colonial Series*, V, 276.

of the question. We are sure it will be against us, no one will be our Bail, not a Lawyer in the Province that has a Salary from the Crown, and any we employ will seem to Act for us, but Secreetly Act against us."[40]

In Massachusetts, the land-bound customs officers were faced with common-law suits for taking fees in excess of their stipulated maximum. Similar cases were soon under way in Rhode Island.[41] These common-law actions reached their greatest height in Rhode Island, when damage suits were combined with common-law prohibitions to deter not only the customs officers, but the vice-admiralty court as well, from enforcement of the revenue and trade laws.

In November 1772, Robert Keeler, commanding H. M. S. *Mercury*, seized a quantity of molasses and coffee in Rhode Island. Nathaniel Straw, Jr., was charged with illegally importing the goods. On the twenty-eighth of November, Judge Andrews decreed the molasses and coffee forfeit but allowed an appeal to Robert Auchmuty's court at Boston if Straw paid the costs of the court trial and security. The merchant decided against the appeal; instead he stopped the proceedings by obtaining a prohibition from the Rhode Island Superior Court.

The sale of the goods was thus postponed until the Superior Court reached a decision on the prohibition. The seized cargo was stored on the *Mercury* until the writ was set aside, sometime in February. Then the marshal of the vice-admiralty court sold the forfeiture at public auction. Within less than two hours after the sale, Straw prevailed upon the common-law court to issue a second prohibition. This time the court issued a writ of restitution, ordering the vice-admiralty court to restore the value of the goods, or the goods themselves, to the owner.

40. George Talbot to John Montagu, June 28, 1772, PRO, Admir. 1, 484.
41. Earl of Hillsborough to Thomas Hutchinson, Feb. 17, 1770, PRO, CO 5, 759; Papers in PRO, Treas. 1, 471.

Charles Dudley, who had succeeded John Robinson as the customs collector at Rhode Island, had received the king's half of the forfeiture, and Captain Robert Keeler, the informer, had received the other share. Dudley did not intend to turn the king's profits over to the owner, and he petitioned the King in Council to stay the execution of the common-law writ and review the case. The appeal was admitted and the execution stayed, but the council did not reach a decision until the Revolution had begun.

Andrews reported the case to the Admiralty. He was determined to keep the Superior Court from issuing indiscriminate prohibitions on his decrees. As he wrote, he was "very sensible that a writ of prohibition may issue from the Justices of the Superior Court, upon any proceedings in . . . [the vice-admiralty] court, not cognizable therein." But he claimed that this cause was "fairly within the cognizance and jurisdiction of the Court of Vice Admiralty and out of reach of the Superior Court to stop or prohibit." "Such a precedent," he believed was "warranted, neither by Law, usage, or custom."[42]

The litigious Rhode Islanders remained untamed by the new provisions for the vice-admiralty and customs establishments. Probably no other justice of a provincial common-law court would have dared to issue a prohibition on such thin legal grounds. But the Superior Court of the little charter government continued to harass both Judge Andrews and the customs officers. Captain Robert Keeler soon found himself charged by the captain and mate of a brig he had seized with actions of trespass, assault, and illegal imprisonment. The sailors had supposedly been assaulted and imprisoned when the vessel entered Newport from the West Indies. The owner of the brig brought charges of embezzle-

42. John Andrews to Admiralty, Apr. 20, 1773 and enclosures, PRO, Admir. 1, 3884; *Acts of the Privy Council: Colonial Series*, V, 383-84.

ment against Keeler for the alleged theft of salt, sugar, and rum which had been "legally entered at the Custom House."

The Superior Court listened to the charges and left the verdict to the jury. They found for each of the plaintiffs: £94 for the captain, £11 for the mate, and £44 for the owner. The naval officer was forced to pay the costs of all three suits. When Keeler petitioned the King in Council to reverse the action of the Superior Court, the council's committee decided that it would not be "proper to comply with the prayer."[43]

Collector Dudley, this same year of 1773, was faced with an even more damaging suit in the Superior Court. The schooner *Industry* had entered Newport Harbor in June 1772 and paid duties on the molasses which she carried. Later the same day, John Linzie, the commander of H.M.S. *Beaver,* seized additional molasses and sugar on board the schooner and prosecuted them to condemnation in the vice-admiralty court. The owners, two Rhode Island merchants named Clark and Nightingale, later attempted to win back the forfeited goods by paying the duties on them, but Dudley refused to accept their offer. Thereupon, they sued the collector in the Superior Court at Providence. Their charge against the officer was that he refused "to admit to Post Entry." Certainly, there was nothing in any of the acts of trade or revenue that instructed the collector to such action, and he was clearly within his rights to refuse the offer. The jury, however, decided the case in favor of the merchants and awarded them over £500 in damages, in addition to the costs of the trial. Such flagrant abuse of the customs official did not stand. Dudley appealed to the King in Council, and in 1775 the judgment against him was reversed.[44]

Extreme actions were not general throughout the colonies.

43. Robert Keeler to Admiral Montagu, Oct. 2 and 5, 1772, PRO, Admir. 1, 484; *Conn. Courant,* Mar. 23-30, 1773; *N.Y. Jour.,* Apr. 1, 1773.
44. *N.Y. Jour.,* Apr. 15, 1773.

In most of the provinces, the judges did their daily work, whether it involved seizures for illegal trading or ordinary marine disputes, without undue interference from any quarter. As the months passed, the judges' chores in deciding the cases brought before them were eased to some extent. The Stamp Act and the Townshend duties were in the past, and the judges had established reasonable rules of interpretation for the disputed clauses of the statutes that remained. However, one type of dispute before the vice-admiralty courts at Boston and New York remained to cause the judges difficulty. Unknown to the judges further south, these cases involved trespass against the king's white pine reserves in New England. They took the judges far afield from their customary duties and involved them in the ever-increasing squabble between the crown and land-hungry settlers and squatters.

The King's Broad Arrow

In their jurisdiction over violations of the revenue and trade laws, the vice-admiralty courts shared their authority with the common-law courts. At the election of the prosecutor or informer, an offense might be prosecuted in any colonial "court of record" or in the vice-admiralty court having jurisdiction in the area. However, the prosecution of violators of the statutes reserving the great white pine trees of New England to His Majesty was, and had been since 1729, one realm of British control in which the vice-admiralty courts had been granted exclusive jurisdiction.

Attempts in the last part of the seventeenth and early eighteenth centuries to form a policy and program for securing these mast pines for the use of the Royal Navy had met with only indifferent success. Finally, in 1729, Parliament passed a statute "for the better preservation of his Majesty's woods in America," combining the provisions of earlier statutes with new regulations and enforcement machinery. No white pine tree, not on private property, growing within the provinces of Nova Scotia, New England, New York, or New Jersey, could legally be cut without a special license if it measured over twenty-four inches in girth, three feet from the ground. The royal licensing for cutting was reserved for those who secured mast contracts from the navy. The forests were watched over by the surveyor general of the king's woods and his deputies. Trees which they surveyed, measured, and reserved for the king's use, were marked with the "Broad Arrow," "the old sign of naval property, shaped like a crow's track and made with three blows of a marking hatchet."[45] Illegal cuttings of woods so marked, or of trees larger than the minimum size, were confiscated, and the violators were fined. Prosecutions were under the sole jurisdiction of the vice-admiralty courts at Boston and New York.

Such cases led these sea-court judges far away from their usual realm of litigation. A legion of disputes and problems arose from the enforcement of the 1729 statute. Crown officers and defending lawyers, alike, scrutinized each clause of the statute for their own meaning, and the vice-admiralty judges at Boston and New York were called upon for interpretation and definition, often in areas of knowledge quite foreign to their regular duties.

New Hampshire and Maine were, by 1760, the two great logging regions in the northern colonies. The mast trade centered at Portsmouth, New Hampshire, where the agent for the mast contractors, Mark Hunking Wentworth, was the surveyor general of His Majesty's woods, as well as governor of New Hampshire. Mark's son John succeeded him in both

45. Albion, *Forests and Sea Power*, 241. Chapter Six, "The Broad Arrow in the Colonies," is an excellent discussion of the woods policy and its enforcement in America.

of these offices. The mast trade, the woods, and New Hampshire were all family preserves of the Wentworth clan. In defending those preserves against trespassers, they relied on the legal interpretations of the judges of the vice-admiralty courts at Boston and New York.

One of the most dangerous attacks on the family monopoly was made in the early 1760's by a group of Connecticut promoters. Knowing that Connecticut had never developed a great staple export crop, these men found that the lands lying on either side of the Connecticut River (upstream where the boundaries of New York, Massachusetts, and New Hampshire overlapped) were capable of producing masts and other marine timbers. To tap this forest and divert the mast trade from Portsmouth to New London would be no easy task. The first obstacle was a contract for the masts from the Royal Navy. Presumably over the protests of the Wentworth family, the Navy Board must be persuaded that the Connecticut River and New London was a more logical avenue for the ship timber and mast trade than the Piscataqua and Portsmouth.

A Connecticut vice-admiralty court was equally important. Only with a friendly judge sitting at New London to determine cases of violations against the contractors, could the Connecticut men hope to beat the Wentworths. Connecticut was then, as she had been since the beginning of the century, included in the jurisdiction of the New York Vice-Admiralty Court. Lewis Morris, the New York judge, provided a deputy for a Connecticut court. This situation was precarious. The Connecticut promoters believed that only with a judge and a court of their own choosing and under their own control could they succeed.

To gain both a contract and a court would be difficult, but perhaps not impossible. Jared Ingersoll, the colony's agent had been privy to the plans from the beginning; he was now in London and would exert a vigorous effort to win the mast contract. Governor Fitch and the General Assembly were quickly won over and proceeded to direct their pleas to the Board of Trade. As for the vice-admiralty court, neighboring Rhode Island provided the example. Only a few years earlier she had successfully petitioned for jurisdictional independence from the Massachusetts court. In winning their own court, Rhode Islanders had freed themselves from the wartime restrictions and the Boston tribunal. If Connecticut were as successful in divorcing herself from the New York jurisdiction, there would be no further obstacle to a flourishing mast trade.

Ingersoll won the mast contract in 1761. The Navy Board contracted with the promoters to supply one shipload of masts, an experiment to test the New Englanders' contention that the natural route from the pinelands to Britain lay through the Connecticut River and the port of New London. But Ingersoll failed to obtain an independent vice-admiralty court. The Board of Trade, after considering his arguments, decided it could give no opinion as to the necessity of the proposed court; nor could it suggest any names for possible judges if the Admiralty Board decided it was expedient to erect a court in Connecticut. The Admiralty took no action, and Ingersoll found himself completely stymied.[46]

There was an alternative to the new court, and at this moment the death of Lewis Morris in New York opened the doors of opportunity to Ingersoll. If he could persuade Morris' son Richard, now named judge of New York, to appoint him his deputy in Connecticut, perhaps the lagging plan could still succeed. At first, the new judge was pleased with the suggestion and promised to deputize Ingersoll as

46. John Pownall to John Cleveland, May 26, 1761, PRO, CO 5, 1296; Arthur Herbert Basye, *The Lords Commissioners of Trade and Plantations Commonly Known as the Board of Trade, 1748-1782* (New Haven, 1925), 117.

soon as he came to New London to publish his commission. But before he arrived in Connecticut, the Wentworth defense had quashed the scheme. The surveyor general's deputies not only inspected and seized some of the logs that the Connecticut men had cut to supply their mast contract, but also had some of the cutters prosecuted in Morris' court at New York. The new judge, who had earlier claimed himself "proud" to appoint Ingersoll his deputy, changed his mind and chose another man.[47]

The vice-admiralty court was not gained; the mast contract proved difficult to fulfill. Even after the logs were ready, it was months before the navy sent a mast ship to New London to carry the "experiment" to England. Ingersoll busied himself with other affairs, particularly the coming Stamp Act crisis. In the meantime, John Wentworth had gone to London to watch over the family interests, and returned with commissions to succeed his Uncle Benning, now aged and desirous of retirement, as both governor of New Hampshire and surveyor general of the king's woods. It was he who now became the central figure in the royal endeavor to keep the king's woods from destruction.[48]

To stamp out illegal cuttings in the king's woods was a task superhuman in size. The great stretches of pineland to the north and the west provided an impossibly large area for Wentworth's small staff to survey and inspect. In the areas which they did penetrate, they were often molested by frontier settlers and cutters who had their own brand of

47. See deposition of Gideon Lyman before Richard Morris, Apr. 2, 1764, Ingersoll Papers, Force Transcripts, Lib. Cong.

48. The following correspondence, all printed in New Haven Colony Hist. Soc., *Papers,* 9 (1918), 255-66, 272-73, 275, describes this episode: Ingersoll to Benning Wentworth, Nov. 14, 1761, Apr. 3, 1764; Ingersoll to Navy Board, Feb. 13, May 13, Oct. 12, 1762, Mar. 1, June 8, 1763, Feb. 7, 1764; Ingersoll to Colonel Symes, Mar. 3, 1763; Navy Board to Ingersoll, Jan. 26, July 5, 1762; William Livingston to Ingersoll, July 28, 1762; Richard Morris to Ingersoll, Dec. 23, 1762. See also Gipson, *Jared Ingersoll,* 79-110; *Board of Trade Journal* [*1759-1763*], 118-19.

swamp law to deter the crown officials. Intimidation and violence accompanied the seizure or threatened seizure of cuttings. The backwoods common-law courts, often crude and ill-managed, offered another remedy to the loggers and settlers who found themselves "victimized" by surveyors and seizers.[49]

It was not only in the frontier areas that Wentworth encountered opposition. Seaboard men of wealth found their land grants in the west threatened under interpretations of the private-property clause of the 1729 statute. The whole complicated question of legal title to lands granted before and after the 1691 charter of Massachusetts came into dispute. The surveyor general found himself at odds with powerful men in the Bay province.[50]

In the difficult job of enforcing the statute, Wentworth was forced to depend upon all the help he could summon. He invoked the aid of the colonial governors, who responded with proclamations admonishing officers of every rank to aid him. He employed the assistance of sheriffs and law officers. But, above all, Wentworth was dependent on the advocates and judges in the vice-admiralty courts at Boston and New York, where seizures had to be prosecuted. There was no specially constituted advocate general in the province of New York, but John Tabor Kempe, the attorney general, prosecuted Wentworth's cases before Judge Morris' court. In Boston, Auchmuty, Sewall, and Fitch, in turn, provided the legal counsel for the surveyor general.[51]

49. John Wentworth to Admiralty, Sept. 3, 1767, and Jan. 16, 1773, PRO, Admir. 1, 3819, 3820; Thomas Scammel to Admiralty, July 20, 1772, *ibid.*, 4287; *Conn. Courant*, Apr. 28-May 5, 1772; *Mass. Gazette*, Apr. 30, 1772.

50. Including James and William Bowdoin, James Potts, Silvester Gardiner, and Benjamin Hallowell. See *Acts of the Privy Council: Colonial Series*, V, 401. James Bowdoin to Thomas Pownall, Nov. 12, 1770, Mass. Hist. Soc., *Collections*, 6th ser., 9 (1897), 234-35.

51. Proclamations in *Mass. Gazette*, Aug. 13, 1767; *Conn. Courant*, Jan. 30, 1769. See also petition of John Tabor Kempe to the King, Feb. 24, 1768, PRO, CO 5, 1073.

The distance of both the Boston and New York courts from the pinelands made prosecutions especially difficult. Wentworth and his deputies employed the services of Auchmuty's Boston court more often than the New York tribunal. In both places, they frequently encountered little opposition in trial; the causes were frequently decreed in their favor by default because the offenders failed to appear in court. The penalties for cutting included both confiscation and forfeiture of the logs, and a fine of £50 for each tree felled. These, added to the cost of defending an action in either of the courts, forced the frontiersmen to drastic action.

One of the most extreme and celebrated prosecutions for illegal pine-cutting was heard by Judge Morris in New York in 1769. Wentworth had seized three men, William Dean and his two sons, William and Willard, near Windsor, a town on the west bank of the Connecticut River. The Deans had felled seventeen trees larger in size than the legal limit. Wentworth relied upon Attorney General Kempe to begin prosecutions in the New York Vice-Admiralty Court. The three were imprisoned, and Judge Morris refused to allow them freedom on bail. Despite a vigorous defense by their attorney, James Duane, they were each found guilty and fined £50 per tree, a total of £850 sterling. The two sons were without resources or property and could not satisfy the judgment against them. Attorney Duane persuaded Judge Samuel Welles of Brattleborough to accept a conveyance of the father's personal property and thereby secure it against the judgment of the vice-admiralty court. Unable to pay the stipulated fines, Dean was sentenced to prison for four months, while his sons drew terms of three months each. At the end of their confinement, they gave security for good behavior before the New York chief justice, in accordance with Judge Morris' decree.[52]

Wentworth thus proved himself capable of punishing some of the trespassers against the woods he watched over. But for every conviction, there were innumerable violations that went unpunished. Even with the aid of his staff, the law officers, and the vice-admiralty courts, the task was too great for the surveyor general. Penalties were inflicted for only a small proportion of the violations, and the program for saving all of the large white pines for His Majesty's navy was doomed from the beginning.[53]

In the long run, the timber policy only created more antagonism between crown officials and the colonists. In those New England regions where the surveyor general and his staff tramped the woods, marking the broad arrow on mast trees and seizing illegal cuttings, they became as much hated as any customs officer along the seacoast. And the prosecution of violations in the Boston and New York Vice-Admiralty Courts contributed to the opposition to those courts in a region where they would otherwise have been little known and less opposed.

52. The records of the case are in Records of New York Vice Admiralty Court, Lib. Cong. Photostats, and are printed in Hough, *N.Y. Reps.*, 227-33. See also Governor Moore to Hillsborough, Apr. 14, 1769, and John Wentworth to Hillsborough, Dec. 4, 1771, PRO, CO 5, 1100, and 73 and 228; Wentworth to John Temple, Nov. 18, 1770, Mass. Hist. Soc., *Collections*, 6th ser., 9 (1897), 37; and Edward P. Alexander, *A Revolutionary Conservative: James Duane of New York* (N.Y., 1938), 28.

53. Various proposals for changes in the regulations and enforcement came to nothing. See PRO, Treas. 1, 454; *Board of Trade Journal* [1764-1767], 367-70, 407, 409, 412, 430; Albion, *Forests and Sea Power*, 268-70.

8

New Courts for Old

ON THE SECOND day of June 1774, the Honorable Joseph Gerrish, judge surrogate of the Admiralty, died at Halifax, and Jonathan Sewall, still residing in Massachusetts, found himself in need of a new deputy. Sewall had no more intention of taking up the duties of his court himself than he had five years before when he appointed Gerrish as his surrogate. It would be pleasant to be out of Boston, but the "inhospitable, Lilliputian Region of Halifax" did not interest him. The climate was cold, the winters long, "provisions poor, scarce, & dear." Besides, the "flame" might "catch there notwithstanding the coldness of the climate."

The flame in Boston was burning brighter than ever. Tea dumping had been bad enough, but now as the months passed, each day brought news of more dreadful matters. Words were no longer of any use; the pattern of attack and counterattack had gone too far. September saw a congress at Philadelphia; blood ran on the green common at Lexington in April; May brought another Philadelphia congress. Bunker Hill in June proved—if by then proof was needed—that the flame had broken into wildfire. Sewall knew that he must flee from Boston and the "Mal conduct" of his countrymen. In July 1775, he decided to "retreat" to the "renouned seat" of his "maritime jurisdiction," a place that would afford peace, at least, because it was "not worth quarreling about."

But the next month brought rumors of smallpox in Nova Scotia, and Sewall arranged passage to England. He left Boston, which he was never to see again, and transported himself and his "wife, children, man servant, & maid servant . . . to London." There he stayed for twelve long years, watching the war from the other side. When he at last came to Halifax, in the summer of 1787, the "Rebellion & Fanaticism" that he so despised had triumphed over the crown. Thirteen of His Majesty's American dominions had become free and independent.[1]

The Rift Widens

The news of the repeal of the Townshend duties reached the colonies in the spring of 1770. Once again, the ministry had retracted offensive legislation. But the surrender was not total; the duty on tea was continued, and the Board of Customs Commissioners and the vice-admiralty courts were unchanged. The patriot press pointed out these facts, labeling them "engines ready prepared by law to work in the cause of tyranny and oppression, when the mandates

1. *Mass. Gazette,* June 16, 1774; Sewall to Edward Winslow, Jan. 10, 1776, W. O. Raymond, ed., *The Winslow Papers* (St. John, 1901), 14; Sewall to Thomas Robie, July 15, Aug. 12, 1775, Mass. Hist. Soc., *Proceedings,* 2nd ser., 10 (1896), 413, 415-16.

. . . are issued out; one would imagine a snake in the grass, from the duty's being left to Tea."[2]

The "snake in the grass" lay quiet for three years, until 1773; then the prophecy came true. The right to sell tea directly on the American market, granted to the East India Company in the Tea Act of April 1773, provided the long-sought issue for the American radical leaders. None of the tea ever reached the hands of the consignee merchants in America. New York and Philadelphia sent the cargoes back across the Atlantic. The Charleston tea was stored in government warehouses for nonpayment of duties and was later sold by the Revolutionary government at public auction. And the Boston patriots answered the threat with their celebrated tea party.

The British replied to these actions with a series of measures designed to punish insurgent Massachusetts. The Boston Port Act, the Administration of Justice Act, the Massachusetts Government Act, and the Quartering Act were the severest measures, short of war, that Lord North's ministry could muster to teach the Bay Colony the necessity of obedience. The Americans countered the following autumn when the fifty-six delegates to the First Continental Congress, after much debate, agreed upon a Declaration of Rights and Grievances and a Continental Association to halt commercial intercourse with the British Isles.

This nonintercourse scheme was a much more ambitious program than the nonimportation agreements against the Stamp Act and the Townshend taxes had been. After the first of December 1774, importation of British goods ceased in all the American colonies, and the tenth day of September of the following year was chosen as inaugural day for prohibiting exports to the homeland, unless Britain had by

2. *N.Y. Jour.,* May 10, 1770.

then granted the concessions prayed for in the Declaration
and Resolves. Enforcement of the Association was handed
to local committees, with the right to inspect all commerce,
seize goods in any way illegally imported, and punish the
offenders.

Thus, as in the days of the earlier nonimportation agreements, again arose along the Atlantic seacoast a dual set of
customs officers. The royal establishment watched for
breaches in the trade laws, while the patriots uncovered and
punished violations of the Continental Association. The
former depended upon the vice-admiralty courts to condemn
and sell their seizures, the latter upon the local committees of
safety.[3]

Throughout these difficult months, the four new district
judges discovered themselves suspect. Their every action
was closely watched, and the conduct of their courts carefully
scrutinized. In Philadelphia, the tea troubles had just ended
when the seizure of a small shallop employed in the coasting
trade between Philadelphia and New Castle County on the
Delaware "threw the Town into a fret."[4] The charge against
the boat, as set forth in the information filed in Judge Ingersoll's vice-admiralty court, was that of sailing without bond
from one British plantation to another. David Van Dyke,
the owner of the boat, had experienced such difficulties before. In 1767, another of his shallops had been prosecuted
on the same charge. Edward Shippen, the judge of the
provincial vice-admiralty court, had then pronounced acquittal, decreeing the lower Delaware counties part of the
colony of Pennsylvania. James Biddle, Ingersoll's deputy,
had ruled to the same effect in a similar cause. But this
time, before the judge heard the case in court, a barrage of

3. See advertisement for sale of the ship *Hester, N.Y. Jour.,* Dec. 8, 1774.
4. Jared Ingersoll to Jonathan Ingersoll, Mar. 12, 1774, New Haven Colony
Hist. Soc., *Papers,* 9 (1918), 446.

newspaper comments instructed him about the opinions of
the merchants and the citizens of Philadelphia.[5]

Judge Ingersoll's decrees had thus far brought forth only
minor criticism in the Pennsylvania capital.[6] Now, suddenly
his whole institution and its legal foundations were openly
attacked. Of course, the issue involved much more than the
cause of David Van Dyke, as the attackers admitted. They
claimed it the "cause of the public," and they answered
defenders of the trade laws and their enforcers with positive statements about the injustices committed in the
vice-admiralty courts. Many of the arguments were not
new; they had been used again and again in other places at
other times. But it was in the Philadelphia newspapers, in
the first two months of 1774, that the whole question of the
vice-admiralty jurisdiction was thrashed out in great detail.
For every letter, a corresponding answer appeared, the
authors concealing themselves behind such names as "Mentor," and "Russell," "Cato" and "Civis." Jacob Rush, a
young lawyer and brother of Doctor Benjamin Rush, led
the band of attackers under the signature "Russell." Ingersoll appropriated the name "Civis" to help formulate and,
in part, write the defense of his court.

Van Dyke and his boat were soon forgotten in the controversy over Ingersoll's court. The attack was four-headed,

5. Letters of "Mentor," "A.N.," "Cato," "Russell," "Civis," and "Veritas,"
Penn. Jour., Jan. 5, 12, 26, and Feb. 2, 1774; "Russell" letter in *Penn.
Gazette*, Feb. 9, 1774; *Mass. Gazette*, Feb. 10, 1774; Gipson, *Jared Ingersoll*,
303-13.

6. The sloop *Ruby* and her cargo had been seized in Aug. 1772, and
prosecution had begun in the district court before James Biddle, Ingersoll's
deputy. Biddle issued a writ of delivery, allowing the owners of the sloop
custody of their vessel upon payment of proper security, until the cause
was decided. PRO, Treas. 1, 491. Ingersoll heard the cause in November
and condemned both the sloop and her cargo. The *Penn. Jour.*, Dec. 9,
1772, claimed that this decree caused "the utter astonishment of all those
who attended the hearing . . . and indeed, of every other person acquainted
with the merits of it," and pointed out that Ingersoll's salary was "payable
out of the American Revenue," suggesting his interest in the forfeiture.

aiming blows at the difference between the American and
the English admiralty courts, the extension of jurisdiction
granted to the new courts, the elevation of Ingersoll's court
above and beyond the powers of the provincial common-law
courts, and the method of paying the new judges' salaries.
Early in this verbal combat, the attackers printed Ingersoll's
commission, italicizing the words and phrases which they
interpreted as being dangerous to colonial liberty.[7] With
this as a basis, both sides argued the provisions of the commission, summoning legal authorities from Blackstone to
Beawes' *Lex Mercatoria.*

Rush and his fellow writers began their charge against
the court by describing the differences between the English
and the American admiralty establishments. In the mother
country, they claimed, the common-law courts and Parliament had combined to reduce these civil-law courts to their
proper status. In America, on the other hand, the vice-
admiralty courts were constantly gaining authority by whole-
sale grants of power from Parliament and the Admiralty.
This point might have been effectively illustrated if the attackers had then listed the recent additions to the vice-
admiralty courts' jurisdiction in the trade and revenue laws.
These grants of power could not have been denied, and the
inequality between Englishmen and Americans could have
been emphasized, for parallel powers in the homeland were
entrusted to the common-law Court of the Exchequer.

But the attackers took a different line of approach, summoning other arguments to prove the extension of the vice-
admiralty jurisdiction. Relying on the terms of the judge's
commission as strong evidence, they cited the authority given
to Ingersoll to try cases of marine agreements "contracted on
land," crimes committed on the high seas, and disputes involving shipyard workers. They contended that in these

7. *Penn. Jour.,* Jan. 20, 1774.

areas of litigation the process of jury trial was guaranteed, by
long usage and common agreement, in the common-law
courts of England. But now, in America, a single judge of
the civil law had been granted the right to try such cases.

To refute these assertions, Ingersoll argued that his commission was almost identical with the commissions which
had been traditionally issued to vice-admiralty judges. Both
in England and in the provinces, the judges had always
determined marine contracts entered into on the seas or the
shores and banks of oceans and rivers. This was quite different from a blanket authority to try causes of agreements
contracted "on land." And if some minor discrepancy had
found its way into the new commissions, it was subject, as
was the entire commission, to the qualification, "according
to the civil and maritime laws and customs of our High
Court of Admiralty in England."

As for authority to determine "crimes" committed on the
high seas, Ingersoll defended his commission by explaining
the legal difference between "felonies" and "crimes." Felonies, that is, crimes involving the death penalty, were not
mentioned in the commission. Since the reign of Henry VII,
such felonies, including murder and treason, if committed
on the high seas, had been cognizable only before a court
employing a jury, whether the Admiralty Sessions of Oyer
and Terminer in England, or the specially commissioned
admiralty courts for piracy and murder in the colonies.
Nothing had been changed by Ingersoll's commission. His
opponents had merely misinterpreted the general word
"crime" to include the specific term "felony."

The third example of the courts' "extended" jurisdiction
concerned the authority over shipwrights and laborers in
shipyards. The attackers claimed that shipworkers were now
denied their heritage of trial by jury. But Ingersoll quoted
authorities to show that the identical jurisdiction was en-

trusted to the admiralty courts in England, and he explained
the reason. A similar situation had brought about the
rights granted to seamen to sue for wages in the vice-admiralty courts. For, said Ingersoll and his defenders, "suppose a
foreign vessel . . . should come into this power, in order to
refit . . . and the Captain should employ a number of shipwrights . . . [and] refuse to pay their bills,—in this case, the
Court of Admiralty . . . might issue process whereby the ship
might be arrested . . . until the shipwrights . . . obtain a
decree, have the ship sold, and their dues paid." Such a
procedure, capable of such speedy justice, was unknown to
the common-law courts. And thus the "law has taken care
to put it in the power of a Court of Admiralty, to lend its
aid . . . where a Common Law Court cannot so well do it."
The court's defenders thus denied any extension of the vice-
admiralty jurisdiction and any difference, in terms of commissions, between the American and the English admiralty
courts.

Both parties paid homage to the common law and its procedures. Ingersoll himself declared that no one could have
"a higher idea, or a more favourable opinion of Trials by
Jury" than he. But the two sides viewed the relations between the two legal systems differently. The men attacking
the new court claimed that it was not known whether a writ
of prohibition from the Supreme Court of Pennsylvania
could stop the proceedings in the new court, and that, even
if it could, there was still more doubt about cases brought
from other colonies to the district court. The defenders of
the new tribunal answered with assurance that the common
law in the colonies had always exercised the right to issue
prohibitions, and there was nothing in the commission or
the statute authorizing the new court that in any way interfered with that right.

The final argument, concerning the payment of Ingersoll's

salary, was largely academic, centering in the charge that his pay was to come from the seizures and forfeitures he condemned in his court. The attackers admitted that the salary was fixed, and that when, and if, the fund proved too small, the remainder would come from the sale of old naval stores in England. Nevertheless, they charged that in order to ensure his salary, a judge would condemn all seizures brought to him. This, they said, "looks too much like being party, judge, and jury. The administration of justice should not only be pure, but like Caesar's wife, should not even be suspected."

Ingersoll explained that "when the four Vice Admiralty Courts were . . . appointed, in order to free them from those objections which had been made against the mode of paying the former Judges . . . it was concluded to give these Judges fixt sums by way of salary, in lieu of all other fees and perquisites." The salaries were permanent and would be paid regardless of the number of forfeitures, for the old naval stores fund was large and permanent and "would not fail, so long as the nation itself should last." These new judges were, therefore, less interested than any of the provincial vice-admiralty judges in the number and value of the forfeitures they decreed. Nothing could modify their salaries in the least. As for Caesar's wife, she "ought, no doubt, to be careful not to furnish Caesar with any ground of jealousy; but if from a general discontent, occasioned by the ill treatment of his other friends, he will suspect his wife, without a cause, if she is such a woman as she ought to be, possessed of *virtue* and *honour,* her husband's suspicion, must sensibly touch her *delicacy;* but . . . her pain ought to be considered her misfortune and not her fault."[8]

Such was Philadelphia's debate over the powers of the

8. This account is based on articles by "Civis" in *Penn. Jour.* and "Russell" in *Penn. Gazette,* Feb. 2, 1774.

vice-admiralty courts. Neither of the antagonists admitted truth in their opponents' contentions, and the newspaper readers were left to judge for themselves the merits of each side.[9] After the initial assault, Van Dyke's market boat and the trade and revenue laws were never mentioned. The antagonism was created by the jurisdiction given to these civil-law institutions to determine violations of the trade laws. Not only in Philadelphia, but all along the Atlantic seacoast, the courts had become identified with English revenue measures and were linked in the mind of the public with the customs establishment and the American board at Boston.

Ingersoll summed up this entire argument in a private communication to his brother Jonathan in March 1774. "The people here, as everywhere else, are disposed not over much to like Courts of Admiralty, so far as they have any thing to do with Seizures, upon the late Obnoxious Acts, yet they know that if there should come a war, they would want such Court, and they know their own interest too well to wish to have this Court of Appeal carried away from themselves to New York or elsewhere."[10]

Yet it is understandable why the colonists always coupled the courts with the British revenue establishment. The appointment of the judges was easily seen as compensation to men "who had made themselves obnoxious by their conduct at the time of the Stamp Act." Even more objectionable was the manner in which the courts were staffed. It was common knowledge that the commissioners at Boston controlled the nomination of the deputies. At Philadelphia, when Ingersoll opened his court, "every officer in it was some underling of the custom house. The register was the guager and sur-

9. Newspaper editors in other provinces reprinted parts of the controversy. See *N.Y. Jour.*, Jan. 25, 1773.
10. New Haven Colony Hist. Soc., *Papers*, 9 (1918), 447.

veyor, the marshal one of the principal tidewaiters, &c."[11] While the judges might claim their innocence, pronouncing total disinterest in the cases they tried because of their fixed salaries, the subordinate officers stood to lose or gain their fees and percentages by the decrees of the courts.

Although the Philadelphia newspaper writers did not spell out this connection, and never mentioned the actual causes for the antagonism to the vice-admiralty courts, other men in other colonies were more explicit, if less scholarly, in their attacks. The Customs Commissioners and the courts of vice-admiralty were said to "act in concert," and the courts, no less than the commissioners, were constantly exposed to the vitriolic abuses of the penmen of the patriot press. The anniversary of the coronation of George III was announced with a satirical device: "Rejoice *O America,* in the Blessings of His Auspicious Reign—in which your Property is so wisely Justly & Mercifully taken care of by Courts of Admiralty."[12] A writer in a Massachusetts newspaper pointed out that the provincial charter expressly reserved the power of erecting and exercising admiralty jurisdiction to the crown and charged his opponents with arguing that the charter was contrary to the Constitution. But logic no longer availed. The "unconstitutional" vice-admiralty courts had become "the Grievance of Grievances."[13]

This stream of argument against the vice-admiralty courts culminated in the statement of rights and grievances which the Continental Congress at Philadelphia issued in the fall of 1774. That document proclaimed that "the several Acts

11. Joseph Reed to Earl of Dartmouth, William B. Reed, *Life and Correspondence of Joseph Reed* (2 vols.; Phila., 1847), I, 57-58.

12. *Boston Gazette,* Oct. 5, 1772.

13. *Mass. Gazette,* Oct. 22, 1772, June 4, 1773. The innumerable thrusts at the vice-admiralty courts are illustrated by the following examples: "Beware the ides of March. . . ," *Conn. Courant,* Feb. 16-23, 1773; "Old Truth," "American Solon," and "Cautuius," *Boston Gazette,* Aug. 24, 1772, Feb. 21, 1774, Apr. 11, 1774; "Second Letter to the Inhabitants of the British Colonies in America," *N.Y. Jour.,* June 9, 1774.

. . . which impose duties for the purpose of raising a revenue in America, extend the powers of the admiralty courts beyond their ancient limits, deprive the American subject of trial by jury, authorize the judges' certificate to indemnify the prosecutor from damages, that he might otherwise be liable to, requiring oppressive security from a claimant of ships and goods seized before he shall be allowed to defend his property, and are subversive of American rights."[14]

Once more, as in the days of the Stamp Act and the Townshend duties, the vice-admiralty courts were included in the specific grievances which the colonists intended to right. This time, however, half-answers no longer availed. The musket fire at Lexington and Concord the following April signaled the end not only of the vice-admiralty courts, but of all British rule in America.

The Judges Go Home

After years of controversy, the time for decision was at hand. Every man in America was confronted with the choice between the old and the new. The decision, relatively uncomplicated for some, was not easy for the judges of the vice-admiralty courts. For years they had enjoyed the favors and offices of the crown, interpreting and enforcing the very laws and regulations that were now so violently opposed. On the other hand, their private lives were closely tied to their native provinces, and to seek safety in England would mean a total renunciation of the past. It would be best, perhaps, to remain and wait out the storm, regardless of the consequences. But for royal officeholders, especially vice-admiralty judges, this called for high stamina.

Robert Auchmuty was the first of the four district judges

14. Worthington Chauncey Ford, ed., *Journals of the Continental Congress, 1774-1789* (34 vols.; Washington, 1904-37) , I, 71-72.

to decide the question of his future. In October 1774, he wrote to the Lords of the Admiralty, requesting permission to come to England "for a visit." Auchmuty did not wish to relinquish his salary and asked if he might continue to draw his £600 annually from the cashier of the American Customs Board. The Admiralty had no objection to his coming to Europe if he appointed a proper surrogate to sit for him while he was absent. But they could not "consent to . . . [his] enjoying the Salary . . . during such Absence."[15]

Auchmuty hesitated and then decided to forego his salary and seek the haven of the mother country. He settled in London, becoming a leader of the group of loyal Americans set adrift by the war in the colonies. He was unhappy out of Massachusetts, but he did not know where else to turn. Nor was the news from America cheerful. His country seat of Roxbury, a short distance from Boston, had been confiscated by the Revolutionary government, and all of his colleagues had fled Boston. Auchmuty had no desire to return to America; he stayed on in London and died there in 1788.[16]

Soon after his arrival in England, Auchmuty was joined by Jonathan Sewall, the second of the district judges to flee America. Sewall lived in London until 1777, then moved to Bristol. There he waited for the war to end, hearing reports that his estate, like Auchmuty's, had been seized and sold by the new government. Five years after the peace, he finally sailed for Nova Scotia and his vice-admiralty court there. He established himself in New Brunswick, where he lived until his death in 1796.[17]

The other district judges elected to wait out the war in America, taking their chances with the outcome of the conflict. Augustus Johnston, who had never established

15. Auchmuty to Philip Stephens, Oct. 29, 1774; Stephens to Auchmuty, Jan. 28, 1775, PRO, Admir. 1, 3884, 2, 1058.
16. Davis, *History of Judiciary of Massachusetts*, 78.
17. Donnan, "Jonathan Sewall," *DAB*, XVI, 607-8.

himself permanently in Charleston, remained in his home town of Newport, Rhode Island. He was unmolested until the summer of 1776, when he refused to take the test of allegiance to the new government and was interned at South Kingston. When the British occupied the Rhode Island seaboard a few months later, he was released to perform services for the occupation government. In 1779, the royal troops evacuated Newport, and he moved along with them to New York, where he lived out the rest of his life. His Rhode Island property was confiscated and, like Auchmuty, he died a broken and unhappy man, sometime around 1790.[18]

Of the four judges, Jared Ingersoll was probably the most moderate in his views of the American crisis. John Adams was pleasantly surprised when Ingersoll, then in New Haven, "came over with his neighbors . . . and made his compliments very respectfully" to the Massachusetts delegates to the First Continental Congress as they passed through the city on their way to Philadelphia.[19] After the revolutionary government assumed control of Pennsylvania in the spring of 1776, Ingersoll suspended activities in his court. But he stayed on in the province, a prisoner surrounded by the turmoil of war. He left Philadelphia, under parole, in September 1777, and returned to New Haven where he died four years later.

Both Auchmuty and Sewall left deputies to rule their courts, but after the British evacuated Boston in March 1776, it made little difference who was assigned to the vice-admiralty court. In late February of that year, the court condemned the schooner *Hope* and its cargo of eighty tons of salt for a breach of the trade laws. After that there is no further record of the Boston district tribunal.[20] The court was unable to function without the support of the army and the

18. Bronson, "Augustus Johnston," *ibid.*, X, 138-39.
19. John Adams' Diary, Adams, ed., *Works of John Adams*, II, 343.
20. *Mass. Gazette*, Feb. 22, 1776.

provincial civil government. Only Halifax, of the four district courts, remained in operation throughout the war.

The provincial vice-admiralty judges faced the same decision that confronted the district court judges. Like them,
they chose different solutions. Richard Morris, in New York,
had no desire to join the revolutionists, but neither could
he bring himself to leave his native soil. In the fall of 1775,
after his court had been closed for almost eight months, he
tendered his resignation to Governor William Tryon. The
Governor urged him to reconsider his actions, to wait until
the political crisis had passed. But Morris believed that
he could remain above the struggle, taking no part in it.
He retired from his judgeship to his country seat at Morris-
ania, satisfied to pursue a policy of personal neutrality.[21] In
Philadelphia, Edward Shippen also attempted the role of a
neutral. He left Philadelphia for more quiet parts of the
province and managed to stay out of the conflict. After the
war ended, he again entered political life, and was awarded
several judicial appointments, including the chief justiceship
of the new state.[22] John Randolph, on the other hand, followed the example of Auchmuty and Sewall. He left Virginia in 1775 for the safety of England.[23]

With the collapse of British government in the American
colonies, the vice-admiralty courts no longer had a function.
Without customs men, governors, and other royal officials in
control, there was no occasion for the courts to be used.
Only in those towns occupied by the British army, and in
other areas ruled by a combination of civil and military
government, was there a need for a vice-admiralty judge and
his court.

21. John A. Krout, "Richard Morris," *DAB*, XIII, 218-19; Hough, *N.Y.
Reps.*, 242.
22. William Roy Smith, "Edward Shippen," *DAB*, XVII, 116-17.
23. Maud H. Woodfin, "John Randolph," *ibid.*, XV, 362-63; Dunmore to
Earl of Dartmouth, Sept. 24, 1775, PRO, CO 5, 1353.

Yet the very war that drove the judges from their court-houses and caused the collapse of the vice-admiralty courts created a need for such tribunals. With the outbreak of hostilities, the game of privateering and sea captures recommenced. The Privy Council ordered the courts that were still operating in the spring of 1776 to try the seizures. These were difficult orders to obey, for the regular courts were gone, and the few royal officials remaining in the colonies were directing affairs from men-of-war in the provincial harbors. Governor Josiah Martin of North Carolina, aboard a sloop-of-war in the Cape Fear River, informed Dartmouth that it would be "very difficult if not impracticable to form Courts of Vice Admiralty . . . [in his] Province as well as in other of the Colonies, for want of Communication with the proper Officers." But by the following summer, he had established a court on the warship, and was trying seizures brought before it by the Royal Navy.[24] In New York and other cities controlled by the British, the situation was somewhat easier. Although Richard Morris' New York court ceased to function after March 1775, Governor Tryon established another tribunal, naming Robert Bayard judge.[25] And in the provinces to the north and south that held aloof from the conflict, the vice-admiralty courts continued their operations. They became largely prize courts, determining but few marine or trade law cases.

The end of the British vice-admiralty courts was at hand, but the first American admiralty courts were about to be born.

24. *Acts of the Privy Council: Colonial Series,* V, 422; Governor Martin to Earl of Dartmouth, Oct. 16, 1775, and Martin to Lord Germain, Aug. 7, 1776, Saunders, ed., *N.C. Col. Recs.,* X, 272, 734-35.

25. Although there are no records from Morris' court after March 1775, the judge did not give up his seat this early. In September he was negotiating a commission for a new register with the High Court of Admiralty in England. Morris to Sir Thomas Salisbury, Sept. 7, 1775, and Robert Bayard to Philip Stephens, Nov. 4, 1777, PRO, Admir. 1, 3884.

Congress Creates a Committee

An ironic development of the early days of the American Revolution was the rapidity with which the new state-makers discovered the need for many of the royal institutions they had taken up arms against. Almost as soon as the state governments had granted merchantmen the power to seize and capture British ships and cargoes, it had become obvious that the vice-admiralty courts, despite their alleged unconstitutionality and tyranny, were necessary to the trial and condemnation of the seizures. Therefore, often before the new states drafted constitutions, they erected courts with the powers formerly entrusted to the provincial vice-admiralty courts.[26]

The state-makers attempted, however, to keep these new tribunals free from the evils, as they saw them, of their older counterparts. They experimented with various formulas, but common to most was the prohibition of trial without jury. The absence of jury trial, more than any other procedure, had pointed up the difference between the old courts and common-law tribunals. Thus, the grand experiment of conducting admiralty and prize trials by pseudo common-law procedure began.

The courts erected in the various colonies differed considerably from one another. Massachusetts was one of the first states to establish a court. In November 1775, the provincial council established three prize courts, with a judge for each of three districts. Nathan Cushing presided over the court of the southern district; Timothy Pickering, the middle jurisdiction; and James Sullivan, the eastern. These judges were empowered to determine only the "law"; the

26. Judge Jared Ingersoll was thus proven a good prophet. See his prediction of 1774, above, 188. See also J. Franklin Jameson, "The Predecessor of the Supreme Court," *Essays in the Constitutional History of the United States in the Formative Period, 1775-1789* (Boston, 1889), 1-45.

"facts" of each cause were to be decided by a jury of "twelve good and lawful men."[27]

Virginia soon followed the example of Massachusetts. In December 1775, the provisional government established a maritime court designed to try causes arising from violations of the Continental Association. In an attempt to circumvent the dangers of a single judge, three were chosen: John Blair, James Holt, and Edmund Randolph. Each judge was permitted to appoint a register, an advocate, and a marshal for his court. All trials were to be by jury, with an appeal allowed to the state committee of safety. In May 1776, the court's jurisdiction was enlarged to include trial of captured enemy ships. At the same time, new judges were named, replacing two who had been appointed to other offices, and a third who had resigned.[28]

In October, the new state legislature again reorganized the court by enacting Thomas Jefferson's "Bill for Establishing a Court of Admiralty." This permanent establishment provided a more extensive jurisdiction for the court, allowing it cognizance "of all causes heretofore of Admiralty jurisdiction in this country." The court's procedure was to be governed by the regulations of Congress, the Virginia General Assembly, the English statutes prior to the fourth year of James I's reign, the laws of Oleron, and the Rhodian and Imperial laws as they had been observed by the English courts. But there was a series of exceptions to these precedents. The court was to have no jurisdiction over any

27. Octavius T. Howe, "Massachusetts on the Seas in the War of the Revolution 1775-1783," in Albert Bushnell Hart, ed., *Commonwealth History of Massachusetts* (5 vols.; N.Y., 1929), III, 30-63; Charles Oscar Paullin, *The Navy of the American Revolution: Its Administration, Its Policy, and Its Achievements* (Cleveland, 1906), 322-27.

28. William Hening, comp., *The Statutes at Large, Being a Collection of all the Laws of Virginia from . . . 1619* [to 1792] (13 vols.; Richmond, 1809-1823), IX, 103-5, 131; H. R. McIlwaine, ed., *The Letters of Patrick Henry* (Official Letters of the Governors of the State of Virginia [Richmond, 1926], I), 20, 21n.

capital offense. All matters of fact were to be tried by a jury, except captures from the enemy of the United States, which were to be tried either by court or jury as the Congress directed. Appeals in prize causes involving enemies of the United States were to be made to the body designated by Congress, and in all other cases to the Virginia Court of Appeals.[29]

After several months of appointing temporary courts for each sea capture, North Carolina in the spring of 1776 established tribunals at Edenton, Bath, New Bern, and Wilmington, with a single judge for each. As in the Virginia experiment, the judges were allowed to name their own court officers, and trial was directed to be by jury. Rhode Island erected a court in March; South Carolina in April; Connecticut and Maryland in May; and New Hampshire in midsummer, 1776.[30]

The New York provincial convention offered Richard Morris the bench of a newly created High Court of Admiralty in July 1776; he had conducted the royal vice-admiralty court since the French and Indian War. John McKesson, who had served as register in Morris' old court, was named to the same position in the new tribunal. Morris, however, declined the office, stating that although he was in sympathy with the new government, his family needed his assistance to recover their losses from the British destruction of his Westchester County estate. The convention then turned to Lewis Graham, a distant relative of Morris, who accepted the post.[31]

29. Hening, ed., *Statutes at Large*, IX, 202-6; Julian P. Boyd and others, eds., *The Papers of Thomas Jefferson* (15 vols.; Princeton, 1950 to date), I, 645-49.

30. Saunders, ed., *N.C. Col. Recs.*, X, 542, 547, 580, 634; Thomas Cooper and David J. McCord, comps., *The Statutes at Large of South Carolina, 1662-1838* (10 vols.; Columbia, 1836-1841), IV, 348; Richard F. Upton, *Revolutionary New Hampshire* (Hanover, 1936), 108; Paullin, *Navy of American Revolution*, 365, 423-24, 444, 459, 462, 467, 476.

31. Two years later Morris was chosen to the state assembly, where he served for two years. In 1779 he was appointed chief justice of the New

The preceding November, the Continental Congress had investigated the problem of the trial of sea captures and decided to take the lead in arranging for courts within the colonies. On November 25, 1775, Congress recommended to the colonies the expediency of erecting admiralty courts to determine the legality of prizes taken in the war at sea. The recommendations did not suggest that these courts be given the customary accompanying powers of marine jurisdiction, although several of the colonies had already arranged for this. But Congress did advise that all trials in the new courts be by jury, and it arranged a channel of appeals to Congress or to a committee it would provide.

Two such appellate committees were appointed and discharged before a standing committee of five members was established in October 1777. Any three of its members were empowered to hear and determine in finality the appeals brought from the state admiralty courts. Three additional members were appointed to the committee the following July.[32]

Spurred by the Congressional recommendation, Pennsylvania established a court in 1778. This tribunal included some innovations from the older provincial vice-admiralty courts, including a three-year term for the single judge who was appointed by the Supreme Executive Council of the

York Supreme Court to replace John Jay. He was a vigorous worker for ratification of the Federal Constitution and retained his judgeship until his retirement in 1790. From then until his death in 1812, he lived the life of a retired gentleman. Krout, "Richard Morris," *DAB*, XIII, 218-19; Alfred B. Street, *The Council of Revision of the State of New York: Its History, a History of the Courts with which its Members Were Connected* (Albany, 1859), 77; Alden Chester, ed., *Legal and Judicial History of New York* (3 vols.; N.Y., 1911), I, 342.

32. Paullin, *Navy of American Revolution*, 48-50, 67-68; Edmund C. Burnett, ed., *Letters of Members of the Continental Congress* (8 vols.; Washington, 1921-36), I, 272-73, 275, 280; J. C. Bancroft Davis, *The Committees of the Continental Congress Chosen to Hear and Determine Appeals from Courts of Admiralty: and the Court of Appeals In Cases of Capture, Established by that Body* (N.Y., 1888), 5.

state. The court's procedure was carefully detailed, and included an explicit subjection of its actions to writs of prohibition from the state Supreme Court. Appeals to the Congressional committee were allowed, as in the other state courts. A jury of twelve men was provided to determine all prize cases and all maritime causes except suits for seamen's wages for less than four months' service.[33]

In this manner, the new state courts attempted to do away with the most hated feature of the old provincial vice-admiralty courts—trial without jury. But the experiment soon proved unworkable. Prize law, no less than maritime law, had developed into a highly complex process, and although provisions were made in some of the new institutions to divorce "fact" from "law," only a few months' experience was necessary to prove how disastrous jury trial could be. Men with no knowledge of sea law or sea customs could not be expected to prove able umpires in the causes that were put to them. The pattern soon emerged of local juries being overruled by appeals to the committee created by Congress.

In Pennsylvania, the crisis came to a head over the sloop *Active*. The vessel had been brought into Pennsylvania as a prize by an armed brig belonging to the state. Although the sloop was British, it had been taken from three Connecticut men, former British prisoners who had mutinied and overpowered the crew. The case was tried in the state admiralty court before Judge George Ross and a jury. The jury allowed only one-fourth of the prize money to the Connecticut captors, dividing the remaining three-fourths between the sailors of the Pennsylvania ship and the state of Pennsylvania. The disgruntled Connecticut men appealed the case to Congress, where the Pennsylvania findings were reversed. Judge Ross refused to change the court's

33. Mitchell and Flanders, eds., *Statutes at Large of Pennsylvania,* IX, 277-83.

decision, and the Pennsylvania Assembly declared they would submit to such reversals no longer.[34]

In March 1780, the Pennsylvania legislators re-established the state admiralty court, abolishing the procedure of jury trial. Nor was the Quaker state the only one that made such changes. Two years later, South Carolina repealed her "Admiralty Act" and empowered her court of admiralty "to proceed to a final sentence and decree in all cases . . . without the intervention of a jury." Virginia, in 1779, had altered the procedure of her admiralty court so that trial by jury was mandatory only in causes where both parties were citizens of the state.[35]

Even in Massachusetts, where the patriot press before the Revolution had been most vocal in denouncing the "unconstitutionality" of the vice-admiralty courts, the experiment with jury trial was disappointing. James Sullivan, sitting as judge for one of the three district courts, admitted the difficulties to Elbridge Gerry in December 1779. "When our law was made for erecting the maritime courts," he wrote, "the temper of the people was such, and so greatly were they enraged at the corruption of former admiralty courts, that courts . . . without a jury would have met their universal disapprobation." Only four years under the new experiment had passed, and yet, Sullivan continued, "they are now fully satisfied with the wisdom of all civilized nations in appointing one judge to try, facts as well as law, which certainly, if he is an honest able man will give greater dis-

34. Hampton Laurence Carson, *The Supreme Court of the United States: Its History* (Phila., 1892), 53-54. Years later, in 1803 and again in 1809, this case caused similar controversies between the state of Pennsylvania and the national government. See Charles Warren, *The Supreme Court in United States History*, rev. edn. (2 vols.; Boston, 1935), I, 374-87.

35. *Journals of the [Pennsylvania] Assembly*, Jan. 31, 1780; Mitchell and Flanders, eds., *Statutes at Large of Pennsylvania*, X, 97-106; Cooper and McCord, eds., *Statutes at Large of South Carolina*, IV, 528; Hening, ed., *Statutes at Large*, X, 98-102.

patch and do more justice than can be done in the present mode of trials."[36]

Final defeat was admitted in January 1780, when Congress abolished the committee of appeal and established in its place a permanent court. This appeal court, presided over by three judges, was empowered to hold sessions any place between Williamsburg, Virginia, and Hartford, Connecticut. The trials "were to be . . . according to the usage of nations and not by jury."[37] The experiment had failed; admiralty law and jury trial had been found incompatible.

36. Thomas C. Amory, *Life of James Sullivan* (2 vols.; Boston, 1859), II, 378-79. Gerry and Sullivan authored the establishing legislation.

37. Carson, *History of Supreme Court*, 55.

9

Fact and Fiction

A REVOLUTION is not easily dissected. Men take up arms and fight battles; the armies are victorious or suffer defeat; the cause is triumphant and the leaders become patriots, or the cause is crushed and its propagators are rebels. The battles and the men who fought them are facts, easily detailed in history. But to discover the psychology of a revolution is more difficult, for the revolution must be separated from the image it has engendered. But when each known fact has been duly classified, and we have attempted to relate them, one to the other, we may be confronted by the truth that men fought as much for images as realities.

These are the problems encountered by students who seek out the story of the American Revolution. The colonists waged a successful war against Great Britain because they were, or imagined they were, suffering from the policies by which the mother country ruled them. The course of the

war and the men who led the armies are not difficult facts to
establish. But more careful analysis is required to discover
the motives for taking up arms and to determine how
many of those motives were based on actuality and how
many on fancy. Only when every statement of purpose and
every reported grievance has been carefully examined can
the historian come close to determining accurately the moti-
vations that led to war. Only then can the student express
reasonably correct generalizations as to the relative importance of the propagandists, the blunders of British policy,
the radical leadership in the colonies, and all of the other
suggested causes of the American Revolution.

The vice-admiralty courts were a minor, but persistent,
cause of the American Revolution. Although they never
invoked the opposition that greeted such larger issues of the
times as the Stamp Act and the Townshend Acts, from the
first news of the Revenue Act of 1764, down to the signing
of the Declaration of Independence, colonists constantly
questioned their jurisdiction, authority, and constitutionali-
ty. The preceding chapters have told the story of what
those courts did, how they did it, and the opposition to them
during these crucial years. All that now remains is to sum
up the arguments so effectively charged against the courts,
and by employing the actual history of the institutions, attempt to balance the fact and the fiction.

The American colonists cited four major grievances
against the vice-admiralty courts in the pre-Revolutionary
years. They objected to the methods of paying the vice-
admiralty judges. They expressed alarm when the four
regional courts were headed by men who gained their appointments as rewards for their loyalty to the crown during
the Stamp Act crisis. They complained that Britain was
extending the jurisdiction of the vice-admiralty courts far
beyond their traditional limits, creating an inequality that

would not be tolerated in England. Finally, they argued
that through this extension of jurisdiction they were being
deprived of the right of trial by jury.

The first of these arguments falls most easily into the
category of fiction. The judges of the old provincial courts
received their wages from small fees allowed them by provincial statutes and from percentages and commissions on
the property they condemned. Such a system, in which the
judge was financially interested in the forfeitures he decreed,
was capable of great abuse, although the fact that abuses were
seldom reported suggests that the judges were generally men
of honesty and integrity. Nonetheless, the colonists cited
the system as a basic grievance, and they were not alone in
favoring a change. Royal governors and other crown supporters also favored a method by which the potential conflict
of interest could be removed. They suggested fixed salaries
for the judges, stipends divorced from the forfeited vessels
and cargoes condemned in the courts.

The British ministries, in setting up both Doctor Spry's
court at Halifax and, later, the four district courts, provided
permanent salaries for the judges, specially arranged to
abolish the old evils. Although these salaries were drawn,
in the first instance, from the proceeds of forfeitures imposed
by the judges, the salaries were independent of the number
or value of those penalties. The fund from the sale of old
naval stores in England was available to make up deficien-
cies in the first source. Thus, whether the judges condemned
a thousand vessels, or none at all, their salaries could not be
reduced or enlarged.

Instead of being satisfied by these solutions, the colonists protested against the system through which the new
judges' salaries were derived. They also attacked the size
of the salaries, describing them as "exorbitant" and "enormous." No one could deny, of course, that the £800 annually

bestowed upon William Spry, or the £600 granted to the
four district judges, exceeded the pay of the common-law
chief justices.   But these admiralty judges ruled over courts
with much larger territorial jurisdiction than any common-
law tribunal.   The British assumed that by providing sufficient salaries, the judges would be rescued from all suspicion of corruption.   And, the ministry reasoned, the
judges' salaries, by their very size, would aid in elevating
the courts to the desired status of dignity and power.

The colonists' second protest was that the ministry had
selected four crown supporters as judges of the regional
courts.   Johnston and Ingersoll were obviously being com-
pensated for their losses during the Stamp Act riots; Auchmuty and Sewall were being rewarded for their support of
Governor Bernard and the prerogative.   Yet all four men
seem to have conducted their courts and themselves with
decorum and moderation, and the worst fears of the objectors
never materialized.   It is true, however, that these judges
did submit to the American Customs Commissioners, and
allowed the minor offices of their courts to become political
plums at the disposal of that board.   This itself was a
constant irritation to those who viewed the two institutions
as part of a sinister conspiracy against American commerce.
It afforded another opportunity for the patriots to demon-
strate that the admiralty courts were inseparable from the
other oppressive instruments of British rule.   The governors
continued to control the appointment of the provincial
judges, and they were certain to name supporters and sus-
tainers of royal policies to these posts.   But taken together,
the judges of both the district and the provincial courts were
capable and intelligent.

With three exceptions, the judges remained above the
struggle that finally shaped itself into revolution.   John
Andrews in Rhode Island and Egerton Leigh in South Caro-

lina were undoubtedly the most controversial of the judges. Leigh, who found himself and his court in combat with Henry Laurens and the South Carolina traders, attempted to deliver decrees satisfactory to both merchants and revenue men. But Leigh was too much of a politician, too involved in his other royal offices, to keep his court free from attack. Andrews also found himself caught between two masters. His office had been created to serve the mercantile community of Rhode Island, but he found he could please neither the men who had elevated him to a judgeship, nor their enemies, the royal customs officials. Whether any judge in the same situation could have kept his court from such entangled and complicated difficulties is open to question. In Massachusetts, Robert Auchmuty firmly allied himself with the royal governor, and, in the Hancock prosecutions, allowed his court to become an agency at the disposal of the American Customs Board. But even Auchmuty could not, or would not, miscarry justice enough to win that prosecution.

Excepting these judges, the other provincial officers remained out of the direct line of fire during most of the pre-Revolutionary struggles. Their political views and their private contacts varied considerably, as is shown by their decisions in the actual test of war. Some remained loyal to the crown and withdrew from the colonies. Others attempted to wait out the war as neutrals. Some actively joined the Revolutionary party.

The colonists' third argument against the vice-admiralty courts focused on the extent of the courts' jurisdiction. The vice-admiralty courts in the colonies had exercised jurisdiction over marine disputes since the middle of the seventeenth century. This jurisdiction did not cease with the coming of the Revolution. Cases of seamen's wages, salvage, insurance, charter parties, partnerships, and all the variations of commercial disputes continued to come before the judges. But, as the new regulations for trade and revenue were enforced, the proportion of marine cases diminished. By 1766, the antagonists and defenders of the vice-admiralty courts ceased to consider this jurisdiction important. That it had been important, and still was, cannot be questioned. In exercising their ancient jurisdiction, the courts served the merchants and the sailors they were designed to aid.

But it was their jurisdiction in the realm of imperial control that brought forth the violent demonstrations against the courts. It was this jurisdiction which the Americans claimed was enlarged. The historic facts were not, and could not be, denied. The courts had served the crown as tribunals for determining violations of the trade and navigation acts in the colonies since 1696. They had been granted the sole jurisdiction in white-pine prosecutions in 1729. In British eyes, basing the enforcement of the imperial policies on these tribunals did not break with tradition; rather it was deeply rooted in the scheme of mercantile control.

This explanation the colonists refused to accept. Before 1763, the acts of trade and navigation had been designed as regulatory laws, to direct the commerce of the empire. After 1763, the trade laws were intended as revenue statutes. The Stamp Act of 1765 was the most obvious example. Many of the articles for which stamps were prescribed were completely divorced from the sea and its commerce. Newspapers and real estate were not properly a part of a merchant's or sailor's life. Yet the Stamp Act allowed prosecutions to be brought before the vice-admiralty judges. This, in the colonial viewpoint, was surely an unwarranted extension of civil-law jurisdiction.

The fact that the Stamp Act was never enforced in the mainland colonies, or that it was repealed the year after its enactment, did not diminish the colonists' argument. The

Revenue Act of 1764 and the Townshend Revenue Act also allowed prosecutions in the vice-admiralty courts. The crown might argue that the powers of the courts increased only as the duties, regulations, and restrictions on trade increased; but the Americans were of a different mind. They were convinced that the courts' jurisdiction had been so enlarged that it bore little resemblance to its character in 1763. Given the colonists' assumption that the objectives of the trade laws had changed from regulation to revenue, their complaints of enlarged admiralty jurisdiction were justified.

The Americans also complained about the territorial jurisdiction of the new superior courts. They were especially concerned about the large area over which Doctor Spry's establishment at Halifax held authority. Their protests were echoed in royal governors' letters and in departments of state at home. The unsuccessful attempt to divide the jurisdiction in 1765 and 1766 might have answered their protests. Yet, in 1768, when a division was finally accomplished, the issue was dead. Doctor Spry's court showed itself to be only a theoretical danger long before his commission was revoked and his duties distributed among the four district judges.

Twice within the decade preceding the Revolution, the British attempted to reorganize the vice-admiralty system in the colonies. The first effort, the creation of the Halifax court, caused great apprehension, although in actuality it modified the colonial vice-admiralty courts very little. The second attempt, the creation of the four district courts, changed the older institutions only in minor ways. The new courts displaced the provincial courts in the four colonies in which they were located. But neither their authority to determine causes arising within their districts nor their appellate powers were much used in the few short years before they closed their doors.

It is, of course, conceivable that the colonists could not, or did not care to, discern the ineffectualness of these changes. Some of their grievances against the vice-admiralty courts held as true against the provincial courts as their district counterparts. But much of the writing was specifically directed to these new establishments and was thus founded less on actuality than on assumed or pretended facts.

The final colonial argument, the heart of the dispute over the vice-admiralty courts in the decade before the Revolution, centered in the charge that they denied the colonists their right of trial by jury. The accusation was constantly reiterated: The Americans were denied the "native rights of Englishmen." The charge was included in the Declaration of Rights and Grievances of the First Continental Congress and in the Declaration of Independence. No other argument concerning the courts was more consistently debated, nor more indicative of the gulf separating the British and the colonials.

The British position can be stated simply. Juries could not be relied upon to bring verdicts against fellow colonists for violating the acts of trade and revenue. In seeking to place the prosecution of such offenders out of the hands of juries, the British government had traditionally granted the vice-admiralty courts concurrent jurisdiction, in such causes, with the common-law courts. In no instance, with the exception only of the white-pine laws, were the vice-admiralty courts granted exclusive jurisdiction. In practice, however, they exercised exclusive jurisdiction in most colonies. This was partially the result of admiralty procedures, which allowed customs officials to circumvent the hazards of jury trial. But there were other reasons. The vice-admiralty courts were constantly open to hear causes, observing no schedules or terms. Also, the process of trial and decree was much speedier in the vice-admiralty courts than in the common-law tribunals.

There was, hence, no break with tradition or with the "rights" of the colonists as they had enjoyed these rights throughout the eighteenth century. It was unfortunate for those who placed great value in the system of jury trial that the system was unworkable with the trade laws. On the other hand, no practical observer could logically suggest that Britain relinquish all hope of effectively enforcing her colonial policies because of the breakdown of the jury system in the colonies. As long as the policies were inadequately enforced, there was little or no opposition to the mode of trying violations. After 1763, when the mother country began to enforce the trade laws strictly, the opposition developed.

The Americans viewed the situation differently. They asserted that the shift in the trade laws from regulation to revenue wrenched the mercantile policy from what it had been before 1763 to an unconstitutional position. Americans were refused the right to sanction tax laws through their own chosen representatives, and this wrong was made worse by the inequality between Americans and Englishmen in trials for violating the revenue laws. If fellow subjects in England were tried by juries when apprehended for violations of such laws, that same benefit should extend to the colonists in America. But the arbitrary ministries had denied the Americans this traditional and guaranteed right by allowing prosecutions in the civil-law admiralty courts.

That the colonists came to believe passionately about this loss of jury trial is amply demonstrated. Once the break with Britain was effected, and the Americans were free to establish civil governments as they saw best, in state after state the courts which they substituted for the provincial

vice-admiralty courts were specifically required to proceed
only by jury trial. And the new Congress for the united
colonies recommended trial by jury when it suggested establishing such courts.

That the experiment failed need not detract from the
good intentions of the experimenters. They had seen a
system at work enforcing legislation they opposed, and they
concluded that part of the difficulty was attributable to the
procedures of trial in that system. They set out to correct
the flaws as they understood them. The provincial vice-
admiralty courts were not the complete evils that the patriot
propagandists painted them. Long years of development
had created a system of civil law with a highly complex procedure, and certain attributes beneficial to the colonial merchants in private litigation and to the British government
in enforcing its trade laws. When those laws became oppressive, either in actuality or imagination, the courts which enforced them were mistrusted as oppressive institutions.

The vice-admiralty courts were, after all, tools to be
used, either in the hands of crown officials or state-makers.
A regulatory institution may receive the brunt of an argument, but it is often the regulations entrusted to it for enforcement, and not the institution itself, that is the cause
of the complaint. The history of the sea courts, both before
and after the American Revolution, indicates that it was
the laws they enforced, not the courts themselves, that
required revision to silence the hostile critics.

A Note on Sources

A COMPARATIVELY large quantity of the records of the colonial vice-admiralty courts for the years up to 1763 is available to students. The Library of Congress has compiled photostatic copies of the remaining records of the courts in Massachusetts, New York, Pennsylvania, Maryland, and North and South Carolina. Dorothy S. Towle's edition of the Rhode Island records, and Judge Hough's volume of selected cases from the New York court, supplement these. Unfortunately, with only a few exceptions, these records end either before or at the time of the French and Indian War.

For the years between 1763 and 1776, records from only two of the vice-admiralty courts remain. The New York records, which are now housed in the National Archives in Washington, D.C., and in the New York Public Library (with copies in the Library of Congress), are the most complete. There are minute books, a series of papers from individual cases tried before the court including libels, answers, interrogations, citations, and other processes issued from the court, and a volume compiled about 1916 that consists of papers selected from various files to illustrate admiralty practices. The Massachusetts records for the pre-Revolutionary years include an incomplete volume of entries by the court register in the years 1765 to 1772. On many occasions, little more than the titles of the cases were recorded. The original volume is in the library of the Supreme Judicial Court, Suffolk County, Boston. A photostatic copy is available at the Library of Congress. There is also a manuscript volume from the Massachusetts court, Admiralty Book of Accots of Sales &c., 1743-1765, in the library of the Suffolk County court.

Few records have been found from the Superior Court of Vice-Admiralty at Halifax, Nova Scotia, or from the four district vice-admiralty courts. Part of the Massachusetts register's volume relates to the court of the Boston district, rather than to the provincial court. There are no other known records from the district courts. This study has therefore, of necessity, been compiled more from personal manuscripts, newspapers, and published records, than from court papers.

There is much information about the courts in the official correspondence of the provincial governors and the Admiralty, Colonial, Audit, and Treasury offices in England. Reproduced material from the British Public Record Office and from the British Museum is available at the Library of Congress. For this study, these files have been supplemented by Public Record Office material reproductions owned by Professor Merrill Jensen.

The Microfilm Collection of Early State Records, and most of the colonial newspaper files, were consulted at the Library of the State Historical Society of Wisconsin, but are available at other depositories. Personal papers of judges, lawyers, and merchants have been examined at the Library of Congress, the Historical Society of Pennsylvania, the Boston Athenaeum, the Massachusetts Historical Society, the Harvard University Library, the New-York Historical Society, the New York Public Library, the New Haven Colony Historical Society, and the Connecticut Historical Society.

The bibliography which follows does not include many of the materials searched for information about the vice-admiralty courts. It is, rather, a listing of the manuscript collections and published volumes which have been cited in the text of this study. However, it does include most of the sources of information concerning the colonial vice-admiralty courts for the years between 1763 and 1776.

Bibliography

Manuscripts

Boston Athenaeum:
    Ezekiel Price Papers
    Manuscript Scrapbook
Connecticut Historical Society:
    William Samuel Johnson Papers
Harvard University Library:
    Francis Bernard Letterbooks
Historical Society of Pennsylvania:
    Board of Trade Papers, Plantations General. Transcripts
    Philadelphia Customs House Papers
    John Reynell Letterbook
    Henry Laurens Letterbook
    Etting Manuscripts, Miscellaneous
    Peters Manuscripts
Henry E. Huntington Library:
    Grenville Letterbooks
Library of Congress:
    Jared Ingersoll Papers. Force Transcripts
    Samuel Adams Papers. Photostats

Minutes of the Vice-Admiralty Court of the Province of New York. Photostats

Records of the Court of Vice-Admiralty of Massachusetts Bay. Photostats

House of Lords Manuscripts, Item 226: Papers Concerning the Superior Court of Vice-Admiralty at Halifax, Nova Scotia. Photostats

British Museum, Egerton Manuscripts 2659: Correspondence of the Hutchinson Family. Transcripts

British Museum, Egerton Manuscripts 2671: "Origin and Progress of the Rebellion in America, to 1776" by Peter Oliver. Transcript

Massachusetts Historical Society:
Miscellaneous Manuscript Collection

National Archives:
New York Provincial Vice-Admiralty Records

New-York Historical Society:
Miscellaneous Manuscript Collection
John Tabor Kempe Papers

New York Public Library:
Chalmers Papers

Microfilm Collection of Early State Records:

Maryland E.1c	Executive Records, Appointments and Commissions
Massachusetts A.1b	Journal of the House of Representatives
New Jersey E.1c	Executive Records, Appointments and Commissions
North Carolina E.1	Executive Records, Governor Tryon's Letterbooks
North Carolina F.3	Court Records, Vice-Admiralty Papers
Pennsylvania E.2a	Executive Records, Penn Manuscripts, Official Correspondence

Microfilms of the Adams Papers given by the Adams Manuscript Trust to the Massachusetts Historical Society. Part III, Reel 184. John Adams, Miscellany.

Manuscript Reproductions from the Public Record Office, London, England:
Admiralty 1, 482 Dispatches of Admirals Charles Saunders and Lord Colville. Library of Congress Transcripts.

Admiralty 1, 483 Dispatches of Commodores Samuel Hood and James Gambier. Library of Congress Transcripts.

Admiralty 1, 484 Dispatches of Admirals John Montagu and Molyneaux Shuldham. Library of Congress Transcripts.

Admiralty 1, 3678, 3679 Letters relating to the Solicitor's Department. Library of Congress Photostats.

Admiralty 1, 3818, 3819, 3820 Letters from the governors of Plantations. Library of Congress Transcripts.

Admiralty 1, 3866 Letters from the Customs House, 1757-1780. Private Microfilms of Professor Merrill Jensen.

Admiralty 1, 3878, 3882, 3883 Letters from Doctors Commons. Library of Congress Photostats.

Admiralty 1, 3884 Letters from Doctors Commons. Private Microfilms of Professor Merrill Jensen.

Admiralty 1, 4286, 4287 Letters from the Treasury 1757-1777. Private Microfilms of Professor Merrill Jensen.

Admiralty 2, 1056, 1057, 1058 Letters relating to admiralty and vice-admiralty courts. Library of Congress Photostats.

Audit Office 16, 43 East Florida, General Record Book, 1764-1776. Library of Congress Photostats.

Colonial Office 5, 66, 67, 68, 73 Plantations general, Indian affairs, trade, etc. Library of Congress Transcripts.

Colonial Office 5, 216 Instructions, Reports and Various. Library of Congress Transcripts.

Colonial Office 5, 228 In-letters to the Secretary of State 1700-1774. Library of Congress Photostats.

Colonial Office 5, 250 Out-letters from the Secretary of State for the Colonies. Library of Congress Transcripts.

Colonial Office 5, 378 Board of Trade, Original Correspondence, South Carolina. Private Microfilms of Professor Merrill Jensen.

Colonial Office 5, 755, 757, 758 Secretary of State, Original Correspondence, Massachusetts. Private Microfilms of Professor Merrill Jensen.

Colonial Office 5, 759 Letters from Governor Thomas Hutchinson of Massachusetts to the Secretary of State. Library of Congress Photostats.

Colonial Office 5, 891, 892 Board of Trade, Original Correspondence, New England. Private Microfilms of Professor Merrill Jensen.

Colonial Office 5, 1071, 1073   Board of Trade, Original Correspondence, New York. Library of Congress Transcripts.

Colonial Office 5, 1097, 1100, 1103, 1104   Letters from the governors of New York to the Secretary of State. Library of Congress Transcripts.

Colonial Office 5, 1141   Secretary of State's Out-letters, 1768-1782, New York Entry Book. Library of Congress Transcripts.

Colonial Office 5, 1280, 1282, 1286, 1296   Secretary of State, Original Correspondence, Proprietaries. Library of Congress Transcripts.

Colonial Office 5, 1331   Board of Trade, Original Correspondence, Virginia. Library of Congress Transcripts.

Colonial Office 5, 1347, 1353   Secretary of State, Original Correspondence, Virginia governors. Library of Congress Transcripts.

State Papers Domestic 37, 22   Treasury Correspondence, 1763-1775. Private Microfilms of Professor Merrill Jensen.

State Papers Domestic 42, 65   Lords of the Admiralty, Supplementary, 1764-1775. Private Microfilms of Professor Merrill Jensen.

Treasury 1, 423, 431, 441, 442, 445, 447, 449, 452, 453, 454, 463, 465, 468, 471, 472, 486   Board Papers, Original Correspondence. Library of Congress Transcripts.

Treasury 1, 429, 459, 491   Board Papers, Original Correrespondence. Private Microfilms of Professor Merrill Jensen.

Treasury 1, 501   Board Papers, Original Correspondence. Virginia Records Project. Microfilm, University of Virginia.

Treasury 28, 1   Letters Relating to America. Library of Congress Photostats.

Library, Supreme Judicial Court, Suffolk County, Boston, Massachusetts: Admiralty Book of Accots of Sales &c., 1743-1765.

Published Documents and Records

Andrews, Charles M. *Guide to the Materials for American History, to 1783, in the Public Record Office of Great Britain,* 2 volumes. Washington, 1912-1914.

Journals of the Continental Congress, 1774-1789. Edited by Worthington Chauncey Ford. 34 volumes. Washington, 1904-1937.

Prologue to Revolution, Sources and Documents on the Stamp Act Crisis, 1764-1766. Edited by Edmund S. Morgan. Chapel Hill, 1959.

GREAT BRITAIN:

Acts of the Privy Council of England: Colonial Series, 1613-1783. Edited by W. L. Grant and James Munro. 6 volumes. London, 1908-1912.

Correct Copies of the Two Protests Against the Bill to Repeal the American Stamp Act, of Last Session, with Lists of Speakers and Voters. Paris, 1766.

"Debates on the Declaratory Act and the Repeal of the Stamp Act, 1766," *American Historical Review,* 17 (1912), 563-86.

Journal of the Commissioners for Trade and Plantations, from April 1704 to . . . [May, 1782], preserved in the Public Record Office. 14 volumes. London, 1929-1938.

Opinions of Eminent Lawyers on Various Points of English Jurisprudence, Chiefly Concerning the Colonies, Fisheries and Commerce of Great Britain; Collected and Digested, from the Originals in the Board of Trade, and other Depositories. Edited by George Chalmers. London, 1858.

Reports of Cases Determined by the High Court of Admiralty, 1758-1774. Edited by Reginald G. Marsden. London, 1885.

The Royal Commission on the Loses and Services of American Loyalists 1783 to 1785: Being the Notes of Mr. Daniel Coke, M. P. one of the Commissioners during that Period. Edited by Hugh Edward Egerton. Oxford, 1915.

The Statutes at Large . . . of Great Britain: Continued as Statutes of the United Kingdom of Great Britain and Ireland. 46 volumes. Cambridge and London, 1762-1869.

MASSACHUSETTS:

Acts and Resolves, Public and Private of the Province of
the Massachusetts Bay: To Which are Prefixed the Charters
of the Province; With Historical and Explanatory Notes,
and an Appendix. 21 volumes. Boston, 1869-1922.

"Opinion of Attorney General Jonathan Sewall of Massachusetts in the Case of the Lydia." Edited by Oliver M.
Dickerson, William and Mary Quarterly. 3rd Series, 4
(1947), 499-504.

A Report of the Commissioners of the City of Boston, containing the Boston Town Records 1758 to 1769. Boston,
1886.

Reports of Cases Argued and Adjudged in the Superior
Court of Judicature of the Province of Massachusetts Bay,
Between 1761 and 1772. Edited by Josiah Quincy, Jr.
Boston, 1865.

New York:

Reports of Cases in the Vice Admiralty of the Province of
New York and in the Court of Admiralty of the State of
New York, 1715-1788. Edited by Charles Merrill Hough.
New Haven, 1925.

Select Cases of the Mayor's Court of New York City, 1764-
1784. Edited by Richard B. Morris. Washington, 1935.

The Colonial Laws of New York from the Years 1664 to
the Revolution. 5 volumes. Albany, 1894.

NORTH CAROLINA:

The Colonial Records of North Carolina. Edited by Wil-
liam L. Saunders. The State Records of North Carolina.
Edited by Walter Clark. 26 volumes. Raleigh and
Goldsboro, 1886-1907.

PENNSYLVANIA:

Journals of the Assembly. 1780.

The Statutes at Large of Pennsylvania from 1682 to 1801.
Edited by James T. Mitchell and Henry Flanders. 17
volumes. Harrisburg, 1896-1915.

RHODE ISLAND:

Records of the Colony of Rhode Island and Providence
Plantations in New England. Edited by John Russell
Bartlett. 10 volumes. Providence, 1856-1865.

*The Records of the Vice Admiralty Court of Rhode Island,
1716-1752.* Edited by Dorothy S. Towle. Washington,
1936.

SOUTH CAROLINA:

*Records of the Court of Chancery of South Carolina, 1671-
1779.* Edited by Anne King Gregorie. Washington, 1951.
The Statutes at Large of South Carolina, 1662-1838. Compiled by Thomas Cooper and David J. McCord. 10 volumes. Columbia, 1836-1841.

VIRGINIA:

*The Statutes at Large, Being a Collection of all the Laws
of Virginia from . . . 1619* [*to 1792*]. Compiled by William Hening. 13 volumes. Richmond, 1809-1823.

Newspapers

CONNECTICUT:
Connecticut Courant

GEORGIA:
Georgia Gazette

MARYLAND:
Maryland Gazette

MASSACHUSETTS:
Boston Chronicle
Boston Evening Post
Boston Gazette
Boston Weekly Newsletter
Massachusetts Gazette
O. M. Dickerson, ed., *Boston Under Military Rule, 1768-69,
as Recorded in a Journal of the Times.* Boston, 1936.

NEW YORK:
New York Journal
New York Mercury

PENNSYLVANIA:
Pennsylvania Chronicle
Pennsylvania Gazette
Pennsylvania Journal

RHODE ISLAND:
  Newport Mercury
  Providence Gazette

SOUTH CAROLINA:
  South Carolina Gazette

VIRGINIA:
  Virginia Gazette

Published Letters and Diaries

Adams, John. *The Works of John Adams, Second President of the United States: With a Life of the Author, Notes and Illustrations.* Edited by Charles Francis Adams. 10 volumes. Boston, 1850-1856.

Allen, James. "Diary of James Allen, Esq., of Philadalphia, Counsellor-at-Law, 1770-1778," *Pennsylvania Magazine of History and Biography,* 9 (1885), 176-96, 278-96, 10 (1886), 424-41.

The Barrington-Bernard Correspondence and Illustrative Matter, 1760-1770. Edited by Edward Channing and Archibald Cary Coolidge. Cambridge, 1912.

Bernard, Francis. *Select Letters on the Trade and Government of America: And the Principles of Law and Policy, Applied to the American Colonies; Written by Governor Bernard at Boston in the Years 1763, 4, 5, 6, 7, and 8. Now first Published; To which are added the Petition of the Assembly of Massachusetts Bay against the Governor.* London, 1774.

The Bowdoin-Temple Papers. Massachusetts Historical Society, *Collections.* 6th Series, 9 (1897).

Champion, Richard. *The American Correspondence of a Bristol Merchant, 1766-1776: Letters of Richard Champion.* Edited by G. H. Guttridge. University of California Publications in History, XXII. Berkeley, 1934.

The Correspondence of the Colonial Governors of Rhode Island, 1723-1775. Edited by Gertrude Selwyn Kimball. 2 volumes. Cambridge, 1903.

De Berdt, Dennys. *Letters of Dennys De Berdt.* Edited by Albert Matthews. Publications of the Colonial Society of Massachusetts, XIII. Cambridge, 1911.

Gage, Thomas. *Correspondence of General Thomas Gage with the Secretaries of State, 1763-1775.* Compiled and edited by Clarence E. Carter. 2 volumes. New Haven, 1931.

The Grenville Papers: Being the Correspondence of Richard Grenville Earl Temple, KG., and the Right Hon. George Grenville. 4 volumes. London, 1852-1853.

Henry, Patrick. *The Letters of Patrick Henry.* Edited by H. R. McIlwaine. Official Letters of the Governors of the State of Virginia, I. Richmond, 1926.

Ingersoll, Jared. "Correspondence," New Haven Colony Historical Society, *Papers.* 10 volumes. New Haven, 1865-1951. Volume 9.

Jefferson, Thomas. *The Papers of Thomas Jefferson.* Edited by Julian P. Boyd. 15 volumes. Princeton, 1950-date.

Jenkinson, Charles. *The Jenkinson Papers, 1760-1766.* Edited by Ninetta S. Jucker. London, 1949.

Letters and Papers of Benjamin Franklin and Richard Jackson, 1753-1785. Edited by Carl Van Doren. Philadelphia, 1947.

Letters of Members of the Continental Congress. Edited by Edmund C. Burnett. 8 volumes. Washington, 1921-1936.

Letters to the Ministry from Governor Bernard, General Gage, and Commodore Hood: And Also, Memorials to the Lords of the Treasury, from the Commissioners of the Customs; With Sundry Letters and Papers Annexed to the Said Memorials. Boston, 1769.

Pitt, William. *Correspondence of William Pitt When Secretary of State with Colonial Governors and Military and Naval Commissioners in America.* Edited by Gertrude Selwyn Kimball. 2 volumes. New York, 1906.

Reed, Joseph. *Life and Correspondence of Joseph Reed.* Edited by William B. Reed. 2 volumes. Philadelphia, 1847.

Rowe, John. "Diary of John Rowe," Massachusetts Historical Society, *Proceedings.* 2nd Series, 10 (1896), 11-107.

—— *Letters and Diary of John Rowe, Boston Merchant 1759-1762, 1764-1779.* Edited by Anne Rowe Cunningham. Boston, 1903.

Stiles, Ezra. *Extracts from the Itineraries and Other Miscellanies of Ezra Stiles, D.D., LL.D., 1755-1794.* Edited by Franklin Bouditch Dexter. New Haven, 1916.

Watts, John. *The Letter Book of John Watts.* New-York Historical Society, *Collections* (1928).

The Winslow Papers. Edited by W. O. Raymond. St. John, 1901.

Books and Articles

Adams, James Truslow. *Revolutionary New England, 1691-1776.* Boston, 1927.

—— "William Bollan," *Dictionary of American Biography,* II, 420.

Albion, Robert Greenhalgh. *Forests and Sea Power: The Timber Problem of the Royal Navy, 1652-1862.* Cambridge, 1926.

Alden, Edmund Kimball. "Robert Auchmuty, Sr." and "Robert Auchmuty, Jr.," *Dictionary of American Biography,* I, 421-22.

Alexander, Edward P. *A Revolutonary Conservative: James Duane of New York.* New York, 1938.

Amory, Thomas C. *Life of James Sullivan.* 2 volumes. Boston, 1859.

Andrews, Charles M. "Introduction" to *The Records of the Vice Admiralty Court of Rhode Island, 1716-1752.* Edited by Dorothy S. Towle. Washington, 1936.

—— *The Colonial Period of American History.* 4 volumes. New Haven, 1934-1937.

Basye, Arthur Herbert. *The Lords Commissioners of Trade and Plantations Commonly Known as the Board of Trade 1748-1782.* New Haven, 1925.

Baxter, W. T. *The House of Hancock: Business in Boston, 1724-1775.* Cambridge, 1945.

Beer, George Louis. *British Colonial Policy, 1754-1765.* New York, 1908.

Benedict, Erastus C. *The American Admiralty: Its Jurisdiction and Practice with Practical Forms and Directions.* 6th Edition. 5 volumes. New York, 1940-1941.

Bridenbaugh, Carl. "Charlestonians at Newport, 1767-1775," *South Carolina Historical and Genealogical Magazine,* 41 (1940), 44-45.

Bronson, Elsie M. S. "Augustus Johnston," *Dictionary of American Biography,* X, 138-39.

Carson, Hampton Laurence. *The Supreme Court of the United States: Its History.* Philadelphia, 1892.

Channing, Edward. *A History of the United States.* 6 volumes. New York, 1905-1925.

Chester, Alden, editor. *Legal and Judicial History of New York.* 3 volumes. New York, 1911.

"The Courts of Admiralty in New England Prior to the Revolution," *Massachusetts Law Quarterly,* 17 (1932), 97-100.

Crump, Helen Josephine. *Colonial Admiralty Jurisdiction in the Seventeenth Century.* London, 1931.

Davidson, Philip. *Propaganda and the American Revolution, 1763-1783.* Chapel Hill, 1941.

Davis, J. C. Bancroft. *The Committees of the Continental Congress Chosen to Hear and Determine Appeals from Courts of Admiralty; and the Court of Appeals In Cases of Capture, Established by that Body.* New York, 1888.

Davis, William Thomas. *History of the Judiciary of Massachusetts Including the Plymouth and Massachusetts Colonies, the Province of the Massachusetts Bay, and the Commonwealth.* Boston, 1900.

Dickerson, Oliver M. *The Navigation Acts and the American Revolution.* Philadelphia, 1951.

Donnan, Elizabeth. "Jonathan Sewall," *Dictionary of American Biography,* XVI, 607-8.

Doty, Joseph D. *The British Admiralty Board as a Factor in Colonial Administration, 1689-1763.* Philadelphia, 1930.

Gipson, Lawrence Henry. *Jared Ingersoll: A Study of American Loyalism in Relation to British Colonial Government.* New Haven, 1920.

Harper, Lawrence A. *The English Navigation Laws: A Seventeenth Century Experiment in Social Engineering.* New York, 1939.

Harrington, Virginia D. *The New York Merchants on the Eve of the Revolution.* New York, 1935.

Holdsworth, William. *A History of English Law.* 12 volumes. London, 1925-1938.

Hopkins, Stephen. *The Rights of Colonies Examined.* Providence, 1764. Reprinted in John R. Bartlett, ed. *Records of the Colony of Rhode Island and Province Plantations in New England.* Providence, 1861. VI, 416-27.

Howe, Octavius T. "Massachusetts on the Seas in the War of
    the Revolution, 1775-1783." *The Commonwealth History
    of Massachusetts*, III. Edited by Albert Bushnell Hart.
    5 volumes. New York, 1929.

Hutchinson, Thomas. *The History of the Colony and Province
    of Massachusetts-Bay*. Edited by Lawrence Shaw Mayo.
    3 volumes. Cambridge, 1936.

—— *Strictures Upon the Declaration of the Congress at Phila-
    delphia; In a Letter to a Noble Lord*. London, 1776.

Jameson, J. Franklin. "The Predecessor of the Supreme Court,"
    *Essays in the Constitutional History of the United States in
    the Formative Period, 1775-1789*. Boston, 1889.

Jones, Edward Alfred. *The Loyalists of Massachusetts: Their
    Memorials, Petitions, and Claims*. London, 1920.

Kerr, Wilfred B. "The Stamp Act in Nova Scotia," *New Eng-
    land Quarterly*, 6 (1933), 552-66.

King, Joseph Edward. "Judicial Flotsam in Massachusetts 1760-
    1765," *New England Quarterly*, 27 (1954), 366-81.

Krout, John A. "Richard Morris," *Dictionary of American
    Biography*, XIII, 218-19.

Labaree, Leonard Woods. *Royal Government in America: A
    Study of the British Colonial System Before 1783*. New
    Haven, 1930.

Lovejoy, David S. "Rights Imply Equality: The Case Against
    Admiralty Jurisdiction in America 1764-1776," *William and
    Mary Quarterly*. 3rd Series, 16 (1959), 459-84.

MacPherson, David. *Annals of Commerce, Manufactures, Fish-
    eries, and Navigation, with Brief Notices of the Arts and
    Sciences Connected with Them*. 4 volumes. London, 1805.

Martin, Alfred S. "The King's Customs: Philadelphia 1763-
    1774," *William and Mary Quarterly*. 3rd Series, 5 (1948),
    201-16.

Mayo, Lawrence Shaw. *John Langdon of New Hampshire*. Con-
    cord, 1937.

Miller, John C. *Sam Adams: Pioneer in Propaganda*. Boston,
    1936.

Morgan, Edmund S. "The Postponement of the Stamp Act,"
    William and Mary Quarterly. 3rd Series, 7 (1950), 353-92.

Morgan, Edmund S. and Helen M. *The Stamp Act Crisis: Pro-
    logue to Revolution*. Chapel Hill, 1953.

Mowat, Charles Loch. *East Florida as a British Province 1763-1784.* University of California Publications in History, XXXII. Berkeley, 1943.

Nettels, Curtis P. *George Washington and American Independence.* Boston, 1951.

—— *The Roots of American Civilization.* New York, 1938.

Nicholas, Ray. *The Importance of the Colonies of North America, and the Interest of Great Britain With Regard to Them, Considered Together with Remarks on the Stamp-Duty.* London, 1766.

Observations on Several Acts of Parliament Passed in the 4th, 6th, and 7th Years of his present Majesty's Reign: And Also on the Conduct of the Officers of the Customs, Since those Acts were Passed: And the Board of Commissioners Appointed to Reside in America. Boston, 1769.

Paullin, Charles Oscar. *The Navy of the American Revolution: Its Administration, Its Policy, and Its Achievements.* Cleveland, 1906.

Pitman, Frank Wesley. *The Development of the British West Indies, 1700-1763.* New Haven, 1917.

Register for New England and Nova Scotia . . . for 1769. Mein and Fleming. Boston, n.d.

Root, Winfred Trexler. *The Relations of Pennsylvania With the British Government, 1696-1765.* New York, 1912.

Rowland, Kate Mason. *The Life of George Mason, 1725-1792.* 2 volumes. New York, 1892.

Schlesinger, Arthur M. *Colonial Merchants and the American Revolution.* New York, 1918.

Sellers, Leila. *Charleston Business on the Eve of the Revolution.* Chapel Hill, 1934.

Smith, Joseph Henry. *Appeals to the Privy Council from the American Plantations.* New York, 1950.

Smith, William Roy. "Edward Shippen," *Dictionary of American Biography,* XVII, 116-17.

Street, Alfred B. *The Council of Revision of the State of New York: Its History, a History of the Courts with which its Members Were Connected: Biographical Sketches of Its Members and Its Vetoes.* Albany, 1859.

Thacher, Oxenbridge. *Sentiments of a British American.* Boston, 1764.

Thomas, Leslie J. The Non-Consumption and Non-Importation movements, 1767-1770. Unpublished master's thesis, University of Wisconsin, 1949.

Townsend, Annette. *The Auchmuty Family of Scotland and America.* New York, 1932.

Ubbelohde, Carl. "The Vice-Admiralty Court of Royal North Carolina, 1729-1759," *North Carolina Historical Review,* 31 (October 1954), 517-28.

Upton, Richard F. *Revolutionary New Hampshire.* Hanover, 1936.

Wallace, David D. *The Life of Henry Laurens, with a Sketch of the Life of Lieutenant-Colonel John Laurens.* New York, 1915.

Warren, Charles. *The Supreme Court in United States History.* Revised edition. 2 volumes. Boston, 1935.

Washburn, Emory. *Sketches of the Judicial History of Massachusetts from 1630 to the Revolution in 1775.* Boston, 1840.

Washburne, George Adrian. *Imperial Control of the Administration of Justice in the Thirteen American Colonies, 1684-1776.* New York, 1923.

Wiener, Frederick Bernays. "Notes on the Rhode Island Admiralty, 1727-1790," *Harvard Law Review,* 46 (1932), 44-90.

Woodfin, Maud H. "John Randolph" and "Peyton Randolph," *Dictionary of American Biography,* XV, 367-68.

Index

The word "vice-admiralty" has been used in reference to the courts in the colonies. For the state courts, or English courts, the word "admiralty" has been used.